MILITARY
VEHICLES

MILITARY
VEHICLES

CHRIS McNAB

Grange
BOOKS

Editorial and design by
Amber Books Ltd
Bradley's Close
74–77 White Lion Street
London N1 9PF
www.amberbooks.co.uk

Project Editor: James Bennett
Design: Neil Rigby at Stylus Design
Editor: Conor Kilgallon

Printed in Singapore

Photographs © TRH Pictures

Artworks © Amber Books Ltd except:

Aerospace Publishing: 15, 16, 18, 21, 28, 30, 31, 33, 34, 37, 43, 45, 47, 66, 71, 73, 76, 96, 107,
114, 116, 127, 137, 179, 191, 200, 201, 216, 232, 238, 255, 257, 263, 275, 282, 292, 306, 309

Peter Pusztai: 17, 23, 35, 40, 48, 49, 50, 53, 60, 63, 69, 70, 74, 79, 85, 86, 98, 100, 102, 104, 105,
113, 118, 125, 128, 129, 132, 133, 139, 141, 144, 149, 154, 158, 159, 175, 176, 177, 186, 192,
193, 194, 195, 196, 197, 202, 203, 205, 206, 218, 219, 226, 233, 236, 241, 243, 249, 251, 258,
267, 268, 269, 272, 274, 280, 286, 288, 290, 295, 299, 301, 305

CONTENTS

Introduction

While Main Battle Tanks often capture the attention of media and enthusiasts, their role on the modern battlefield is actually a rather minor one. For of all the factors which contribute to combat success, vehicle logistics always ranks amongst the most important. Without the ability to transport men and material from the industrial base to the actual frontline, an army will be starved of the means to prosecute war.

THE YEARS OF EXPERIMENTATION

World War I began the true mechanization of logistics and infantry manoeuvres. Three particular needs arose. The first was to transport the vast amounts of ammunition required for conducting artillery warfare. Second, trench warfare demanded a constant influx of logistics to maintain the viability of the static positions. Finally, in the last years of the war, tacticians sought ways to speed up assault manoeuvres across no-man's land and reduce high-volume casualties.

None of these problems were adequately solved during the war. Yet the conflict served to challenge the military's outdated ideas of horse-drawn transport towards new conceptions of mechanised logistics and combat. More and more countries developed armoured cars: France the Laffly-White, Germany the A5P and the Daimler/15, Italy the Autoblinda IZ, Russia the Garford-Putilow, and the UK 'Little Willie', the forerunner of the first tanks. Apart from this latter example, most armoured vehicles of World War I were simply civilian machines clad in crude iron and armed with a machine-gun or cannon. Their performance was frequently poor, with top speeds of around 45km/h (28mph) and a limited ability to negotiate the muddy conditions which characterized the Western and Eastern fronts. In addition, industry was not geared up to the mass-production methods required to equip large-scale armies. Consequently the impact of armoured cars on infantry warfare was minimal, though they did find good use as urban security and patrol vehicles where road conditions were less demanding.

Trucks also made an appearance in World War I, though mainly in the form of requisitioned civilian vehicles. Some 825 civilian trucks were put into military service by Germany during the conflict, with 3000 tractors, 7700 heavy trucks and 50,000 cars in reserve. (German citizens received grants and annual subsidies for purchasing a truck, the agreement being that the truck would be requisitioned by the army if necessary.) Four-wheel-drive U.S.

The Ehrhardt BAK 1906 was typical of early armoured vehicles. It consisted of a commercial truck chassis with bolt-on armour and a crude turret mounting a 50mm (1.97in) cannon.

trucks manufactured by FWD Corporation entered service on the Western front in 1917. Yet the trucks still did not have the capability or numbers to threaten horse-drawn logistics. Of greater persuasion were the tracked vehicles entering service. Tracked transporters, in spite of their persistent unreliability, slow speed and inadequate weaponry, demonstrated that vehicles could go where horses couldn't and transport far greater loads. The Renault Cargo Carrier of 1916 only moved at 6.5km/h (4mph) but had a cargo capacity of four or five tons. In 1918, the U.S. Holt Tractor, Caisson Mk VII carried five tons at 11.2km/h (7mph). U.S. designers also elongated British Mk V tanks to create a troop compartment for a squad of soldiers – and the first true Armoured Personnel Carrier was born.

World War I ended not with a mechanization of warfare, but at least mechanized progress. During the inter-war period tacticians such as Major-

General J.F.C. Fuller in the UK and the German army officer Heinz Guderian propounded the mechanization of war as the key way to seize military advantage. The full mechanization of armies was still too much of a cultural change for many nations, Germany later being an exception, but vehicular technology was advancing. Far better engines, suspension systems, and armaments were developed, improving both the off-road mobility and combat performance of military vehicles. More investment was poured into vehicle technologies and by World War II mechanized warfare became a reality.

WORLD WAR II AND THE COLD WAR

World War II is significant in the story of the mechanization of warfare for two main reasons. Firstly, the range of what constituted 'military vehicles' broadened massively to include specialist machines such as radio vehicles, command vehicles, engineer vehicles and self-propelled guns. Secondly, the quantities of vehicles available made the mechanization of large-scale units possible. These two factors were decisive.

During the war, multi-purpose vehicles became common, vehicles which took a standard format as the basis for several specialist roles. Half-tracks, a particular phenomenon of the conflict, were ideally suited for this flexibility, being manoeuvrable, durable and offering troop- and cargo-carrying capacity. The German SdKfz 250, for example, was not only a basic APC but also converted to a communications vehicle (SdKfz 250/2 and 3), a mortar platform (SdKfz 250/7), a self-propelled anti-tank system (SdKfz 250/9), an anti-tank gun carrier (SdKfz 250/8) and a range-finding and artillery survey vehicle (SdKfz 250/12) amongst others.

Trucks became more dependable and capable in World War II, and improved techniques of mass production ensured they were available in sufficient numbers. Horse carriage, though still heavily used, was the transport of default, not of choice. A British 6x4 Leyland Hippo truck could carry 10 tons of cargo at speeds of around 40mph for a distance of 837km (520 miles), a feat well beyond the easy capacity of horse logistics. Each side built up fleets of trucks and made them an intrinsic part of infantry battalions and armoured units.

With the increase in mechanization came an expansion in engineering challenges for the wartime armies, and multifarious engineer vehicles were developed. The Sherman Beach Armoured Recovery Vehicle (BARV) was created from a turretless Sherman tank for the purpose of towing stuck vehicles from deep water or soft sand during amphibious operations. Churchill tanks were mounted with fascine and mat-laying devices to create mobile road-laying or ditch-breaching machines. In Germany, the massive railway-mounted Karl 600mm (23.62in) mortar required a specialist ammunition carrier to transport its 2-ton shells. The result was the Munitionstransporter IV, based on the chassis of the PzKpfw IV Ausf F tank but fitted with a 3000kg (6614lb) capacity crane and racks to carry four shells. The list could go on, but mobile engineering vehicles became a necessary presence for all sides during the war.

Another interesting development in World War II was the rise of amphibious vehicles. These offered many manoeuvre advantages, the principal being that they did not require the assistance of another vehicle or unit to transport their cargo from the water to an inland position. They usually fell into three categories of use: beach assault vehicle, reconnaissance vehicle and APC. The American DUKW – affectionately known as the 'Duck' – was the most famous of the first category, able to carry either a sizeable unit of troops or five tons of cargo from sea to beach at speeds of 9.7km/h (6mph). In the Pacific conflict, experience of aggressive amphibious landings on Japanese-occupied islands led to the development of the U.S. LVT series of vehicles, designed to provide combat influence rather than just cargo-landing. The LVT(A) 1, for example, was fully turreted and armed with a heavy machine

Entering production in 1934, the PzKpfw 1 had a limited operational life owing to weak armour and limited firepower of two 7.92mm (0.3in) MG34 machine guns.

The Warrior is designed to mix the roles of an APC with a light tank. Seven soldiers can be carried in addition to the three-man crew, and defence comes from a 30mm (1.18in) Rarden cannon.

gun and a 37mm (1.45in) cannon for immediate beachhead fire support.

The list of vehicle innovations in World War II could go on and on, but when the war ended a key change had occurred in the nature of modern armies. Mechanization had become essential rather than preferred. As the world entered the Cold War, units had to be fully mechanized to meet the greater speed and mobility of armed conflict. This was assisted by the reduction in size of most armies following World War II, but that reduction in size meant that survivability had to depend on speed and defensive technology rather than physical numbers of troops. The Cold War period did little to change the basic categories of military vehicles. What it did transform, however, was their fighting capability.

The APC is a good example. APCs after World War II became more central to infantry combat. A typical vehicle such as the Soviet BMP-1 could carry eight fully equipped infantrymen, was amphibious and featured NBC protection (qualities which became standard on most post-war APCs) and could travel at 55km/h (34mph) for a range of 300km (186 miles). In addition it was armed with one 73mm (2.87in) smoothbore turret-mounted gun, a 7.62mm (0.3in) PKT machine gun, and one launcher rail for a Sagger ATGW. Such weaponry signalled the shift from the concept of a plain APC to the Mechanized Infantry Fighting Vehicle (MICV). Modern weaponry such as the ATGW and SAM missile systems made even the humble APC a realistic threat to the heaviest MBT or the most modern military aircraft.

Vehicles other than MBTs suddenly had significant combat potential. Nuclear ballistic missiles could be fired from transporter-erector-launcher vehicles such as the Russian Scud B or FROG-7. The Tomahawk Ground-Launched Cruise Missile (GLCM) system could strike at targets 2500km (1553 miles) away with an accuracy capable of striking single buildings. The steady development of self-propelled weapons such as Multiple Launch Rocket Systems has meant that infantry vehicles are now amongst the most powerful instruments of land warfare.

The post-war world also saw a transformation in military logistics, particularly with the advent of new engine and suspension technologies from the 1970s onwards. Many modern military trucks are capable of huge feats of transportation, benefiting from the development of turbocharged powerplants and all-wheel-drive multi-wheel configurations. The Faun SLT 50-2 Elefant, for example, can transport a Leopard 2 Main Battle Tank which weighs 54,981kg (120,960lb). Even smaller trucks now commonly have payloads of 10–15 tons. Their survivability is increased by features such as central tyre-pressure regulation, wheels with run-flat inserts, armoured cabs and mine-resistant chassis design.

A BMP-1 fires a Sagger AT-3 ATGW during training.

Today's military vehicles benefit from advanced vehicle technology, computerised warfare and navigation systems, and exceptional weaponry. One vehicle in particular demonstrates how far we have come. The U.S. Advanced Amphibious Assault Vehicle (AAAV) can travel at 47km/h (30mph) on water and requires no support ship to make amphibious manoeuvres. On land its road speed of 72km/h (45mph) and off-road manoeuvrability matches that of any MBT. Its Bushmaster II 30mm (1.18in) cannon with computerized fire-control system is a real threat to any soft-skinned or lightly armoured vehicle. Behind its advanced armour 18 fully equipped combat troops can travel in relative safety at high speed to the battlefield.

The AAAV represents the amazing technological advances reached by today's military vehicles. The IFV Dardo, Cadillac Cage ASV 150, and M4 C2V, amongst many others, represent similar levels of advance in their own

categories. The irony is that the survivability of military vehicles is more crucial than ever. A single infantryman can now carry weaponry powerful enough to destroy even an MBT. Airborne surveillance detects the slightest vehicular movement, relays the information to ground-attack aircraft, and has the vehicle destroyed by guided missile from well beyond visual range. The mechanization of armies is a constant process of trying to stay ahead of vehicle-destroying technologies. 'Stealth' armour, unmanned configurations, electronic countermeasures, more destructive weaponry and enhanced manoeuvrability may all become essential features of future infantry weapons if infantry mechanization is to remain viable.

A single rocket from a Multiple-Launch Rocket System (MLRS) distributes 644 submunition bomblets over an area of 0.23 sq. km (0.08 sq miles). A full salvo contains 12 such rockets.

An 8x8 USMC LAV-25 cuts through a water obstacle. The LAV-25 is fully amphibious, and is used for both reconnaissance and light combat duties.

Self-Propelled Artillery

Type 54-1

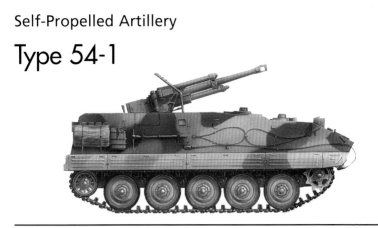

The Type 54-1 consists of a 122mm (4.8in) howitzer mounted on the chassis of the YW 531 armoured personnel carrier, though the Type 54-1 differs in that it has a fifth road wheel on each side. Armoured protection is provided by the shield from the howitzer's towed version. The gun itself is actually a copy of the Soviet M-30 122mm (4.8in) howitzer, an ageing weapon now obsolete amongst modern field artillery. With a maximum gun range of 11.8km (7.33 miles), the Type 54-1 is outclassed by most NATO and Russian artillery. Nonetheless, the simplicity of the Type 54-1 vehicle makes it a dependable weapon, though one now being replaced by the Type 85 self-propelled gun.

Country of origin:	China
Crew:	7 (max)
Weight:	15,400kg (34,000lb)
Dimensions:	Length: 5.65m (18.54ft); width: 3.06m (10.04ft); height: 2.68m (8.79ft)
Range:	500km (310 miles)
Armour:	Not available
Armament:	1 x 122mm (4.8in) howitzer
Powerplant:	1 x Deutz 6150L 6-cylinder diesel, 257hp (192kW)
Performance:	Maximum road speed: 56km/h (35mph)

M-77 Dana

The M-77 Dana is the principal self-propelled gun of the Czech Republic and Slovakia, and also serves in the Libyan and Polish armed forces. It utilizes the modified chassis of a Tatra 815 8x8 truck, but with an armoured cab. The engine is relocated to the rear of the truck and the vehicle has a central tyre-pressure regulation system. The gun is a 152mm (5.98in) howitzer with a range of 18.7km (11.61 miles) and ammunition types which include HE, APHE and smoke. Using base-bleed rounds more than doubles the range to nearly 40km (25 miles). Gun loading is an automatic process and three rounds per minute is the maximum rate of fire.

Country of origin:	Czech Republic/Slovakia
Crew:	4
Weight:	29,250kg (64,500lb)
Dimensions:	Length: (with gun) 10.4m (34.12ft); width: 2.97m (9.74ft); height: 3.52m (11.55ft)
Range:	740km (460 miles)
Armour:	12.7mm (0.5in)
Armament:	1 x 152mm (5.98in) howitzer
Powerplant:	1 x Tatra 2-939-34 12-cylinder diesel, developing 341hp (254kW)
Performance:	Maximum road speed: 80km/h (50mph); fording: 1.4m (4.6ft); gradient: 60 percent

Self-Propelled Artillery

F3

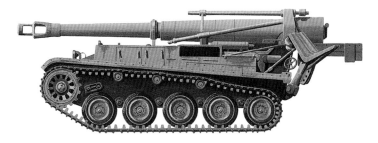

The F3 was a 155mm (6.1in) self-propelled howitzer developed by France in the early 1960s. Like most self-propelled weapons, it used the hull and chassis of a conventional tank – in this case the AMX-13. A space at the rear of the hull was used to mount a 155mm (6.1in) gun manufactured by Atelier de Construction de Tarbes. Depending on ammunition type, this weapon had a maximum range of 21.5km (13.35 miles) and a maximum rate of fire of three rounds per minute. Folding spades at the hull rear were set into the earth prior to firing. No ammunition was carried on board, so the F3 was accompanied by an AMX-VCI support vehicle.

Country of origin:	France
Crew:	2
Weight:	17,400kg (38,400lb)
Dimensions:	Length: 6.22m (20.4ft); width: 2.72m (8.92ft); height: 2.08m (6.82ft)
Range:	400km (250 miles)
Armour:	(Steel) 20mm (0.78in) maximum
Armament:	1 x 155mm (6.1in) howitzer
Powerplant:	1 x SOFAM 8Gxb 8-cylinder petrol, developing 250hp (186kW)
Performance:	Maximum road speed: 60km/h (37mph); fording: 0.65m (2.13ft); gradient: 50 percent; vertical obstacle: 0.6m (2ft); trench: 1.5m (4.9ft)

BAK 1906

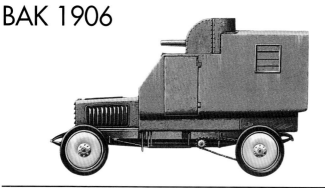

The Ballon-Abwehr-Kanonenwagen (BAK) 1906 was designed by the Ehrhardt company for use against enemy observation balloons in World War I. It was essentially a commercial truck chassis on which was mounted a 50mm (1.97in) cannon firing high-explosive shrapnel shells. The cannon was seated on a rotating turret with a 60 degree traverse and could engage static balloon targets up to several hundred metres in altitude. With the advent of aircraft observation, however, the BAK 1906 was upgraded to a 75mm (2.95in) cannon and became possibly the first self-propelled anti-aircraft vehicle, the BAK 1909. The open crew compartment made the BAK 1906 vulnerable to infantry fire.

Country of origin:	Germany
Crew:	5
Weight:	3200kg (7100lb)
Dimensions:	Length: 5.27m (17.29ft); width: 1.93m (6.33ft); height: 3.07m (10.07ft)
Range:	Not available
Armour:	Not available
Armament:	1 x 50mm (1.97in) cannon
Powerplant:	1 x Ehrhardt 4-cylinder petrol, developing 60hp (45kW)
Performance:	Maximum road speed: 45km/h (28mph)

SIG 33 auf Geschützwagen

The SIG 33 auf Geschützwagen was a self-propelled version of the Geschütz 55 150mm (5.9in) howitzer. In its first incarnation – the SIG 33 auf Geschützwagen I Ausf B – it was nothing more than a basic howitzer (including carriage and wheels) mounted on a turretless PzKpfw I tank. Extra armour plate was added for crew protection. The vehicle went through subsequent improvements, the most successful being the SIG 33 (Sf) auf PzKpfw 38 (t) Bison Sdkfz 138/1. This utilized the Czech PzKpfw 38(t) chassis, and the gun was set lower down into the chassis for greater stability. Introduced in 1943, this vehicle became the standard self-propelled gun of German mechanized infantry units.

Country of origin:	Germany
Crew:	4
Weight:	10,600kg (23,400lb)
Dimensions:	Length: 4.84m (15.88ft); width: 2.15m (7.05ft); height: 2.4m (7.87ft)
Range:	185km (115 miles)
Armour:	(Steel) 28mm (1.1in) maximum
Armament:	1 x Geschütz 55 150mm (5.9in) howitzer
Powerplant:	1 x Praga 6-cylinder petrol, developing 150hp (112kW)
Performance:	Maximum road speed: 35km/h (22mph); fording: 0.91m (3ft)

SdKfz 135/1 15cm Howitzer

The origins of the SdKfz 135/1 actually lay with a French vehicle, the Tracteur Blinde 37L (Lorraine). This served as a French armoured personnel carrier and artillery tractor, and a total of 315 were captured by the Germans when France was occupied in 1940. Initially the vehicles were converted into self-propelled anti-tank guns – the original crew compartment was removed and replaced by a gun shield and a PaK 40/1 L-46 75mm (2.95in) cannon. This vehicle was the SdKfz 135. The 135/1 variant was of similar construction but mounted a 150mm (5.9in) howitzer. All such converted vehicles suffered from thin upper armour, and the crews were especially vulnerable to artillery or air attack.

Country of origin:	Germany
Crew:	5
Weight:	8100kg (17,900lb)
Dimensions:	Length (with gun): 5.31m (17.42ft); width: 1.88m (6.17ft); height: 2.08m (6.82ft)
Range:	135km (85 miles)
Armour:	Not available
Armament:	1 x 150mm (5.9in) howitzer
Powerplant:	1 x Delahaye 103 TT diesel, developing 79hp (59kW)
Performance:	Maximum road speed: 34km/h (21mph)

Self-Propelled Artillery

Rascal

The Rascal is one of a new generation of lightweight fighting vehicles. Produced by Soltam Ltd of Israel, it is a 20-ton 155mm (6.1in) self-propelled howitzer, light enough to be airlifted by modern transport aircraft, including the C-130 Hercules. Its low weight is combined with a powerful engine to provide fast speeds both on- and off-road. When firing, two hydraulically powered spades drop down to the rear of the hull, and the gun is elevated on a turntable, also hydraulically powered. The howitzer has a range of 24km (15 miles). Rascal is armoured throughout, and has sophisticated features such as night-vision devices, armoured shutters for the windows and high-performance brakes.

Country of origin:	Israel
Crew:	4
Weight:	19,500kg (43,000lb)
Dimensions:	Length (with gun): 7.5m (24.6ft); width: 2.46m (8.07ft); height: 2.3m (7.55ft)
Range:	350km (220 miles)
Armour:	Not available
Armament:	1 x 155mm (6.1in) howitzer
Powerplant:	1 x diesel, developing 350hp (261kW)
Performance:	Maximum road speed: 50km/h (31mph); fording: 1.2m (3.9ft); gradient: 22 percent; vertical obstacle: 1m (3.3ft)

M41M90/53

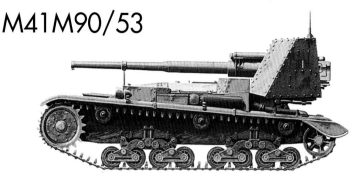

The Semovente M41M90/53 was one of several self-propelled guns developed by Italy during the early years of World War II. Its original purpose was as an anti-aircraft gun, but like the German 88mm (3.46in) Flak weapons it was equally useful against ground targets. The 90mm (3.54in) Model 39 cannon was set to the rear of an M14/41 chassis, the engine relocated to the front of the vehicle. An L.6 light tank accompanied the M41M90/53 as an ammunition resupply vehicle, carrying 26 rounds internally and another 40 in a trailer. The M41M90/53 saw most action in North Africa in 1941 and 1942, but after the Italian armistice, it continued in use in German hands in Italy's mountainous northern regions.

Country of origin:	Italy
Crew:	2
Weight:	17,000kg (37,500lb)
Dimensions:	Length: 5.21m (17.09ft); width: 2.20m (7.22ft); height: 2.15m (7.05ft)
Range:	200km (125 miles)
Armour:	25mm (0.98in)
Armament:	1 x Ansaldo Model 39 90mm (3.54in) cannon.
Powerplant:	1 x SPA 15-TM-41 8-cylinder petrol, developing 145hp (108kW)
Performance:	Maximum road speed: 35km/h (22mph)

Self-Propelled Artillery

2S7

The 2S7 is a massive vehicle stretching to 13.12m (43.04ft) when its long-barrelled 2A44 203mm (7.99in) gun is taken into account. Firing conventional ammunition, the gun has a range of over 37km (23 miles). Coping with the recoil of the 43kg (95lb) shells requires three recoil pistons with maximum travel of 140cm (55.11in). Unusually, no muzzle brake is fitted to the gun. Reloading is fully mechanized using a power-assisted loader. Two rounds per minute is the maximum rate of fire. The vehicle itself has the largest chassis of any Russian armoured vehicle, using seven rubber-tyred road wheels. Its engine sits at the rear, while the crew occupy an enclosed compartment at the front.

Country of origin:	Russia/Soviet Union
Crew:	7
Weight:	46,500kg (102,500lb)
Dimensions:	Length (with gun): 13.12m (43.04ft); width: 3.38m (11.09ft); height: 3m (9.8ft)
Range:	650km (400 miles)
Armour:	Not known
Armament:	1 x 2A44 203mm (7.99in) gun
Powerplant:	1 x V-46I 12-cylinder diesel, developing 839hp (626kW)
Performance:	Maximum road speed: 50km/h (31mph); fording: 1.2m (3.9ft); gradient: 22 percent; vertical obstacle: 1m (3.3ft)

SM-240

The SM-240 self-propelled mortar is a weapon unique to the former Soviet Union. Using the chassis of an SA-4 SAM launcher, Russian designers in the mid-1970s created a moving platform for a massive 2B8 240mm (9.45in) mortar, the vehicle requiring nine crew in total. The mortar is carried on the rear of the hull when in transit, but hydraulically lowered to the ground for firing (though the mortar remains connected to the vehicle). Two 20-round magazines feed the mortar through automatic breech-loading. Ammunition types include HE, fragmentation, smoke and even nuclear warheads. The 2B8 can fire a 131kg (289lb) shell just under 10km (6.2 miles).

Country of origin:	Russia/Soviet Union
Crew:	9
Weight:	27,500kg (60,600lb)
Dimensions:	Length: 7.94m (26.05ft); width: 3.25m (10.66ft); height: 3.22m (10.56ft)
Range:	500km (310 miles)
Armour:	15–20mm (0.59–0.78in)
Armament:	1 x 2B8 240mm (9.45in) mortar
Powerplant:	1 x V-59 12-cylinder diesel, 520hp (388kW)
Performance:	Maximum road speed 45km/h (28mph)

PRAM-S

The Slovakian PRAM-S, also known as the Vzor 85, is a 120mm (4.7in) self-propelled mortar. It is heavily influenced by Russian weapons carriers, and its chassis is that of the Soviet BMP-2 armoured personnel carrier lengthened to incorporate seven road wheels. The 120mm (4.7in) Model 1982 mortar is a potent weapon designed for sustained fire support. It can fire out to a range of 8000m (26,250ft) with a rate of fire of 18 to 20 rounds per minute via an automatic feeder. In addition, a 12.7mm (0.5in) NSV machine gun is mounted on the hull rear, while internally, the PRAM-S carries RPG-75 anti-tank rocket launchers and a 9K113 Konkurz ATGW.

Country of origin:	Slovakia
Crew:	4
Weight:	16,970kg (37,419lb)
Dimensions:	Length: 7.47m (24.5ft); width: 2.94m (9.65ft); height: 2.25m (7.38ft)
Range:	550km (340 miles)
Armour:	(Steel) 23mm (0.9in)
Armament:	1 x 120mm (4.7in) Model 1982 mortar; 1 x 12.7mm (0.5in) NSV MG; RPG-75 anti-tank rocket launchers; 9K113 Konkurz ATGW
Powerplant:	1 x UTD-40 6-cylinder diesel, 300hp (224kW)
Performance:	Maximum road speed: 63km/h (39mph); fording: amphibious; gradient: 60 percent; vertical obstacle: 0.9m (2.9ft); trench: 2.7m (8.9ft)

G6 Rhino

The G6 is a high-mobility, heavily armoured and technologically advanced 155mm (6.1in) self-propelled gun system from South Africa. Its gun can be used in both direct- and indirect-fire roles. Its direct-fire range is 3km (1.9 miles) and its indirect-fire range is 30km (19 miles). Mobility is provided by a purpose-built 6x6 vehicle with run-flat tyres and a central tyre-pressure control system. Turret and hull are both heavily armoured to resist small-arms fire, landmine explosions, and even 20mm (0.78in) cannon fire across the vehicle's 60 degree frontal arc. Full NBC protection is optional. Despite sophisticated features such as night-vision equipment and a muzzle-velocity analyser, export sales have not been good.

Country of origin:	South Africa
Crew:	6
Weight:	47,000kg (103,600lb)
Dimensions:	Length (chassis): 10.2m (33.4ft); width: 3.4m (11.2ft); height: 3.5m (11.5ft)
Range:	700km (430 miles)
Armour:	Not available
Armament:	1 x 155mm (6.1in) gun
Powerplant:	1 x diesel, developing 525hp (391kW)
Performance:	Maximum road speed: 90km/h (56mph); fording: 1m (3.3ft)

Birch Gun Mk II

The Birch Gun was the world's first effective example of self-propelled artillery. It was named after General Sir Noel Birch, Master General of the Ordnance, and it emerged from the Woolwich Arsenal as an experimental model in 1925. The Birch Gun consisted of an unmodified Vickers medium tank chassis on which was mounted an 18-pounder (83.8mm/3.3in) field gun. A second version, the Mk II of 1926, featured better elevation for the gun, allowing it to engage either ground or aerial targets. British high command response to the Birch Gun was not favourable, mainly from prejudice rather than reasoned complaint, and after a third version in 1928, the project was abandoned.

Country of origin:	United Kingdom
Crew:	6
Weight:	12,000kg (26,500lb)
Dimensions:	Length: 5.8m (19ft); width: 2.4m (7.9ft); height: 2.3m (7.6ft)
Range:	192km (119 miles)
Armour:	6mm (0.24in)
Armament:	1 x 75mm (2.95in) gun
Powerplant:	1 x Armstrong-Siddeley 8-cylinder petrol, developing 90hp (67 kW)
Performance:	Maximum road speed: 45km/h (28mph)

T19

The T19 was produced between 1941 and 1944. Its weapon was a 105mm (4.13in) M2A1 howitzer. This had a maximum range of 10,698m (35,097ft) and could fire HE, HEAT, smoke and illumination rounds. The gun was mounted on an M3 half-track to create the T19, and the vehicle chassis required considerable strengthening to cope with the impact of firing. Eight rounds of 105mm (4.13in) ammunition were carried on board, with more being transported in a towed trailer. The T19 saw service in North Africa, Italy and northern Europe, but it was replaced by the M7 GMC during 1944. Existing T19s were often stripped of their howitzers to supply the M7 and converted back to standard M3s.

Country of origin:	United States
Crew:	5 or 6
Weight:	10,500kg (23,150lb)
Dimensions:	Length: 6.18m (20.28ft); width: 2.22m (7.28ft); height: 2.55m (8.37ft)
Range:	282km (175 miles)
Armour:	(Steel) 13mm (0.51in) maximum
Armament:	1 x 105mm (4.13in) M2A1 howitzer
Powerplant:	1 x White 160AX 6-cylinder diesel, developing 128hp (95kW)
Performance:	Maximum road speed: 65km/h (40mph); fording: 0.81m (2.66ft)

Rocket Launchers

XLF-40

The XLF-40 is the largest rocket launcher in the Brazilian arsenal. The vehicular component is a modified version of the US M3A1 light tank chassis. Large numbers of M3s were sold to South America after World War II. In Brazil, 100 subsequently underwent conversion in the 1970s to create the X1A1 vehicle, a lengthened M3 with an additional road wheel. The X1A1 became the basis of the XLF-40. It carries three launcher rails mounting SS-60 missiles and extends three hydraulic stabilizing columns during launching to provide a rigid base. Each rocket weighs 595kg (1312lb), contains either a high explosive or submunition warhead and has a tactical range of 60km (37 miles).

Country of origin:	Brazil
Crew:	4
Weight:	17,070kg (37,639lb)
Dimensions:	Length 6.5m (21.3ft); width: 2.6m (8.5ft); height: 3.2m (10.5ft)
Range:	600km (370 miles)
Armour:	(Steel) 58mm (2.28in)
Armament:	3 x SS-60 rockets
Powerplant:	1 x Saab Scania DS-11 6-cylinder turbo diesel, developing 295hp (220 kW)
Performance:	Maximum road speed: 55km/h (34mph); fording: 1.3m (4.3ft); gradient: 60 percent; vertical obstacle: 0.8m (2.6ft)

Pluton

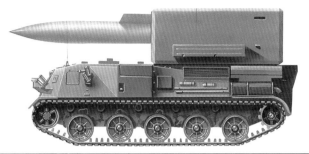

The Pluton is a short-range tactical nuclear weapons system developed by France in the late 1960s. During this period, defence disagreements with the United States and other NATO nations led France to concentrate on producing its own nuclear weaponry. The Pluton was a replacement for the US Honest John battlefield missile, and entered service in 1974. It was a 7.6m (24.9ft) long, 2400kg (5300lb) missile in a power-operated launcher box mounted on an AMX-30 main battle tank chassis. An accompanying Berliet 6x6 truck provided the fire-control centre. The missile had a range of up to 150km (90 miles) and was powered by a single-propellant rocket. Pluton systems were dismantled during the 1990s.

Country of origin:	France
Crew:	4
Weight:	36,000kg (79,400lb)
Dimensions:	Length (with rocket): 7.76m (25.46ft); width: 3.1m (10.17ft); height: 3.64m (11.94ft)
Range:	600km (370 miles)
Armour:	80mm (3.14in) max
Armament:	1 x short-range nuclear missile
Powerplant:	1 x Renault-Saviem HS110 12-cylinder diesel, developing 691hp (515kW)
Performance:	Maximum road speed: 65km/h (40mph); fording: 2m (6.5ft); gradient: 60 percent; vertical obstacle: 0.93m (3.05ft)

28/32cm Wurfkörper SdKfz 251

The Wurfkörper was one of the earliest German rocket systems, entering service in 1940. It offered two sizes of rocket, the Wurfkörper Spreng with a 28cm (11in) high-explosive rocket and the Wurfkörper M F1 50, a 32cm (12.6in) rocket with liquid incendiary warhead. Crude, inaccurate, and underpowered – maximum range was around 2000m (6600ft) – the rockets nonetheless proved useful in action, particularly in urban combat. Mobility for the Wurfkörper system was achieved by mounting the missiles in their packing crates on the side of a SdKfz 251 half-track. Aiming the rockets was a simple matter of aligning the vehicle with the target. The mobile Wurfkörper tended to operate within Panzer units.

Country of origin:	Germany
Crew:	Up to 12
Weight:	8000kg (17,600lb)
Dimensions:	Length: 5.8m (19ft); width: (without rockets) 2.1m (6.9ft); height: 1.75m (5.74ft)
Range:	300km (190 miles)
Armour:	(Steel) 15mm (0.59in)
Armament:	6 x 28cm (11in) or 32cm (12.6in) Wurfkörper rockets; 1 x MG
Powerplant:	1 x Maybach HL 42 6-cylinder petrol, developing 101hp (75kW)
Performance:	Maximum road speed: 53km/h (33mph); fording: 0.6m (2ft); gradient: 24 percent

LARS II

The Light Artillery Rocket System II (LARS II) was an upgrade to the 110mm (4.33in) LARS I which entered service with the West German Army in 1969. Whereas the LARS I rocket launcher was mounted on a simple 4x4 truck, the upgrade in 1980 placed it on the back of a MAN 6x6 truck and gave it an updated fire-control system. The weapon itself consists of two banks of launcher tubes situated side by side, each bank having 18 tubes. Munitions include DM-711 mine dispensers, DM-21 HE-fragmentation and DM-701 anti-tank mine dispenser. All 36 rockets can be fired in 17.5 seconds and have a maximum range of up to 14km (9 miles). A cab-mounted 7.62mm (0.3in) machine gun provides crew defence.

Country of origin:	Germany
Crew:	2
Weight:	19,100kg (42,100lb)
Dimensions:	Length: 8.26m (27.09ft); width: 2.49m (8.17ft); height: 2.99m (9.8ft)
Range:	450km (280 miles)
Armour:	Not applicable
Armament:	36 x 110mm (4.33in) rockets; 1 x 7.62mm (0.3in) MG
Powerplant:	1 x Deutz BF8L 413F V8 turbo diesel, developing 315hp (235kW)
Performance:	Maximum road speed: 90km/h (56mph)

Type 75

The Type 75 is the mobile rocket-launching version of the Type 73 Japanese armoured personnel carrier. This was developed in the late 1960s by Mitsubishi Industries, and became the standard armoured personnel carrier of the Japanese Ground Self-Defence Force. It has an all-welded hull made of lightweight aluminium armour. The conversion to rocket launcher took place in 1975. A 130mm (5.12in) hydraulically operated rocket-launching battery was mounted on the rear of the hull. In addition, a Type 75 ground-wind measuring vehicle was developed to operate alongside the attack system. It is fitted with a 12.5m (41ft) vertical mast for measuring wind speeds up to 30km/h (19mph).

Country of origin:	Japan
Crew:	3
Weight:	16,500kg (36,400lb)
Dimensions:	Length: 5.78m (18.96ft); width: 2.8m (9.19ft); height: 2.67m (8.76ft)
Range:	300km (190 miles)
Armour:	Aluminium (details classified)
Armament:	1 x 130mm (5.12in) rocket-launcher system
Powerplant:	1 x Mitsubishi 4ZF 4-cylinder diesel, developing 300hp (224kW) at 2200rpm
Performance:	Maximum road speed: 53km/h (33mph); fording: amphibious; gradient: 60 percent; vertical obstacle: 0.7m (2.3ft); trench: 2m (6.6ft)

BM-13

The BM-13, or 'Katyusha', consisted of a battery of 16 M-13 fin-stabilized rockets which could be launched over a 8500m (27,900ft) maximum range. Though individually inaccurate, as an area saturation weapon the rockets created a terrifying HE salvo. The missiles were launched from a simple iron rail system mounted on the back of a truck and manually targeted. The first truck used in this role was the Russian ZiS-5 (pictured here), of which over 83,000 units were produced between 1942 and 1945. As the war went on, Katyushas were mounted on any available truck, including the Russian ZiS-6 STZ-5 artillery tractor, and US Lend-Lease Fords, Studebakers and Chevrolets.

Country of origin:	Soviet Union
Crew:	2
Weight:	8900kg (19,600lb)
Dimensions:	Length: 6.55m (21.49ft); width: 2.24m (7.35ft); height: 2.76m (9.06ft)
Range:	370km (230 miles)
Armour:	Not applicable
Armament:	16 x 132mm (5.2in) M-13 rockets
Powerplant:	1 x Hercules JXD 6-cylinder petrol, developing 87hp (65kW)
Performance:	Maximum road speed: 72km/h (45mph)

BM-31-12 on ZiS-6

In late 1942, the M-31 rocket was introduced to enhance the performance of the earlier M-8 and M-13 weapons. These were deemed to contain too little explosive force, so whereas the M-13 had a 4.9kg (10.8lb) warhead, the M-31 contained 28.9kg (63.7lb) of explosive. Mobile launchers for the M-31 did not emerge until March 1944. The best vehicles for the job were ZiS-6 6x6 or Studebaker US-6 6x6 trucks. Twelve rockets were held in the rack mounted upon the rear. While the US trucks received armoured shutters to protect the cab windows during firing, the Soviet vehicles tended to be naked against the backblast. Over 1200 BM-31-12s were produced in 1944 alone, and another 600 in 1945.

Country of origin:	Russia/Soviet Union
Crew:	2
Weight:	8900kg (19,600lb)
Dimensions:	Length: 6.55m (21.49ft); width: 2.24m (7.35ft); height: 3.2m (10.49ft)
Range:	350km (220 miles)
Armour:	Not applicable
Armament:	1 x M31 rocket-launcher system
Powerplant:	1 x 6-cylinder petrol, developing 87hp (65kW)
Performance:	Maximum road speed: 70km/h (43mph)

FROG-7

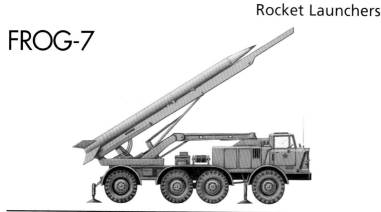

The ZIL-135 has become one of Russia's most successful missile-launch vehicles, exported to Algeria, Egypt, Cuba, Iraq, North Korea, Yemen, Yugoslavia and many other countres. It was chosen to carry battlefield missile systems because its 8x8 configuration gives decent off-road mobility, and also because it is relatively cheap at around $25,000 (£15,600) per vehicle. The FROG-7 is the last unguided nuclear-capable battlefield rocket produced by the Soviet Union, and has a range of up to 69km (43 miles). The circular error probability of the rocket is 500–700m (1650–2300ft). Having entered service in 1965, FROG-7s are now mostly replaced in the Russian Federation by the guided SS-21.

Country of origin:	Russia/Soviet Union
Crew:	4
Weight:	20,300kg (44,900lb)
Dimensions:	Length: 10.69m (35.07ft); width: 2.8m (9.19ft); height (with missile): 3.35m (11ft)
Range:	650km (400 miles)
Armour:	Not applicable
Armament:	1 x FROG-7 rocket
Powerplant:	2 x ZIL-375 8-cylinder petrol, each developing 177hp (132kW)
Performance:	Maximum road speed: 40km/h (25mph)

SS-1c Scud B Launcher

The Scud B is a medium-range tactical missile with nuclear or conventional high-explosive warheads. Introduced in 1961, it has a poor operational record. Its gyroscopic guidance system is only active for the first 80 seconds of flight. After this period, the warhead detaches and makes an unguided flight to the target at speeds of up to Mach 9. The Scud is consequently extremely inaccurate, as was demonstrated by Iraqi Scud attacks against Israeli cities during the Gulf War. A single Scud is carried on a modified MAZ-543 truck acting as a transporter-erector-launcher. Initially a JS-3 tracked chassis was used, but the MAZ-543 was introduced from 1965 to give improved off-road mobility.

Country of origin:	Russia/Soviet Union
Crew:	4
Weight:	37,400kg (82,500lb)
Dimensions:	Length: 13.36m (43.83ft); width: 3.02m (9.91ft); height: 3.33m (10.93ft)
Range:	450km (280 miles)
Armour:	Not applicable
Armament:	1 x Scud B tactical ballistic missile
Powerplant:	1 x D12A-525A 12-cylinder diesel, developing 525hp (391kW) at 2100rpm
Performance:	Maximum road speed: 45km/h (28mph)

BM-22 Uragan

The BM-22 Uragan was one of the later generation of Soviet multiple rocket launchers. It entered active service with Soviet artillery regiments and tank units in the mid-1970s. Sixteen missiles can be launched in one salvo, the number of launch tubes configured 4-6-6 from top to bottom of the three-layer stack. Reloading the entire system takes around 20 minutes. Transportation is provided by a ZIL-135 8x8 truck chassis. Designed in the ZIL Moscow Automobile Plant, the ZIL-135 was produced for various battlefield haulage tasks, particularly missile carriage. It carried the Soviet Union's first tactical battlefield missile system, the Luna, as well as the Uragan MLRS, and features a 70-ton carrying capacity.

Country of origin:	Russia/Soviet Union
Crew:	4
Weight:	20,000kg (44,100lb)
Dimensions:	Length: 9.63m (31.59ft); width: 2.8m (9.19ft); height: 3.22m (10.56ft)
Range:	570km (350 miles)
Armour:	Not applicable
Armament:	16 x 220mm (8.66in) rockets
Powerplant:	2 x ZIL-375 8-cylinder petrol, each developing 177hp (132kW)
Performance:	Maximum road speed: 65km/h (40mph)

Rocket Launchers

DR-3 Reys

The DR-3 unmanned aerial reconnaissance vehicle (UAV) was developed by the Tupolev aircraft company in the early 1970s. It is launched from the back of an 8x8 BAZ-135 TZM transloader vehicle. The UAV is contained in a cylindrical container mounted on the back of the lorry. This is raised to an angle of around 35 degrees for launching, a booster jet ejecting the UAV from the container for 550m (1800ft) before the DR-3's main jet ignites. The DR-3 flies for 150km (90 miles) at which point the main engine cuts out and the aircraft descends to earth by parachute. Intelligence is gathered by a PA-1 wet-film camera or a Chibis-B television camera mounted in the nose at the aircraft.

Country of origin:	Russia/Soviet Union
Crew:	3
Weight:	15,000kg (33,100lb)
Dimensions:	Length: 11.5m (37.73ft); width: 3m (9.84ft); height: 3.35m (11ft)
Range:	500km (310 miles)
Armour:	Not applicable
Armament:	Not applicable
Powerplant:	2 x ZIL-375 8-cylinder petrol, each developing 177hp (132kW)
Performance:	Maximum road speed: 70km/h (43mph)

SS-23 Spider

The SS-23 Spider was a tactical ballistic missile deployed in 1985, but scrapped in 1989 under the Intermediate-Range and Shorter-Range Nuclear Forces (INF) Treaty. Destroyed with them were the SS-23s' transport-erector-launcher vehicles – modified BAZ-6944 8x8 trucks. Unusually for mobile tactical-missile launchers, the BAZ-6944 was fully amphibious and could travel at 10km/h (6mph) in the water. On land, its maximum speed was 70km/h (43mph) and a central tyre-pressure regulation system allowed it to maintain good cross-country speeds. In a four-year service life, 239 SS-23s were produced. With a range of 500km (310 miles) and accurate to 100m (328ft), the SS-23s were of genuine concern to NATO forces.

Country of origin:	Russia/Soviet Union
Crew:	3
Weight:	29,000kg (63,900lb)
Dimensions:	Length: 11.76m (38.58ft); width: 3.19m (10.47ft); height: 3m (9.84ft)
Range:	1000km (620 miles)
Armour:	Not available
Armament:	1 x SS-23 ballistic missile
Powerplant:	1 x UTD-25 8-cylinder diesel, developing 394hp (294kW)
Performance:	Maximum road speed: 70km/h (43mph)

Rocket Launchers

9A52 Smerch

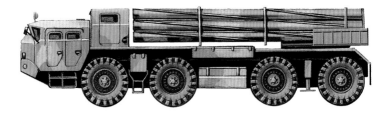

The 9A52 Smerch is Russia's equivalent to the US Multiple Launch Rocket System. Twelve launch tubes can fire salvos of 300mm (11.81in) rockets to distances of 70km (43 miles). Specialist munitions include the Bazalt parachute-retarded warhead which hangs in the air, detects armoured targets and shoots a 1kg (2.2lb) penetrator through the weaker upper armour. The Smerch is carried on a MAZ-543 series 8x8 truck. This vehicle was developed from the MAZ-535/537 series as a specialist carrier vehicle for missile and rocket systems such as the SS-1 Scud and SS-3 Scaleboard. For its size, the MAZ-543 has good cross-country capability owing to ground clearance of 0.45m (1.48ft).

Country of origin:	Russia/Soviet Union
Crew:	4
Weight:	43,700kg (96,400lb)
Dimensions:	Length: 12.1m (39.7ft); width: 3.05m (10ft); height: 3.05m (10ft)
Range:	850km (530 miles)
Armour:	Not applicable
Armament:	12 x 300mm (11.81in) rockets
Powerplant:	1 x D12A-525 12-cylinder diesel, developing 517hp (386kW)
Performance:	Maximum road speed: 60km/h (37mph)

Honest John

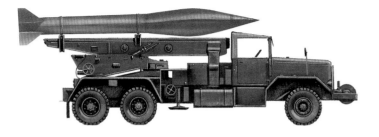

The Douglas MGR-1A Honest John was the earliest of the US tactical battlefield nuclear weapons. It received its first test firing in 1951 at the White Sands testing range and entered service two years later. Both the MGR-1A and the improved MGR-1B (introduced in 1960) were unguided rockets used in a similar manner to conventional tube artillery. Range was up to 19km (12 miles). Besides 2-, 20-, or 40-kiloton W31 nuclear warheads, conventional warheads could be fitted, including 680kg (1500lb) HE and 564kg (1243lb) chemical. The Honest John was launched from the chassis of a 6x6 truck TEL vehicle. Being an unguided missile, it was fired from a simple hydraulically raised rail.

Country of origin:	United States
Crew:	3
Weight:	16,400kg (36,200lb)
Dimensions:	Length: 9.89m (32.45ft); width: 2.9m (9.51ft); height: 2.67m (8.76ft)
Range:	480km (300 miles)
Armour:	Not applicable
Armament:	4 x tactical battlefield missiles supplied from independent transport truck
Powerplant:	1 x AM General 6-cylinder petrol, developing 139hp (104kW)
Performance:	Maximum road speed: 90km/h (56mph)

Pershing

The Martin Marietta MGM-31A Pershing tactical nuclear missile was conceived in 1958 and introduced in 1963. Its primary purpose was to deliver 60- to 400-kiloton W50 airburst nuclear warheads at ranges of between 160 and 740km (100 and 460 miles). Initially, deployment of the Pershing was made using an M474 tracked launch vehicle. On firing, this would hydraulically raise the missile into position and extend a blast plate with two hydraulic stabilizers out of the rear of the vehicle. In 1985, when the MGM-31B Pershing II was introduced, the launcher vehicle was changed to an M656 series truck with faster road speed. Under nuclear weapon treaties, the last Pershings were destroyed in 1991.

Country of origin:	United States
Crew:	1
Weight:	8100kg (17,900lb)
Dimensions:	Length (with rocket): 10.6m (34.78ft); width: 2.5m (8.2ft); height: 3.79m (12.43ft)
Range:	320km (200 miles)
Armour:	Not applicable
Armament:	1 x Pershing tactical nuclear missile
Powerplant:	1 x Chrysler A-710-B 8-cylinder petrol, developing 215hp (160kW)
Performance:	Maximum road speed: 65km/h (40mph)

Lance

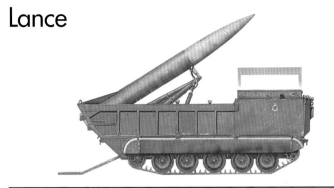

The Vought MGM-52C Lance entered the US arsenal as the replacement for the Honest John and Sergeant battlefield missiles in 1972. Between then and 1992, when the Lance was phased out of service, it relied upon two vehicles: the M752 launch vehicle and the M688 loader-transporter. Both were built upon the M548 cargo carrier, in turn developed from the chassis of the M113 armoured personnel carrier. The M548 was produced as a general support vehicle for the US Army Signal Corps. It had fully amphibious capabilities and was equipped with night-vision equipment for the driver. The design has proved sound, and is still in production in the US and in service around the world in differing configurations and variants.

Country of origin:	United States
Crew:	1 + 3
Weight:	8300kg (18,300lb)
Dimensions:	Length: 6.55m (21.49ft); width: 2.69m (8.83ft); height: 2.72m (8.92ft)
Range:	480km (300 miles)
Armour:	44mm (1.73in)
Armament:	1 x tactical nuclear missile
Powerplant:	1 x Detroit-Diesel Model 6V-53 6-cylinder diesel, developing 215hp (160kW)
Performance:	Maximum road speed: 64km/h (40mph); fording: amphibious; gradient: 60 percent; vertical obstacle: 0.61m (2ft); trench: 1.68m (5.52ft)

MLRS

The Vought Multiple Launch Rocket System (MLRS) is amongst the most powerful land weapons of NATO forces today. Using the chassis of the M2 Infantry Fighting Vehicle, Vought created a Self-Propelled Launcher Loader (SPLL) vehicle which mounted 12 M26 unguided free-flight rockets in two six-missile pods (together known as the M270 launcher unit). Each standard rocket contains 644 M77 submunitions which scatter widely over the area of impact. Consequently, each M26 is able to assault an area of 0.23 sq km (0.09 sq miles). During the Gulf War, Iraqi units nicknamed the MLRS 'steel rain' on account of its terrible inescapability. Other warheads include biological or chemical munitions and anti-tank mines.

Country of origin:	United States
Crew:	3
Weight:	25,191kg (55,546lb)
Dimensions:	Length: 6.8m (21.31ft); width: 2.92m (9.58ft); height: 2.6m (8.53ft)
Range:	480km (300 miles)
Armour:	Details classified
Armament:	12 x MLRS rockets
Powerplant:	1 x Cummins VTA-903 8-cylinder turbo diesel, developing 500hp (373kW)
Performance:	Maximum road speed: 64km/h (40mph); fording: 1.1m (3.6ft); gradient: 60 percent; vertical obstacle: 1m (3.3ft)

BMG-109 Tomahawk GLCM

The BMG-109 Tomahawk cruise missile was developed in the 1970s by General Dynamics, and successfully submarine-launched in 1981. Land- and air-launched variants were subsequently produced, the Ground-Launched Cruise Missile (GLCM) entering service in 1983. The GLCM is a towed launcher unit capable of firing four Tomahawks from a 2500km (1550-mile) range. Even at this distance, the Tomahawk will hug the terrain throughout its flight using TERRCOM (Terrain Contour Matching) and DSMAC (Digital Scene Matching Area Correlation) systems. The launcher vehicle is commonly towed by a MAN Cat I AI 8x8 truck. These vehicles also carry Patriot missile systems and Roland air defence missile systems.

Country of origin:	United States
Crew:	4
Weight:	(Vehicle only) 13,400kg (29,550lb)
Dimensions:	Length: (vehicle only) 10.27m (33.7ft); width: 2.5m (8.2ft); height: 2.93m (9.61ft)
Range:	600km (370 miles)
Armour:	Not applicable
Armament:	4 x BMG-109 Tomahawk cruise missiles
Powerplant:	1 x Deutz BF8L 413 8-cylinder turbo diesel, developing 339hp (253kW)
Performance:	Maximum road speed: 90km/h (56mph)

M-77 Oganj

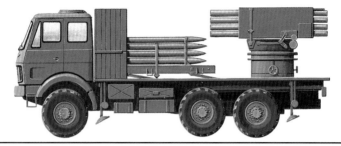

The M-77 Oganj consists of a YMRL 32 (Yugoslav Multiple Rocket Launcher, 32-barrel) rocket system mounted on the back of a FAP-2026 6x6 truck. Each M-77 rocket carries a 19.5kg (43lb) high-explosive warhead which it fires to a distance of 20km (12.5 miles). A full salvo can devastate an area 167 x 213m (548 x 699ft). The truck can carry 32 missiles preloaded in the launcher tubes, and another 32 in a reloading pack just behind the cab. The Oganj has recently received a new M-91 cluster-warhead missile, which dramatically increases the kill zone for a single salvo. Each missile contains 48 bomblets or four anti-tank mines. The new warheads were combat tested during the civil war in Yugoslavia.

Country of origin:	Yugoslavia
Crew:	5
Weight:	22,400kg (49,400lb)
Dimensions:	Length: 11.5m (37.56ft); width: 2.49m (8.17ft); height: 3.1m (10.17ft)
Range:	600km (370 miles)
Armour:	Not applicable
Armament:	32 + 32 x M-77 or M-91 rockets; 1 x 12.7mm (0.5in) MG
Powerplant:	1 x 8-cylinder diesel, developing 256hp (191kW)
Performance:	Maximum road speed: 80km/h (50mph)

VBL

By definition, the Panhard Véhicule Blindé Léger (Lightly Armoured Vehicle) is technically an armoured scout car, but tank-hunting capabilities were a major part of its design brief. A single Anti-tank Guided Weapon (ATGW) is mounted on the roof and operated by the crew member using a roof hatch. The ATGW is usually a MILAN, but TOW and HOT missile systems are also used. Other armament includes a 7.62mm (0.3in) GPMG as standard, and a Mistral SAM launcher as an option. The VBL is fully amphibious and features lightweight steel armour 11.5mm (0.45in) thick. The driver has night-vision devices and the ability to control tyre pressure from a central console.

Country of origin:	France
Crew:	3
Weight:	3550kg (7828lb)
Dimensions:	Length: 3.87m (12.69ft); width: 2.02m (6.63ft); height: 1.7m (5.58ft)
Range:	600km (370 miles)
Armour:	(Steel) 11.5mm (0.45in)
Armament:	1 x MILAN ATGW; 1 x 7.62mm (0.3in) GPMG
Powerplant:	1 x Peugeot XD3T 4-cylinder turbo diesel, developing 105hp (78kW) at 4150rpm
Performance:	Maximum road speed: 95km/h (59mph); fording: 0.9m (2.9ft); gradient: 50 percent; trench: 0.5m (1.6ft)

Anti-tank vehicles

Raketenjadgpanzer 1

The Raketenjadgpanzer 1 was a ground-breaking anti-tank vehicle which entered service with the German Federal Armed Forces in 1961. It was a combination of a Hispano-Suiza HS-30 chassis used for the Schützenpanzer SPz 12-3 APC, and two French SS-11 ATGW launchers. When one missile was ready to fire, the other would be withdrawn inside the hull for rearming (this explains why only one launcher is visible in pictures). The SS-11 missile has a range of 3000m (9800ft). It is guided to its target using wire-command, which is controlled by a crew member using a periscope. Mobile ATGW launchers were a new concept in warfare at this time, and the Raketenjadgpanzer 1 had a large impact on military thinking.

Country of origin:	Germany
Crew:	4
Weight:	13,000kg (28,665lb)
Dimensions:	Length: 5.56m (18.24ft); width: 2.25m (7.38ft); height: 1.7m (5.58ft)
Range:	270km (170 miles)
Armour:	(Steel) 30mm (1.18in)
Armament:	10 x SS-11 ATGWs
Powerplant:	1 x Rolls-Royce B81 Mk80F 8-cylinder petrol, developing 235hp (175kW) at 3800rpm
Performance:	Maximum road speed: 51km/h (32mph); fording: 0.7m (2.3ft); gradient: 60 percent; vertical obstacle: 0.6m (2ft); trench: 1.6m (5.2ft)

Raketenjadgpanzer 2

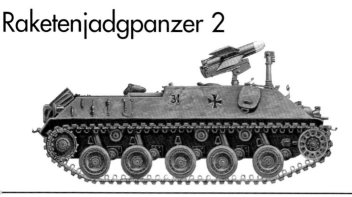

The Raketenjadgpanzer 2 (RJPZ 2) replaced its predecessor, the RJPZ 1, in 1967, using updated missile technology and boasting improved vehicle performance. The same SS-11 ATGW missile launchers were fitted, though the vehicle could carry 14 missiles as opposed to the 10 carried by the RJPZ 1. TOW and HOT ATGWs could also be fitted. Two SS-11 launchers at the front of the hull created a 180-degree arc of traverse to the front of the vehicle. A 7.62mm (0.3in) MG3 machine gun was mounted on the top right-hand side of the hull, and another in the bow. The hull itself was the same as that used for the Jadgpanzer Kanone 4-5 self-propelled anti-tank gun.

Country of origin:	Germany
Crew:	4
Weight:	23,000kg (50,700lb)
Dimensions:	Length: 6.43m (21.09ft); width: 2.98m (9.78ft); height: 2.15m (7.05ft)
Range:	400km (250 miles)
Armour:	(Steel) 50mm (1.97in)
Armament:	14 x SS-11 ATGWs; 2 x 7.62mm (0.3in) MG3 MGs
Powerplant:	1 x Daimler-Benz MB 837A 8-cylinder diesel, developing 500hp (373kW) at 2000rpm
Performance:	Maximum road speed: 70km/h (43mph); fording: 1.4m (4.6ft); gradient: 60 percent; vertical obstacle: 0.75m (2.46ft); trench: 2m (6.6ft)

Jadgpanzer Jaguar 1 and 2

The Jadgpanzer Jaguar 1 self-propelled anti-tank vehicle was the result of the standardized upgrading of the Raketenjadgpanzer 2 to accommodate more advanced anti-tank missile technologies. Chassis structure remained the same – that of the Jadgpanzer Kanone 4-5 self-propelled anti-tank gun – though the glacis plate received extra armour to protect against modern MBT shells. The SS-11 missiles were exchanged for the new Euromissile K3S HOT ATGW. HOT is a command-to-line-of-sight system with an effective range of 4000m (13,100ft), and has penetrative capability even against modern explosive-reactive armour. The Jaguar 2 was simply the Jaguar 1 fitted with a TOW ATGW instead of the HOT.

Country of origin:	Germany
Crew:	4
Weight:	25,500kg (56,200lb)
Dimensions:	Length: 6.61m (21.69ft); width: 3.12m (10.24ft); height: 2.55m (8.37ft)
Range:	400km (250 miles)
Armour:	(Steel) 50mm (1.97in) maximum
Armament:	1 x HOT ATGW system; 1 x 7.62mm (0.3in) MG3 MG
Powerplant:	1 x Daimler-Benz MB837A 8-cylinder diesel, developing 500hp (373kW) at 2000rpm
Performance:	Maximum road speed: 70km/h (43mph); fording: 1.4m (4.6ft); gradient: 60 percent; vertical obstacle: 0.75m (2.46ft); trench: 2m (6.6ft)

Wiesel TOW

The Wiesel was specifically designed to be air-portable, and consequently weighs in at only 2750kg (6063lb) and measures a mere 3.26m (10.69ft) in length. It was mainly designed to carry the Hughes TOW 1 ATGW weapon, and so give air-landed units immediate anti-armour support. Eight TOW missiles are carried on board, with two set for immediate use. The TOW 1 is the standard ATGW used by over 20 nations worldwide. It is a wire-guided missile with a range of up to 3750m (12,300ft) and has the ability to defeat most MBT armour using High-Explosive Anti-tank (HEAT) warheads. Because of its small size and low weight, the Wiesel can reach speeds of 80km/h (50mph) even in off-road environments.

Country of origin:	Germany
Crew:	3
Weight:	2750kg (6063lb)
Dimensions:	Length: 3.26m (10.7ft); width: 1.82m (5.97ft); height: 1.89m (6.2ft)
Range:	200km (125 miles)
Armour:	Not available
Armament:	1 x TOW 1 ATGW system
Powerplant:	1 x Volkswagen Type 069 5-cylinder turbo diesel, developing 98hp (73kW)
Performance:	Maximum road speed: 80km/h (50mph); gradient: 60 percent; vertical obstacle: 0.4m (1.3ft); trench: 1.5m (4.9ft)

Centauro

The Centauro is officially described as a tank hunter. Its armour, however, is light compared to an MBT, and a Centauro crew would rarely tackle an enemy tank in open battle. On top of an IVECO chassis is an OTOBREDA turret armed with a 105mm (4.13in) gun. This weapon is capable of penetrating over 700mm (27.56in) of armour at a range of around 2000m (6550ft) using armour-piercing fin-stabilized discarding-sabot (APFSDS) rounds. Gun handling and targeting are assisted by laser range-finding and a fully computerized fire control system like that used on the Ariete MBT. As an 8x8 vehicle, the Centauro has good off-road mobility assisted by hydropneumatic suspension and central tyre-pressure regulation.

Country of origin:	Italy
Crew:	4
Weight:	25,000kg (55,100lb)
Dimensions:	Length (with gun): 8.55m (28.05ft); width: 2.95m (9.68ft); height: 2.73m (8.96ft)
Range:	800km (500 miles)
Armour:	Steel (details classified)
Armament:	1 x 105mm (4.13in) gun; 1 x 7.62mm (0.3in) coaxial MG; 1 x 7.62mm (0.3in) AA MG; 2 x 4 smoke grenade launchers
Powerplant:	1 x Iveco MTCA 6-cylinder turbo diesel, developing 520hp (388kW)
Performance:	Maximum speed: 108km/h (67mph); fording: 1.5m (4.9ft); gradient: 60 percent; vertical obstacle: 0.55m (1.8ft); trench: 1.2m (3.9ft)

Type 60

Despite showing its age compared to modern ATGW launchers, the Komatsu Type 60 is still in service with the Japanese Ground Self Defence Force, though its future is uncertain. Its main tank-hunting armament comprises of two RCL 106mm (4.17in) recoilless rifles mounted on top of a low-tracked carrier. The guns are only able to traverse 10 degrees either side, so much targeting is reliant upon the driver aligning the vehicle with the target. The effective range of the RCL weapon is a little over 1000m (3280ft). Even with HEAT warheads, the Type 60 is really only suitable for engaging light armoured vehicles rather than modern MBTs, as the penetrative power of the 106mm (4.17in) gun is generally inadequate.

Country of origin:	Japan
Crew:	3
Weight:	8000kg (17,600lb)
Dimensions:	Length: 4.3m (14.1ft); width: 2.23m (7.32ft); height: 1.59m (5.22ft)
Range:	130km (80 miles)
Armour:	(Steel) 12mm (0.47in)
Armament:	2 x RCL 106mm (4.17in) recoilless rifles; 1 x 12.7mm (0.5in) MG
Powerplant:	1 x Komatsu 6T 120-2 6-cylinder diesel, developing 120hp (89kW) at 2400rpm
Performance:	Maximum road speed: 55km/h (34mph); fording: 0.7m (2.3ft) gradient: 60 percent; vertical obstacle: 0.6m (2ft); trench: 1.8m (5.9ft)

Anti-tank vehicles

Panzerjäger 90

The MOWAG Piranha APC has produced many specialist variants since it entered production in 1976. In 1989, an ATGW launcher version was introduced in the Piranha's 6x6 configuration, and acted as a replacement for the Swiss Army's 106mm (4.17in) recoilless rifle carriers. Called the Panzerjäger 90, the first versions were armed with a single Tube-Launched Optically Tracked Wire-Guided (TOW) 2 ATGW, but subsequent versions have received a turret-mounted twin TOW launcher. The commander of the vehicle can stand between the two launchers via a hatch, though the missiles can be launched with all crew inside the vehicle. The TOW 2 missile has a range of 4000m (13,100ft) and armour penetration of 800mm (31.5in) in its latest models.

Country of origin:	Switzerland
Crew:	5
Weight:	11,000kg (24,300lb)
Dimensions:	Length: 6.23m (20.44ft); width: 2.5m (8.2ft); height: 2.97m (9.74ft)
Range:	600km (370 miles)
Armour:	10mm (0.39in)
Armament:	1 x 76.2mm (3in) cannon; 1 x 7.62mm (0.3in) coaxial MG
Powerplant:	1 x Detroit Diesel 6V-53T 6-cylinder diesel, developing 215hp (160kW)
Performance:	Maximum road speed: 102km/h (63mph); fording: amphibious; gradient: 60 percent; vertical obstacle: 0.5m (1.6ft)

FV102 Striker

The FV102 Striker is actually a turretless Scorpion reconnaissance vehicle, its turret replaced by a hydraulically raised launcher box containing five BAC Swingfire anti-tank guided weapons. Five further missiles are stored internally. The Swingfire has an effective range of 4000m (13,100ft). The missile controller of the FV102 uses an Automatic Command Line of Site (ACLOS) system to target an enemy vehicle, at which point the launcher box is raised to a 35-degree angle before firing. Guidance during flight is by command wire. Eight periscopes provide good all-round visibility when the vehicle is in hatch-down position, and the missile controller has a x1 and x10 power monocular sight. The FV102 went into production in 1975.

Country of origin:	United Kingdom
Crew:	3
Weight:	8221kg (18,127lb)
Dimensions:	Length: 4.76m (15.62ft); width: 2.18m (7.15ft); height: 2.21m (7.25ft)
Range:	483km (300 miles)
Armour:	Classified
Armament:	5 + 5 x Swingfire anti-tank missiles; 1 x 7.62mm (0.3in) MG
Powerplant:	1 x Jaguar J60 No.1 Mk100B 6-cylinder petrol, developing 195hp (145kW)
Performance:	Maximum road speed: 100km/h (60mph); fording: 1m (3.3ft); gradient: 60 percent; vertical obstacle: 0.6m (2ft)

M50 Ontos

The M50 Ontos was a tank destroyer designed mainly for use as an air-portable vehicle for the US Marine Corps. Its chassis was developed in the early 1950s by GMC, and its weaponry consisted of six RCL 106mm (4.17in) recoilless rifles, three mounted either side of a small central turret. Attached to the top four guns were 12.7mm (0.5in) spotting rifles. These would fire tracer rounds to assist targeting. Six 106mm (4.17in) rounds were pre-loaded and a further eight were kept inside the vehicle. A major disadvantage of the M50 was that the rifles could only be reloaded from the outside, thus exposing the crew to small arms fire. Production ceased in 1970.

Country of origin:	United States
Crew:	3
Weight:	8640kg (19,051lb)
Dimensions:	Length: 3.82m (12.53ft); width: 2.6m (8.53ft); height: 2.13m (6.99ft)
Range:	240km (150 miles)
Armour:	13mm (0.51in) maximum
Armament:	6 x RCL 106mm (4.17in) recoilless rifles; 4 x 12.7mm (0.5in) M8C spotting rifles
Powerplant:	1 x General Motors 302 petrol, developing 145hp (108kW)
Performance:	Maximum road speed: 48km/h (30mph)

M901

The 1970s and 1980s saw many military forces combining APCs with ATGW weapons systems. In the United States, the enormously successful M113A1 APC received its ATGW upgrade in the mid-1970s, and the M901 entered production in 1978. The vehicle body is the standard APC model, but mounted with the two-tube M27 TOW 2 cupola on the roof. The M901 must come to a stop before it can fire, though it only takes 20 seconds for the TOW system to target and fire. Two TOW missiles are pre-loaded and 10 more are carried internally. Reloading only takes around 40 seconds, the rear of the cupola sinking down to the hull for the convenience and protection of the crew.

Country of origin:	United States
Crew:	4 or 5
Weight:	11,794kg (26,005lb)
Dimensions:	Length: 4.88m (16.01ft); width: 2.68m (8.79ft); height: 3.35m (10.99ft)
Range:	483km (300 miles)
Armour:	(Aluminium) 44mm (1.73in)
Armament:	1 x TOW 2 ATGW system
Powerplant:	1 x Detroit Diesel 6V-53N 6-cylinder diesel, developing 215hp (160kW)
Performance:	Maximum road speed: 68km/h (42mph); fording: amphibious; gradient: 60 percent; vertical obstacle: 0.61m (2ft); trench: 1.68m (5.51ft)

Austro-Daimler

Developed in 1904, the Austro-Daimler armoured car was the first military application of four-wheel drive. Typical of the period, it combines a standard car chassis with crude bolt-on armour, in the Austro-Daimler's case 4mm (0.16in) thick. The engine was situated in the front of the vehicle with the driver sitting just behind using a viewing slit in the frontal armour for visibility. Combat potential was provided by a Maxim machine gun or, in later models, two Schwarzlose machine guns mounted in the turret over the rear section of the vehicle. Although the Austro-Daimler gave a respectable on- and off-road performance (by turn-of-the-century standards) the vehicle never entered into military service.

Country of origin:	Austria
Crew:	4
Weight:	2500kg (5500lb)
Dimensions:	Length (hull): 4.86m (15.94ft); width: 1.76m (5.77ft); height: 2.74m (8.99ft)
Range:	250km (150 miles)
Armour:	4mm (0.16in)
Armament:	1 x 7.92mm (0.31in) Maxim MG or 2 x 7.92mm (0.30in) Schwarzlose MGs
Powerplant:	Daimler 4-cylinder petrol, developing 40hp (30kW)
Performance:	Maximum road speed: 45km/h (28mph)

ADGZ

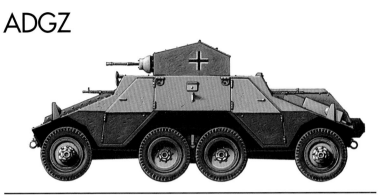

The Daimler ADGZ was in production in Austria between 1935 and 1937, though only very small numbers were ultimately delivered for service – 26 in total. Twelve were delivered to the Austrian Army and 14 were issued to the police and gendarmerie. As an 8x8 vehicle, it had excellent off-road mobility, a fact recognized by the German forces that occupied Austria in 1938. Austrian ADGZs were soon pressed into German Army service and redesignated PzKpfw Steyr ADGZ. Most of these vehicles were deployed by the SS and special police detachments, and they were used heavily on the eastern front. Production continued under German auspices until the end of 1941.

Country of origin:	Austria
Crew:	6 or 7
Weight:	12,000kg (26,500lb)
Dimensions:	Length: 6.26m (20.54ft); width: 2.16m (7.09ft); height: 2.56m (8.39ft)
Range:	70km (43 miles)
Armour:	Not available
Armament:	1 x 20mm (0.78in) automatic cannon; 3 x 7.92mm (0.30in) MG
Powerplant:	Austro-Daimler M612 6-cylinder petrol, developing 150hp (112kW)
Performance:	Maximum road speed: 70km/h (43mph)

Armoured Combat Vehicles

Pandur

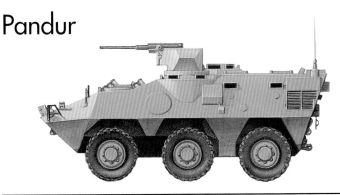

The Pandur 6x6 armoured vehicle was developed by Steyr-Daimler-Puch in the mid-1980s. It entered service with the Austrian Army in 1994 and many other armies since. A common chassis is produced in either 'A' or 'B' variants: 'A' with a raised centre roof and 'B' with a flat roof. Both house a two-man crew. The APC variant has additional space for eight personnel. Pandurs come in a range of variants according to turret or armament configuration. The Pandur Armoured Reconnaissance Fire Support Vehicle, for example, has a Mark 8 90mm (3.5in) gun mounted in a Cockerill LCTS turret, while the Light Armoured Vehicle features the MultiGun Turreted System with 25, 30 or 35mm (0.98, 1.18 or 1.38in) cannon.

Country of origin:	Austria
Crew:	2 + 8
Weight:	13,500kg (29,800lb)
Dimensions:	Length: 5.7m (18.7ft); width: 2.5m (8.2ft); height: 1.82m (5.97ft)
Range:	700km (430 miles)
Armour:	8mm (0.31in)
Armament:	1 x 12.7mm (0.5in) MG; 2 x 3 smoke grenades launchers; various other configurations
Powerplant:	Steyr WD 612.95 6-cylinder turbo diesel, developing 240hp (179kW)
Performance:	Maximum road speed: 100km/h (60mph); fording: 1.2m (3.9ft); gradient: 70 percent; vertical obstacle: 0.5m (1.6ft)

EGESA EE-9 Cascavel

The EE-9 was produced by the Brazilian armaments company ENGESA in the early 1970s as an attempt to replace obsolete US 6x6 M8 Greyhound armoured cars. It is itself a 6x6 vehicle, and originally utilized the M8 turret on the Mk I Cascavel. Subsequent indigenous models featured an ENGESA turret with 90mm (3.54in) gun, though the Mk II export model had the French Hispano-Suiza H-90 turret. Most modern Cascavels are fitted with computerized fire-control systems and laser range-finders. NBC protection is a further option. The Cascavel also has excellent lightweight armour developed by ENGESA and the University of São Paulo in a joint programme.

Country of origin:	Brazil
Crew:	3
Weight:	13,400kg (29,500lb)
Dimensions:	Length (with gun): 6.2m (20.34ft); width: 2.59m (8.5ft); height: 2.68m (8.79ft)
Range:	880km (545 miles)
Armour:	16mm (0.62in)
Armament:	1 x 90mm (3.54in) cannon; 1 x coaxial MG, some versions 1 x 12.7mm (0.5in) or 7.62mm (0.3in) turret-mounted MG
Powerplant:	1 x Detroit Diesel 6V-53 6-cylinder diesel developing 212hp (158kW)
Performance:	Maximum road speed: 100km/h (60mph); fording: 1m (3.3ft); gradient: 60 percent; vertical obstacle: 0.6m (2ft)

Cougar

The Cougar is essentially a Swiss MOWAG Piranha produced by the Diesel Division of General Motors of Canada between 1979 and 1982. Three basic variants exist. The Cougar Gun Wheeled Fire Support Vehicle (WFSV) is fitted with the turret of an Alvis Scorpion with 76mm (2.99in) gun. An APC variant, the Grizzly APC, has the capacity to carry three crew and six other personnel. Finally, the Husky Wheeled Maintenance and Recovery Vehicle features a roof-mounted crane for engineering projects. All variants are amphibious. The Cougars are still in service today with the Canadian Army, though most have been upgraded to an 8x8 configuration. Specifications relate to the Wheeled Fire Support Vehicle variant.

Country of origin:	Canada
Crew:	3
Weight:	9526kg (21,004lb)
Dimensions:	Length: 5.97m (19.59ft); width: 2.53m (8.3ft); height: 2.62m (8.6ft)
Range:	602km (374 miles)
Armour:	10mm (0.39in)
Armament:	1 x 76.2mm (3in) cannon; 1 x 7.62mm (0.3in) coaxial MG
Powerplant:	1 x Detroit Diesel 6V-53T 6-cylinder diesel developing 215hp (160kW)
Performance:	Maximum road speed: 102km/h (63mph); fording: amphibious; gradient: 60 percent; vertical obstacle: 0.5m (1.6ft)

Cardoen Piranha 6x6D

The Chilean Piranha is a Swiss MOWAG Piranha produced under licence by Carlos Cardoen since the early 1980s (FAMAE are also heavily involved with Piranha production). The Swiss and Chilean versions are almost the same, though Cardoen has upgraded its vehicle to a 400-litre (106-gal) fuel capacity instead of the Swiss model's 250 litres (66gal). Though most 6x6 Piranhas in Chile are APCs, a small number are produced as Fire Support Vehicles. These have a Cockerill 90mm (3.54in) MK3 gun mounted on an ENGESA ET-90 90mm turret or a Cardoen 90mm turret. Other trial versions have been fitted with ATGW launchers and even Oerlikon Contraves 20mm (0.78in) GAD-AOA anti-aircraft turrets.

Country of origin:	Chile
Crew:	3 or 4
Weight:	10,500kg (23,200lb)
Dimensions:	Length: 5.97m (19.59ft); width: 2.5m (8.2ft); height: 2.65m (8.69ft)
Range:	700km (435 miles)
Armour:	Not available
Armament:	1 x 90mm (3.54in) cannon; 1 x 12.7mm (0.5in) coaxial MG
Powerplant:	1 x Detroit Diesel 6V-53T diesel, developing 300hp (224kW) at 2800rpm
Performance:	Maximum road speed: 100km/h (60mph); fording: amphibious; gradient: 70 percent; vertical obstacle: 0.5m (1.6ft)

PA-II

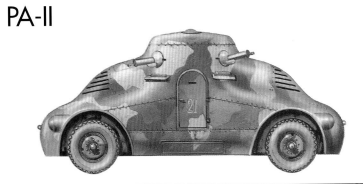

The PA-II was the second in a series of armoured vehicles made by Skoda in the inter-war years. The first, the PA-I, was a prototype weighing 7.3 tons and armed with two 7.92mm (0.31in) Maxim 08 machine guns. Though only two PA-Is were produced, they laid the foundations for the 12 PA-IIs produced between 1924 and 1925 and nicknamed the 'Zelva' (turtle) after their carapace shape. Ten of the units were armoured, the remaining two being unarmoured and used for driver training. Three of the armoured vehicles were used by the Austrian police from 1927. PA-IIs were undoubtedly heavily armed – four Maxim MGs – but they were totally obsolete by the beginning of World War II.

Country of origin:	Czechoslovakia
Crew:	5
Weight:	7360kg (16,229lb)
Dimensions:	Length (hull): 6m (19.68ft); width: 2.16m (7.08ft); height: 2.44m (8ft)
Range:	250km (150 miles)
Armour:	3–5.5mm (0.12–0.21in)
Armament:	4 x 7.92mm (0.31in) Maxim 08 MGs
Powerplant:	1 x Skoda 4-cylinder, petrol, developing 70hp (52kW)
Performance:	Maximum road speed: 70km/h (43mph)

CGV 1906

The French automobile company of Charron, Giradot & Voigt (CGV) was, at the turn of the 20th century, a producer of racing cars. With the growth in demand for military vehicles, however, CGV took a touring-car chassis and fitted it with an armoured barbette mounting an 8mm (0.31in) rear-facing machine gun. This vehicle was presented at the Paris Car Exhibition in 1902. Tests conducted on a new model in Russia in 1905 brought it up to production standard. Only about 12 CGV cars were produced between 1905 and 1908. Russia was a significant export market; indeed, in 1905, one of the vehicles was used to put down rioting in St Petersburg.

Country of origin:	France
Crew:	4
Weight:	3500kg (7700lb)
Dimensions:	Length: 4.46m (14.96ft); width: 1.85m (6ft); height: 2.47m (8.1ft)
Range:	600km (370 miles)
Armour:	6mm (0.23in)
Armament:	1 x 8mm (0.31in) MG
Powerplant:	1 x GCV 4-cylinder petrol, developing 30hp (22kW)
Performance:	Maximum road speed: 45km/h (28mph)

Autoblindé Peugeot

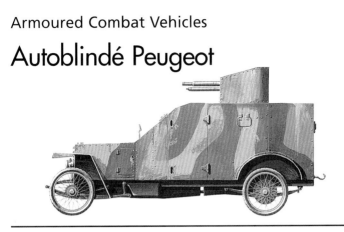

The Autoblindé Peugeot entered service in WWI as one of the first generation of armoured cars. Armoured cars is literally what they were – French commercial road cars covered with armoured panels. Two such vehicles emerged in late 1914: the AM Renault 20CV and the AC Peugeot 18CV. The Renault vehicle was armed with a 7.62mm (0.3in) machine gun, while the Peugeot received a 37mm (1.46in) cannon, but the design of the cars was so similar that both armament and armour were interchangeable. About 150 Peugeots were produced during WWI. Post-war service included combat with the French Army in Africa, and service with the Polish Army in the 1920s against Russia.

Country of origin:	France
Crew:	4 or 5
Weight:	4900kg (10,800lb)
Dimensions:	Length (hull): 4.8m (15.75ft); width: 1.8m (5.9ft); height: 2.8m (9.19ft)
Range:	140km (85 miles)
Armour:	5.5mm (0.21in)
Armament:	1 x 37mm (1.46in) cannon or 1 x 7.62mm (0.3in) MG
Powerplant:	Peugeot 146 4-cylinder petrol, developing 45hp (34kW)
Performance:	Maximum road speed: 40km/h (25mph)

Laffly-White Auto-Mitrailleuse

The Laffly-White Auto-Mitrailleuse ('machine-gun car') was created by combining an armoured body designed by the French company Laffly with the truck chassis from the US company White. White trucks were imported into France from 1915, and in 1918, Laffly began production of its armoured car. In spite of cumbersome dimensions, the Laffly-White served into WWII after active use in the Levant and North Africa in colonial police roles. By 1939, its reliability and durability had made it popular, but its slow speed, largely ineffective 37mm (1.46in) gun and high profile rendered it obsolete against German vehicle technology. By 1940, most were replaced by new Panhard vehicles.

Country of origin:	France
Crew:	4
Weight:	6000kg (13,200lb)
Dimensions:	Length: 5.6m (18.4ft); width: 2.1m (6.9ft); height: 2.75m (9ft)
Range:	250km (150 miles)
Armour:	8mm (0.31in)
Armament:	1 x 37mm (1.46in) cannon; 2 x 8mm (0.31in) MGs
Powerplant:	1 x White 4-cylinder petrol, developing 35hp (26kW)
Performance:	Maximum road speed: 45km/h (28mph)

Berliet VUDB

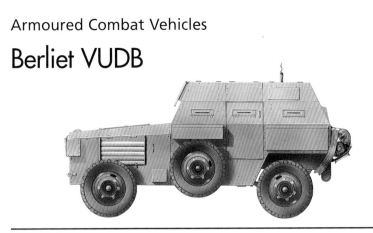

The Lyons based French firm Berliet began producing armoured cars between the wars. Its initial output included the Berliet VUDB, a 4x4 vehicle which saw extensive use in France's North African colonies. The VUDB was produced as a prototype in 1929. In tests, French military officers were impressed with its range of over 350km (220 miles) and speed of 75km/h (47mph), both ideally suited to operations in the North African terrain. In 1930, it entered into service with the French Army. Another 12 vehicles were also built for the Belgian Army. The VUDB featured windows which could be shuttered with armoured plates when under fire, and was armed with three machine guns.

Country of origin:	France
Crew:	3
Weight:	4000kg (8800lb)
Dimensions:	Length: 4.3m (14.11ft); width: 1.96m (6.43ft); height: 2.15m (7ft)
Range:	350km (220 miles)
Armour:	Not available
Armament:	3 x MGs
Powerplant:	1 x Berliet 6-cylinder petrol, developing 49hp (37kW)
Performance:	Maximum road speed: 75km/h (47mph)

Panhard et Levassor Type 178

The Panhard 178 was designed in the mid-1930s as a 4x4 armoured reconnaissance vehicle for the French Army. Its most common armament was a single 25mm (0.98in) cannon or two 7.5mm (0.29in) machine guns. French production of the Panhard 178 ended with the German occupation in 1940. The Germans, however, were impressed with the design and used large numbers under the designation Panzerspähwagen P 204(f). Some of these were turned into anti-aircraft platforms by fitting them with 37mm (1.46in) anti-aircraft guns. French production of the 178 recommenced in August 1944 after the liberation of Paris, though with a larger turret and 47mm (1.85in) gun. These endured in French Army service until 1960.

Country of origin:	France
Crew:	4
Weight:	8300kg (18,300lb)
Dimensions:	Length: 4.8m (15.74ft); width: 2.01m (6.59ft); height: 2.33m (7.64ft)
Range:	300km (190 miles)
Armour:	18mm (0.7in)
Armament:	1 x 25mm (0.98in) cannon; 1 x 7.5mm (0.29in) MG
Powerplant:	1 x Renault 4-cylinder petrol, developing 180hp (134kW)
Performance:	Maximum road speed: 72km/h (45mph); fording: 0.6m (2ft); gradient: 40 percent; vertical obstacle: 0.3m (1ft); trench: 0.6m (2ft)

Panhard EBR/FL-11

The distinction between the FL-10 and the FL-11 variants of the Panhard EBR lies in the turrets. The FL-10 turret is fitted to the AMX-13 light tank, and features a 75mm (2.95in) cannon fed from two revolver-type magazines, each holding six rounds. Gun elevation is +13 degrees and depression is -6 degrees. The FL-11 turret is specific to the EBR. Initial FL-11 models were armed with a 75mm (2.95mm) gun conventionally loaded and had an elevation of +15 degrees and a depression of -10 degrees. However, in the 1960s, the FL-11 turret received a new 90mm (3.54in) gun. The gun had the advantage of firing fin-stabilized rounds with better accuracy and an armour penetration of up to 320mm (12.6in).

Country of origin:	France
Crew:	4
Weight:	13,500kg (29,800lb)
Dimensions:	Length (gun forwards): 6.15m (20.17ft); width: 2.42m (7.94ft); height: 2.32m (7.61ft)
Range:	600km (370 miles)
Armour:	40mm (1.57in)
Armament:	1 x 75mm (2.95in) cannon or 1 x 90mm (3.54in); 2 x 7.5mm (0.29in) or 7.62mm (0.3in) MGs
Powerplant:	1 x Panhard 12-cylinder petrol, developing 200hp (149kW)
Performance:	Maximum road speed: 105km/h (65mph); fording: 1.2m (3.9ft); gradient: 60 percent; vertical obstacle: 0.4m (1.3ft)

Panhard EBR/FL-10

Panhard and Levassor of Paris began producing armoured car designs in 1937. The first successful prototype was revealed in 1939. It was distinguished by its unusual wheel configuration. It had eight wheels, the four centre ones being fitted with steel rims for improved off-road traction. When on-road, these four wheels were raised and the vehicle driven on the usual four corner wheels. After WWII, Panhard reused the idea, and won a French Army competition for a new heavy armoured car with the EBR. EBRs were armed with a 75mm (2.95in) cannon as standard, and the FL-10 received the turret of the AMX-13 light tank which had a 12-round auto-feed mechanism. Production of EBRs ceased in 1960.

Country of origin:	France
Crew:	4
Weight:	15,200kg (33,500lb)
Dimensions:	Length (gun forwards): 7.33m (24ft); width: 2.42m (7.94ft); height: 2.58m (8.46ft)
Range:	600km (370 miles)
Armour:	40mm (1.57in)
Armament:	1 x 75mm (2.95in) cannon; 1 x 7.62mm (0.3in) coaxial MG
Powerplant:	1 x Panhard 12-cylinder petrol, developing 200hp (149kW)
Performance:	Maximum road speed: 105km/h (65mph); fording: 1.2m (3.9ft); gradient: 60 percent; vertical obstacle: 0.4m (1.3ft)

Panhard AML 90

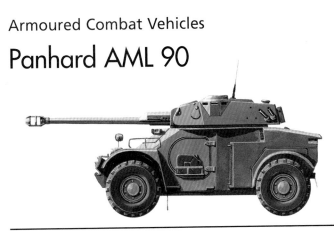

The Panhard Automitrailleuse Legére (AML) is currently in service worldwide in over 40 countries. It was originally developed in the late 1950s, entering service in 1961. The AML is a versatile vehicle, lighter in weight than the EBR, simple to maintain and drive, and easily modified with new turret configurations. Typical of French armoured cars, the basic AML with a H90 or Lynx turret has heavy firepower – a 90mm (3.54in) gun. Other turret versions include the HE-60-7 fitted with a 60mm (2.36in) mortar and the S 530 featuring twin 20mm (0.78in) anti-aircraft guns. The AML is also manufactured under licence in South Africa where it is called the Eland.

Country of origin:	France
Crew:	3
Weight:	5500kg (12,100lb)
Dimensions:	Length (gun forwards): 5.11m (16.76ft); width: 1.97m (6.46ft); height: 2.07m (6.79ft)
Range:	600km (370 miles)
Armour:	8–12mm (0.31–0.47in)
Armament:	1 x 90mm (3.54in) cannon; 1 x 7.62mm (0.3in) coaxial MG; 2 x 2 smoke grenade launchers
Powerplant:	1 x Panhard Model 4 HD 4-cylinder petrol, developing 90hp (67kW)
Performance:	Maximum speed: 90km/h (56mph); fording: 1.1m (3.6ft); gradient: 60 percent; vertical obstacle: 0.3m (1ft); trench: 0.8m (2.6ft)

AMX-10RC

The 6x6 AMX-10RC was developed in France during the 1970s as a replacement for the 8x8 Panhard EBR. The centrepiece of its weaponry is a turret-mounted 105mm (4.13in) semi-automatic gun with computerized fire-control system and laser range-finder. The gun allows it to engage other armoured vehicles, and armour-piercing fin-stabilized discarding-sabot (APFSDS) rounds give it penetrative ability even against MBT armour. A useful feature of the AMX-10RC is its fully amphibious capability. When floating, it is powered by two waterjets at the rear of the hull. The AMX-10RC is currently undergoing extensive upgrading, including fitting of a Land Battlefield Management System.

Country of origin:	France
Crew:	4
Weight:	15,880kg (35,015lb)
Dimensions:	Length (hull): 6.36m (20.87ft); width: 2.95m (9.68ft); height: 2.66m (8.7ft)
Range:	1000km (620 miles)
Armour:	Classified
Armament:	1 x 105mm (4.13in) cannon; 1 x 7.62mm (0.3in) coaxial MG; 2 x 2 smoke grenade launchers
Powerplant:	1 x Badouin Model 6F 11 SRX diesel, developing 280hp (209kW)
Performance:	Maximum road speed: 85km/h (53mph); fording: amphibious; gradient: 50 percent; vertical obstacle: 0.8m (2.6ft)

Renault VBC 90

The Renault Vehicule Blindé de Combat 90 (VBC 90) was produced mainly for export markets. Sales of the vehicle have, however, been disappointing and it is currently in service with only the French gendarmerie and Omani military forces. Unlike many other nations, France commonly fits large-calibre guns to its armoured cars. The VBC 90 mounts a powerful 90mm (3.54in) weapon on its Giat TS-90 turret. Computerized fire-control systems and laser range-finders are also fitted, and today, VBC 90s in service have NBC technology and night-vision devices. Production of the VBC 90 is complete and no variants other than the basic model have been produced.

Country of origin:	France
Crew:	3
Weight:	13,500kg (29,800lb)
Dimensions:	Length (gun forwards): 8.8m (28.87ft); width: 2.5m (8.2ft); height: 2.55m (8.37ft)
Range:	1000km (620 miles)
Armour:	Classified
Armament:	1 x 90mm (3.54in) cannon; 1 x 7.62mm (0.3in) coaxial MG; 1 x 7.62mm (0.3in) turret-mounted MG (option); 2 x 2 smoke grenade launchers
Powerplant:	1 x Renault MIDS 06.20.45 turbo diesel, developing 220hp (164kW)
Performance:	Maximum speed: 92km/h (57mph); fording: 1.2m (3.9ft); gradient: 50 percent; vertical obstacle: 0.5m (1.6ft); trench: 1m (3.3ft)

RPX-90

The Lohr RPX-90 is a 4x4 armoured car with a powerful Hispano-Suiza CNMP 90mm (3.54in) cannon as standard. This weapon enables it to tackle MBTs and fortified positions at close ranges, though armoured reconnaissance remains its primary role. Other turrets are available for the RPX-90, including variants with 20mm (0.78in) cannon, 60mm (2.36in) mortar and MATRA SATCP surface-to-air missiles. The vehicle has an all-welded steel hull and large low-pressure tyres to give good off-road traction. Wide bulletproof windows at the front provide the driver with broad visibility. These can be shuttered in combat. Despite its boat-like shape, the RPX-90 is not amphibious.

Country of origin:	France
Crew:	3
Weight:	11,000kg (24,300lb)
Dimensions:	Length (gun forwards): 7.41m (24.31ft); width: 2.56m (8.39ft); height: 2.54m (8.33ft)
Range:	1000km (620 miles)
Armour:	Classified
Armament:	1 x 90mm (3.54in) cannon; 1 x 7.62mm (0.3in) coaxial MG
Powerplant:	1 x BMW 6-cylinder turbo diesel, developing 310hp (231kW)
Performance:	Maximum road speed: 105km/h (65mph); fording: 1.4m (4.6ft); gradient: 40 percent; vertical obstacle: 0.6m (2ft)

ERC 90 F4 Sagiae

Production of the Panhard ERC 90 F4 Sagiae armoured car began in 1979, and remains in production today with successful export sales. The Panhard ERC F4 Sagiae belongs to the French Army, whose own particular configuration of the ERC features a long-barrelled 90mm (3.54in) cannon. Twenty rounds of 90mm ammunition are stored on board. The latest ERCs have computerized fire contro full NBC systems, and a computerized land-navigation system. The ERC hull can fitted with various turrets. The ERC 90 F1 Lynx, for example, has the Hispano-Sui Lynx 90mm (3.54in) turret as used on the AML armoured car. An 81mm (3.19in) mortar and 20 or 25mm (0.78 or 0.98in) twin anti-aircraft turrets are also availab

Country of origin:	France
Crew:	3
Weight:	8300kg (18,300lb)
Dimensions:	Length (gun forwards): 7.69m (25.23ft); width: 2.5m (8.2ft); height 2.25m (7.38ft)
Range:	700km (430 miles)
Armour:	10mm (0.39in)
Armament:	1 x 90mm (3.54in) cannon; or 1 x 7.62mm (0.3in) coaxial MG; 2 x 2 smoke grenade launchers
Powerplant:	1 x Peugeot V6 petrol, developing 155hp (116kW)
Performance:	Maximum speed: 100km/h (62mph); fording: amphibious; gradient 60 percent; vertical obstacle: 0.8m (2.6ft); trench: 1.1m (3.6ft)

ssing A5P

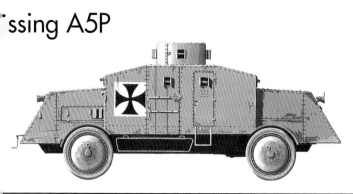

e Büssing company originally specialized in heavy farm vehicles, which then
ecame models for several German military machines. The firm received its
orders for military vehicles in 1910, producing artillery tractors and supply
ers. In November 1914, Büssing, Daimler and Ehrhardt were requested to
lop an armoured car with all-wheel drive. Two years later, Büssing's A5P was
n production. It was powered by one of Büssing's legendary 6-cylinder truck
nes, and featured a large steel armoured body. Inside the vehicle were
ew, six of them working three machine guns. Some A5Ps received two 20mm
in) cannon. The A5P served in Romania and Russia until the end of 1917.

untry of origin:	Germany
ew:	10
eight:	10,250kg (22,600lb)
mensions:	Length: 9.5m (31.17ft); width: 2.1m (6.89ft); height: not available
nge:	250km (150 miles)
mour:	Not available
mament:	3 x 7.92mm (0.31in) MG
werplant:	1 x Büssing petrol, developing 90hp (67kW)
rformance:	Maximum road speed: 35km/h (21mph)

Daimler/15

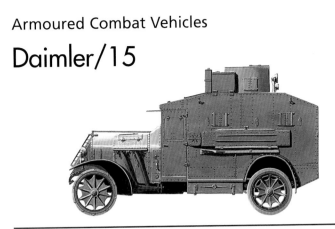

In late 1914, the companies Daimler, Büssing and Ehrhardt were commissioned to develop a prototype armoured car for Germany. Because of other production commitments, Daimler was not able to field its prototype until December 1915, but following testing, prototype models of the Daimler/15 went on to serve on all fronts with reasonable success. The Daimler/15 consisted of an all-wheel-drive car chassis with an armoured structure of Krupp riveted chromium-nickel stainless steel plate. Dual tyres at the rear and sand rims on the front wheels prevented the vehicle sinking into soft ground. Armament was provided by three machine guns. In many ways the Daimler/15's carrying capacity of 10 men made it an incipient APC.

Country of origin:	Germany
Crew:	10
Weight:	9800kg (21,600lb)
Dimensions:	Length: 5.61m (18.4ft); width: 2.03m (6.66ft); height: 3.85m (12.63ft)
Range:	250km (150 miles)
Armour:	Not known
Armament:	3 x 7.92mm (0.31in) MG
Powerplant:	1 x Daimler Model 4-cylinder petrol, developing 80hp (60kW)
Performance:	Maximum road speed: 38km/h (24mph)

Daimler DZVR 1919

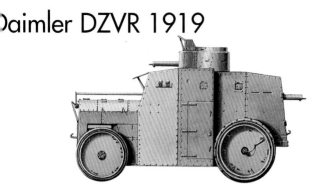

The Daimler DZVR was one of several German vehicles created after the end of World War I under the terms of the Treaty of Versailles. Inter-war Germany required security vehicles to police internal civil unrest and problems on its eastern borders, and 38 DZVR vehicles were ordered for this purpose. The DZVR was based on the chassis of the KD1 artillery tractor, and 1000 of these vehicles were left over from the war. Armour plate, 12mm (0.47in) thick, encased the six-man crew compartment, and a revolving turret at the top held a searchlight. During the 1920s, the searchlight was replaced by a Maxim machine gun. The DZVR remained in police use until the early 1940s.

Country of origin:	Germany
Crew:	6
Weight:	10,500kg (23,200lb)
Dimensions:	Length: 5.9m (19.36ft); width: 2.1m (6.89ft); height: 3.1m (10.17ft)
Range:	150km (100 miles)
Armour:	(Steel) 12mm (0.47in)
Armament:	2 x 7.92mm (0.31in) Maxim MGs
Powerplant:	1 x Daimler M1574 4-cylinder petrol, developing 100hp (75kW)
Performance:	Maximum road speed: 43km/h (27mph)

Schupo-Sonderwagen 21

Though the Treaty of Versailles (1919) did not permit the Weimar Republic to equip itself with armoured units, the Allied victors did permit the construction of 150 armoured cars for German police service. Consequently between 1921 and 1925 three companies – Daimler, Ehrhardt and Benz – were engaged in the production of the Schupo-Sonderwagen 21. The Schupo was a huge vehicle weighing in at 11,000kg (24,300lb). Its extreme weight was caused by large amounts of chromium-nickel plated armour, steel-shod wheels, three Maxim 08 machine guns, and nine crew. The front end of the vehicle was designed to batter its way through street barricades. Around 100 Schupo vehicles were produced.

Country of origin:	Germany
Crew:	9
Weight:	11,000kg (24,300lb)
Dimensions:	Length: 6.5m (21.33ft); width: 2.41m (7.9ft); height: 3.45m (11.32ft)
Range:	350km (220 miles)
Armour:	Chromium-nickel plated
Armament:	3 x 7.92mm (0.31in) Maxim 08 MGs
Powerplant:	1 x Ehrhardt 4-cylinder petrol, developing 80hp (60kW)
Performance:	Maximum road speed: 56km/h (35mph)

Panzerspähwagen SdKfz 232 (8 Rad)

The SdKfz 232 (8 Rad) was essentially the same as the SdKfz 231 (8 Rad), except that it was fitted with a long-range aerial antenna over the top of the turret. A 6x4 SdKfz 231 was produced between 1932 and 1935, but this had limited off-road performance. The SdKfz 231 (8 Rad) solved this problem admirably with its 8x8 configuration – they could even travel through the infamous autumnal muds of the eastern front and the sands of North Africa without impediment. Yet they were very expensive and complicated to produce, and fewer than 1500 were manufactured. Both the SdKfz 231 and 232 have the suffix 8 Rad (8-wheel) to distinguish them from their six-wheel counterparts.

Country of origin:	Germany
Crew:	4
Weight:	9100kg (20,100lb)
Dimensions:	Length: 5.58m (18.3ft); width: 2.2m (7.22ft); height: 2.9m (9.51ft)
Range:	300km (190 miles)
Armour:	15–30mm (0.59–1.18in)
Armament:	1 x 20mm (0.78in) cannon; 1 x 7.92mm (0.31in) MG
Powerplant:	1 x Büssing-NAG L8V-Gs petrol, developing 160hp (119kW) at 3000rpm
Performance:	Maximum road speed: 85km/h (53mph); fording: 1m (3.3ft); gradient: 30 percent; vertical obstacle: 0.5m (1.6ft); trench: 1.25m (4.1ft)

Schützenpanzer SPz 11-2 kurz

The SPz kurz is actually a German version of a French vehicle, the Hotchkiss SP 1A. During the 1950s, Hotchkiss produced tracked armoured vehicles intended for the French Army, though ultimately the army placed no orders. West Germany, however, was at this time seeking to develop its armoured military forces. After testing the Hotchkiss prototypes, the German Army received 2374 Hotchkiss vehicles between 1958 and 1962. Redesignated the SPz 11-2, it featured an all-welded hull of APC type, with twin doors in the rear and escape hatch underneath. The SPz kurz was a reconnaissance vehicle variant of the 11-2, with the small turret carrying a Hispano-Suiza 20mm (0.78in) cannon.

Country of origin:	Germany
Crew:	5
Weight:	8200kg (18,100lb)
Dimensions:	Length: 4.51m (14.8ft); width: 2.28m (7.23ft); height: 1.97m (6.46ft)
Range:	400km (250 miles)
Armour:	15mm (0.59in)
Armament:	1 x Hispano-Suiza 820/L35 20mm (0.78in) cannon; 3 x smoke grenade launchers
Powerplant:	1 x Hotchkiss 6-cylinder petrol, developing 164hp (122kW) at 3900rpm
Performance:	Maximum speed: 58km/h (36mph); fording: 1m (3.3ft); gradient: 60 percent; vertical obstacle: 0.6m (2ft); trench: 1.5m (4.9ft)

Autoblinda Lancia IZ

The Autoblinda IZ was an early foray into armoured-car manufacturing by the Lancia company of Italy. It was based on the chassis of the Lancia IZ light truck but armoured with 6mm (0.24in) steel plates. Originally it had a double-turret construction with three 7.92mm (0.30in) Maxim or 8mm (0.31mm) St Etienne machine guns. The small cupola mounting a single gun at the top was later removed and the gun located in a ball mounting at the rear of the vehicle. In 1915, the first production year, 20 such vehicles were built. Subsequently, the IZ served throughout World War I, and in World War II could still be found in Italian East Africa and Libya.

Country of origin:	Italy
Crew:	6 or 7
Weight:	3700kg (8200lb)
Dimensions:	Length: 5.4m (17.72ft); width: 1.82m (5.97ft); height: 2.4m (7.87ft)
Range:	300km (190 miles)
Armour:	Steel 6mm (0.24in)
Armament:	3 x 7.92mm (0.30in) Maxim or 8mm (0.31in) St Etienne machine guns
Powerplant:	1 x Lancia 4-cylinder petrol, developing 70hp (52kW) at 2200rpm
Performance:	Maximum road speed: 60km/h (37mph)

Pavesi 35 PS

The Pavesi 35 PS emerged from Italian inter-war experiments as an alternative to tracked armoured vehicles. It was developed by the agricultural vehicle company Pavesi-Tolotti of Milan, and consisted of a small armoured car driven by four outsize spoked wheels. Each wheel had a 1.55m (5.09ft) diameter with broad metal rims for powerful cross-country movement. The clearance provided by the wheels was 0.75m (2.46ft) and trenches of 1.4m (4.6ft) width could be crossed. Armament was provided by a single machine gun mounted in the central rotating turret, and later experiments incorporated a 57mm (2.24in) cannon. In use until the late 1920s, it was manufactured in later years by the Fiat company.

Country of origin:	Italy
Crew:	2
Weight:	5000kg (11,000lb)
Dimensions:	Length: 4m (13.12ft); width: 2.18m (7.15ft); height: 2.2m (7.22ft)
Range:	Not available
Armour:	Not available
Armament:	1 x 8mm (0.31in) MG
Powerplant:	1 x Pavesi 4-cylinder petrol, developing 35hp (26kW)
Performance:	Maximum road speed: 30km/h (19mph)

Fiat-Ansaldo L3/35Lf

In 1929, the Italian Army purchased 25 British Carden Lloyd Mk VI tankettes for use in mountainous terrain. Subsequently, Fiat-Ansaldo produced their own version, the Carro Veloce 29 (CV 29), which began an entire series of Italian tankettes. In 1938, the variants numbered CV 3/33 and 3/35 were redesignated as L3. The most basic L3s were armed with a Breda 13.2mm (0.52in) machine gun, but the L3/35Lf flame-thrower version became the most prevalent of the L3 series. The flamethrower barrel extended from the left of the barbette, and the L3/35Lf had its own internal flame-liquid tank. L3s served extensively in North Africa and during the later Italian campaign.

Country of origin:	Italy
Crew:	2
Weight:	3300kg (7300lb)
Dimensions:	Length: 3.2m (10.5ft); width: 1.42m (4.66ft); height: 1.3m (4.27ft)
Range:	120km (75 miles)
Armour:	Not available
Armament:	1 x flame-thrower
Powerplant:	1 x Fiat 4-cylinder petrol, developing 40hp (30kW)
Performance:	Maximum road speed: 42km/h (26mph)

Fiat-OTOBREDA Type 6616 Armoured Car

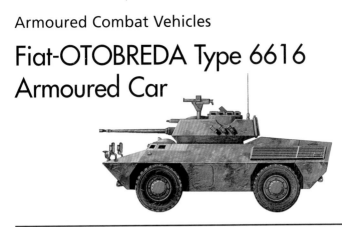

The Type 6616 began its production life in 1972 as a joint venture between Fiat and OTO-Melara. Despite the end of production in the late 1980s, it is still in service today with the Italian Carabinieri and several Latin American and African countries. The three-man crew are seated in an amphibious all-welded steel armoured hull with a maximum thickness of 8mm (0.31in). Vision is provided in a 200-degree arc by five vision blocks, while the driver has a dedicated hatch and a roof aperture for a night-vision periscope. Standard main armament is a Rheinmetall 20mm (0.78in) Mk 20 Rh 202 cannon. A further option is a 90mm (3.54in) gun mounted in an OTOBREDA OTO T 90 CKL turret.

Country of origin:	Italy
Crew:	3
Weight:	8000kg (17,600lb)
Dimensions:	Length: 5.37m (17.62ft); width: 2.5m (8.2ft); height: 2.03m (6.66ft)
Range:	700km (450 miles)
Armour:	(Steel) 6–8mm (0.24–0.31in)
Armament:	1 x Rheinmetall 20mm (0.78in) Mk 20 Rh 202 cannon;1 x 7.62mm (0.3in) coaxial machine gun
Powerplant:	1 x Fiat Model 8062.24 supercharged diesel, developing 160hp (119kW) at 3200rpm
Performance:	Maximum road speed: 100km/h (75mph); fording: amphibious; gradient: 60 percent; vertical obstacle: 0.45m (1.47ft)

OTO Melara R3 Capraia

The R3 Capraia is a heavily armoured Italian reconnaissance vehicle which entered production in 1982. The basic vehicle is 4x4 configuration, with a hull that features welded aluminium armour with a thickness up to 32mm (1.26in), strong enough to deflect small-arms rounds of 7.62mm (0.3in) calibre. Many optional turrets and externally mounted weapons are available for the R3. Seen here is the T20 FA-HS turret fitted with an Oerlikon KAD-B17 20mm (0.78in) cannon. Other turret configurations include the T 7.62 FA (7.62mm (0.3in) machine gun), T 12.7 FA (12.7mm (0.5in) machine gun), T 106x2 FA (twin M40 106mm (4.17in) recoilless rifles) and a TOW turret (mounted launcher for a Hughes TOW ATGW).

Country of origin:	Italy
Crew:	4 or 5
Weight:	3200kg (7100lb)
Dimensions:	Length: 4.86m (15.94ft); width: 1.78m (5.84ft); height: 1.55m (5.09ft)
Range:	500km (300 miles)
Armour:	(Aluminium) 32mm (1.26in)
Armament:	(T 20 FA-HS turret) 1 x Oerlikon KAD-B17 20mm (0.78in) cannon
Powerplant:	1 x Fiat Model 8144.81.200 4-cylinder diesel, developing 95hp (71kW) at 4200rpm
Performance:	Maximum road speed: 120km/h (75mph); fording: amphibious; gradient: 75 percent

VCC-80/Dardo IFV

The Dardo IFV emerged on the world scene in 1998, but is actually derived from an earlier vehicle, the VCC-80 MICV. This entered production 10 years earlier, and is a tracked infantry vehicle armed with a 25mm (0.98in) Oerlikon Contraves KBA cannon. The Dardo is little different. Its main modification lies in the turret, which was adapted to mount TOW anti-tank missiles on either side. Sophisticated technology runs throughout the VCC-80/Dardo, though it has yet to be proven in combat. The armour is of the latest layered aluminium/steel type and laser range-finding and night-vision systems are standard. A highly sloped glacis plate at the front of the vehicle provides maximum deflection against projectiles.

Country of origin:	Italy
Crew:	2 + 7
Weight:	23,000kg (50,700lb)
Dimensions:	Length: 6.7m (21.98ft); width: 3m (9.84ft); height: 2.64m (8.66ft)
Range:	600km (370 miles)
Armour:	Layered aluminium/steel (details classified)
Armament:	1 x 25mm (0.98in) Oerlikon Contraves KBA cannon;1 x 7.62mm (0.3in) coaxial machine gun; 2 x TOW launchers; 2 x 3 smoke grenade launchers
Powerplant:	1 x IVECO 8260 V-6 turbo diesel, developing 520hp (388kW)
Performance:	Maximum speed: 70km/h (43mph); fording: 1.5m (4.9ft); gradient: 60 percent; vertical obstacle: 0.85m (2.79ft); trench: 2.5m (8.2ft)

Sumida M.2593

One of the most ingenious armoured vehicles of the inter-war period was the Japanese Sumida M.2593. Produced from 1933 by the Ishikawajima Motor Works, it had the option of travelling by either road or rail. Solid road wheels could be exchanged for railway wheels carried on the side of the vehicle, the front and rear wheels adaptable to different rail gauges. After the swap it could drive at 60km/h (37mph) on rails, powered by its four-cylinder petrol engine. The Sumida proved useful in covering the great distances of mainland China during the Japanese invasion of the late 1930s, but its solid wheels made it unsuitable for off-road manoeuvre.

Country of origin:	Japan
Crew:	6
Weight:	7000kg (15,400lb)
Dimensions:	Length: 6.57m (21.55ft); width: 1.9m (6.23ft); height: 2.95m (9.68ft)
Range:	240km (150 miles)
Armour:	10mm (0.39in)
Armament:	1 x MG
Powerplant:	1 x 4-cylinder petrol, developing 45hp (34kW)
Performance:	Maximum road speed: 40km/h (25mph); maximum rail speed: 60km/h (37mph)

Armoured Combat Vehicles

Type 89

The Mitsubishi Type 89 Mechanised Infantry Combat Vehicle is a true fighting machine. With the dimensions of a small tank, it boasts one 35mm (1.38in) Oerlikon Contraves cannon, a coaxial 7.62mm (0.3in) machine gun, and two preloaded ATGWs (usually Jyu-MAT medium-range missiles). A crew of three man the forward section (which includes the engine) and turret of the vehicle, and seven other combat personnel can be transported in the rear. Six firing ports are provided around the sides and rear of the Type 89 to allow small arms to be deployed against infantry attack. Production of the Type 89 began in 1991, and continues today.

Country of origin:	Japan
Crew:	3 + 7
Weight:	26,500kg (58,400lb)
Dimensions:	Length: 6.8m (22.3ft); width: 3.2m (10.49ft); height: 2.5m (8.2ft)
Range:	400km (250 miles)
Armour:	Classified
Armament:	1 x 35mm (1.38in) Oerlikon Contraves cannon; 1 x coaxial 7.62mm (0.3in) machine gun; 2 x ATGWs (Jyu-MAT anti-tank missiles)
Powerplant:	1 x 6-cylinder diesel developing 600hp (447kW)
Performance:	Maximum road speed: 70km/h (43mph); fording: 1m (3.3ft); gradient: 60 percent; vertical obstacle: 0.8m (2.6ft); trench: 2.4m (7.9ft)

M39 Armoured Car

The M39 was produced by the DAF company in the build-up to World War II, resisting Dutch Army requests to license-build British armoured cars. It was a well-made 6x4 armoured car with an all-welded hull, a rear-mounted Ford Mercury V8 engine and a well-sloped glacis plate. A useful set of driving controls at the rear of the vehicle allowed the rear machine-gunner to control the vehicle in reverse in an emergency. At the front of the hull, two small wheels prevented the forward edge of the glacis plate digging into the ground on rough terrain. After the fall of the Netherlands in 1940, M39s were pressed into German service as Pz. SpWg L202h.

Country of origin:	Netherlands
Crew:	5
Weight:	6000kg (13,200lb)
Dimensions:	Length: 4.75m (15.58ft); width: 2.03m (6.66ft); height: 2.16m (7.09ft)
Range:	320km (200 miles)
Armour:	12mm (0.47in)
Armament:	1 x 37mm (1.46in) cannon; 3 x 8mm (0.31in) MGs
Powerplant:	1 x Ford Mercury V8 petrol, developing 95hp (71kW)
Performance:	Maximum road speed: 60km/h (37mph)

Armoured Combat Vehicles

WZ/34

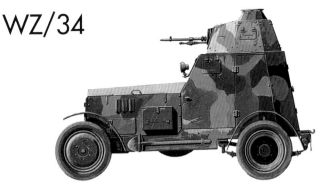

Prior to 1933, Poland's armoured car was the WZ/28, an unsatisfactory halftrack design using the chassis of the French Citroën-Kegresse B2 10CV. Ninety such vehicles were made, but by 1938, 87 of them had been converted into a wheeled 4x2 configuration and renamed the WZ/34. The WZ/34 shape had a recognizable c heritage, though the rear of the vehicle was built up into a high turret mounting either a 37mm (1.46in) SA-18 Puteaux L/21 gun or a 7.92mm (0.31in) Hotchkiss wz.25 machine gun. Neither the armament nor the meagre 6mm (0.23in) riveted armour plate provided any realistic defence against German panzers during the Polish invasion in September 1939.

Country of origin:	Poland
Crew:	2
Weight:	2200kg (4900lb)
Dimensions:	Length: 3.62m (11.87ft); width: 1.91m (6.27ft); height: 2.21m (7.25ft)
Range:	250km (150 miles)
Armour:	6mm (0.23in)
Armament:	1 x 37mm (1.46in) SA-18 Puteaux L/21 gun; or 1 x 7.92mm (0.31in) Hotchkiss wz.25 machine gun
Powerplant:	1 x Citroën B-T4 6-cylinder petrol, developing 20hp (15kW); or 1 x Fiat 6-cylinder petrol developing 25hp (19kW)
Performance:	Maximum road speed: 40km/h (25mph)

AB-72

he TAB-72 made its first appearance in 1972 and still forms an antiquated part of
the Romanian and Serbian military. It is a reasonably straightforward copy of
8x8 Soviet BTR-60PB. The main difference is that the TAB-72's two engines are
able of generating 140hp (104kW) instead of the Soviet vehicle's 90hp (67kW),
xtra output which dramatically improves the TAB-72's cross-country mobility.
e the BTR-60PB, the TAB-72 features a frontal turret mounting two machine guns
4.5mm (0.57in) KPV and a 7.62mm (0.3in) PKT. These are used to engage both
al and ground targets. The only variant of the TAB-72 is a mortar carrier, which
ries an 82mm (3.23in) mortar.

ountry of origin:	Romania
rew:	3 + 8
Veight:	11,000kg (24,300lb)
imensions:	Length: 7.22m (23.69ft); width: 2.83m (9.28ft); height: 2.7m (8.8ft)
ange:	500km (310 miles)
rmour:	9mm (0.35in)
rmament:	1 x 14.5mm (0.57in) KPV MG; 1 x 7.62mm (0.3in) PKT MG
owerplant:	2 x 6-cylinder petrol, developing 140hp (104kW) each
erformance:	Maximum road speed: 95km/h (60mph); fording: amphibious; gradient: 60 percent; vertical obstacle: 0.4m (1.3ft); trench: 2m (6.6ft)

Garford-Putilow

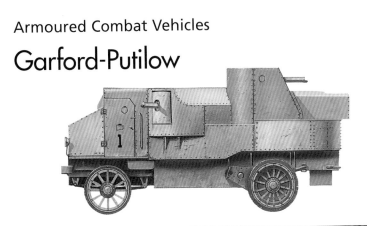

The monstrous Garford-Putilow armoured car hailed from the Putilow factory in St Petersburg in 1914, and 70 such vehicles fought in World War I, the Russian Civil War and the Polish–Soviet campaign of 1939. Chassis were provided by the US Garford Motor Truck Company, and a huge armoured structure was built on the foundation of this standard truck chassis. Total weight was 11,000kg (24,300lb). Consequently the Garford-Putilow had no off-road capability and on-road was slow. Its main armament was a 76.2mm (3in) gun mounted on a 270-degree traversable turret, and three machine guns. During World War II, many Garford-Putilow armoured bodies were subsequently used on armoured trains.

Country of origin:	Russia
Crew:	8
Weight:	11,000kg (24,300lb)
Dimensions:	Length: 5.7m (18.7ft); width: 2.3m (7.55ft); height: 2.8m (9.19ft)
Range:	120km (75 miles)
Armour:	5mm (0.19in) approx.
Armament:	1 x 76.2mm (3in) gun; 3 x Maxim 7.92mm (0.31in) MGs
Powerplant:	1 x Garford 4-cylinder petrol, developing 35hp (26kW)
Performance:	Maximum road speed: 20km/h (13mph)

BMP-1

The BMP-1 is one of the more heavily armed Russian APCs, and the first of the BMP series designed to replace the BTR-50. Its primary armament is a turret-mounted 73mm (2.87in) short-recoil gun, fed with fin-stabilized rocket-assisted ammunition from a 40-round magazine. This weapon features a low-pressure system which negates excessive backblast into the cabin. In addition, the BMP-1 carries a single Sagger ATGW missile and a 7.62mm (0.3in) coaxial machine gun. Equal attention is paid to armour, the all-welded steel hull capable of stopping 12.7mm (.5in) machine gun rounds. The BMP-1 is fully amphibious and propelled in water by its tracks.

Country of origin:	Russia/Soviet Union
Crew:	3 + 8
Weight:	13,900kg (30,650lb)
Dimensions:	Length: 6.74m (22.11ft); width: 2.94m (9.65ft); height: 1.9m (6.23ft)
Range:	600km (370 miles)
Armour:	(Steel) 33mm (1.29in)
Armament:	1 x 73mm (2.87in) gun; 1 x Sagger ATGW missile; 1 x 7.62mm (0.3in) coaxial MG
Powerplant:	1 x UTD-20 6-cylinder diesel, developing 300hp (223kW)
Performance:	Maximum road speed: 80km/h (50mph); fording: amphibious; gradient: 60 percent; vertical obstacle: 0.8m (2.6ft); trench: 2.2m (7.2ft)

BTR-80

The BTR-80 was part of the steady development of the BTR family which entered production in 1984. Its key contribution to the series was to switch from the two petrol engines of the BTR-60 and BTR-70 to a single powerful V8 diesel. Seven fully laden soldiers can travel in the BTR-80 as well as the three-man crew, and the troop compartment has a total of six firing ports. The main weaponry is a turret-mounted 14.5m (0.57in) KPVT machine gun and a coaxial 7.62mm (0.3in) PKT machine gun. Sophisticated features of the BTR-80 include central tyre-pressure regulation, NBC fittings, and front four wheels steering. It is also fully amphibious, powered by a single waterjet.

Country of origin:	Russia/Soviet Union
Crew:	3 + 7
Weight:	13,600kg (23,000lb)
Dimensions:	Length: 7.65m (25.09ft); width: 2.9m (9.51ft); height: 2.46m (8.07ft)
Range:	600km (370 miles)
Armour:	(Steel) 9mm (0.35in)
Armament:	1 x 14.5m (0.57in) KPVT MG; 1 x coaxial 7.62mm (0.3in) PKT MG
Powerplant:	1 x V8 diesel, developing 260hp (193kW)
Performance:	Maximum road speed: 90km/h (56mph); fording: amphibious; gradient: 60 percent; vertical obstacle: 0.5m (1.6ft); trench: 2m (6.6ft)

BMP-3

The BMP-3 entered service in 1990, and is the latest in the BMP range. Classified as an Infantry Combat Vehicle, its extensive armament almost places it in the category of small tank. Its turret boasts a 100mm (3.93in) gun which can fire either conventional shells or AT-10 laser-guided ATGWs. Alongside this weapon is a 30mm (1.18in) cannon, and the turret also bears a 7.62mm (0.3in) PKT coaxial machine gun. Another machine gun is set in the forward hull. Despite the increase in stored ammunition and the consequent extra space this takes up, the BMP-3 takes only one less soldier than the BMP-1 (seven instead of eight), though it is almost a metre (3.3ft) longer.

Country of origin:	Russia/Soviet Union
Crew:	3 + 7
Weight:	18,700kg (41,200lb)
Dimensions:	Length: 7.14m (23.42ft); width: 3.23m (10.59ft); height: 2.65m (8.69ft)
Range:	600km (370 miles)
Armour:	Steel (details classified)
Armament:	1 x 100mm (3.93in) gun; 1 x 30mm (1.18in) cannon; 2 x 7.62mm (0.3in) PKT MG
Powerplant:	1 x UTD-29M 10-cylinder diesel, developing 500hp (373kW)
Performance:	Maximum speed: 70km/h (43mph); fording: amphibious; gradient: 60 percent; vertical obstacle: 0.8m (2.6ft); trench: 2.5m (8.2ft)

BTR-90

The BTR-90 is Russia's next generation of Infantry Combat Vehicles, and its service status is only just being defined. It is similar to the BTR-80 in general appearance, and can carry 10 fully armed soldiers within its armoured and amphibious hull. What makes it distinctive is its armament. All its weaponry is mounted in a single turret located towards the front of the vehicle, and it consists of one 30mm (1.18in) 2A42 automatic cannon, a coaxial 7.62mm (0.3in) PKT machine gun, an automatic grenade launcher, and four AT-5 Spandrel anti-tank missiles. The spectrum of weaponry allows it to engage the enemy infantry, armour and aircraft equally.

Country of origin:	Russia/Soviet Union
Crew:	3 + 10
Weight:	17,000kg (37,500lb)
Dimensions:	Length: 7.64m (25ft); width: 3.2m (10.49ft); height: 2.97m (9.74ft)
Range:	600km (370 miles)
Armour:	Not disclosed
Armament:	1 x 30mm (1.18in) 2A42 automatic cannon; 1 x coaxial 7.62mm (0.3in) PKT MG; 1 x automatic grenade launcher; 4 x AT-5 Spandrel ATGWs
Powerplant:	1 x V8 diesel, developing 210hp (157kW))
Performance:	Maximum road speed: 80km/h (50mph); fording: amphibious

Bionix 25

The Bionix 25 IFV entered service in 1997 with the Singapore Armoured Forces. It is one of the new generation of armoured combat vehicles – fast, manoeuvrable and with enhanced survivability. The tracked configuration supports six road wheels on each side, and the front-drive system can power the Bionix 25 to a 70km/h (43mph) maximum speed. While the vehicular technology is produced by Singapore Technologies Automotive, the turret-mounted 25mm (0.98in) cannon is from the Boeing Company. This is stabilized for accuracy in rough terrain while a thermal sight enables night firing. Seven infantry can ride in the Bionix 25, access provided by a power-operated ramp in the hull rear.

Country of origin:	Singapore
Crew:	3 + 7
Weight:	23,000kg (50,700lb)
Dimensions:	Length: 5.92m (19.42ft); width: 2.7m (8.86ft); height: 2.53m (8.3ft)
Range:	415km (260 miles)
Armour:	Classified
Armament:	1 x 25mm (0.98in) Boeing M242 cannon; 1 x coaxial 7.62mm (0.3in) MG; 1 x turret-mounted 7.62mm (0.3in) MG; 2 x 3 smoke grenade launchers
Powerplant:	1 x Detroit Diesel Model 6V-92TA diesel, developing 475hp (354kW)
Performance:	Maximum speed: 70km/h (43mph); fording: 1m (3.3ft); gradient: 60 percent; vertical obstacle: 0.6m (2ft); trench: 2m (6.6ft)

Eland Armoured Car

The Eland armoured car is actually the French Panhard AML, though modified for the South African Army. Production of the Mk 1 Eland began in 1962. Since then, the vehicle has been steadily updated. Marks 2 to 4 had improved brakes, fuel delivery and clutch. The Mark 5 of 1972 introduced a South African diesel engine and suspension and tyres more suited to the South African terrain. The latest model, the Mk 7, entered service in 1979. It features a turbo diesel engine of standard commercial type, thus reducing the logistical problems of finding spare parts. It works in permanent 4x4 mode and is armed with either a 90mm (3.54in) gun or a 60mm (2.36in) breech-loading mortar.

Country of origin:	Singapore
Crew:	3
Weight:	5300kg (11,700lb)
Dimensions:	Length: 3.79m (12.43ft); width: 2.02m (6.63ft); height: 1.88m (6.17ft)
Range:	500km (310 miles)
Armour:	Classified
Armament:	1 x 90mm (3.54in) gun; or 1 x 60mm (2.36in) breech-loading mortar; 2 x 7.62mm (0.3in) MG
Powerplant:	1 x 4-cylinder turbo diesel, developing 103hp (79kW)
Performance:	Maximum road speed: 85km/h (53mph)

Rooikat

The Rooikat is one of the world's most potent armoured cars. Its development programme began in 1978, but it took 12 years before it was ready to enter service in 1990. Two main versions are available. The Rooikat 76 has a stabilized 76mm (2.99in) gun, and the Rooikat 105 has an even more powerful 105mm (4.13in) anti-tank gun which can fire six rounds per minute. Such firepower allows the Rooikat to make aggressive seek-and-destroy missions as well as combat reconnaissance. The classified armoured type protects the crew from anti-tank mines and small arms ammunition up to 24mm (0.94in) calibre. All tyres have run-flat inserts – mobility is maintained even with loss of pressure in all eight tyres.

Country of origin:	South Africa
Crew:	4
Weight:	28,000kg (61,700lb)
Dimensions:	Length: 7.09m (23.26ft); width: 2.9m (9.51ft); height: 2.8m (9.19ft)
Range:	1000km (620 miles)
Armour:	Classified
Armament:	1 x 76mm (2.99in) gun (Rooikat 76); 1 x 105mm (4.13in) gun (Rooikat 105); 1 x coaxial 7.62mm (0.3in) MG; 1 x turret-mounted 7.62mm (0.3in) MG; 2 x 4 smoke grenade launchers
Powerplant:	1 x V-10 diesel, developing 563hp (420kW)
Performance:	Maximum road speed: 120km/h (75mph); fording: 1.5m (4.9ft); gradient: 70 percent; vertical obstacle: 1m (3.3ft); trench: 2m (6.6ft)

VEC Cavalry Scout Vehicle

The Vehículo de Exploracíon de Caballereía (VEC) emerged in prototype stage in the late 1970s, before entering service with the Spanish Army in 1980. It is a fairly standard armoured car design, with an all-welded aluminium armour providing protection across its frontal section against small arms ammunition up to 7.62mm (0.3in) armour-piercing rounds. The VEC holds five crew comfortably; the engine is set at the rear to conserve interior space. The vehicle is defended by either a 20mm (0.78in) cannon in a FIAT-OTO Melara turret, or a 25mm (0.98in) Oerlikon cannon in an Oerlikon-Bührle GDB-COA turret. NBC options are available and the VEC is also fully amphibious.

Country of origin:	Spain
Crew:	5
Weight:	13,750kg (30,300lb)
Dimensions:	Length: 6.1m (20ft); width: 2.5m (8.2ft); height: 3.3m (10.83ft)
Range:	800km (500 miles)
Armour:	Aluminium (details classified)
Armament:	1 x 20mm (0.78in) cannon; or 1 x 25mm (0.98in) cannon; 1 x coaxial 7.62mm (0.3in) MG; 2 x 3 smoke grenade launchers
Powerplant:	(latest models) 1 x Scania DS9 diesel, developing 310hp (231kW)
Performance:	Maximum road speed: 103km/h (64mph); fording: amphibious; gradient: 60 percent; vertical obstacle: 0.6m (2ft); trench: 1.5m (4.9ft)

Landsverk 180

The Landsverk 180 armoured car was produced from 1938. Its foundation was the chassis of a Scania-Vabis truck with 6x4-wheel drive, though the Landsverk 180 had twin wheels on the rear axles, 10 wheels in total. Armour plate was riveted to the chassis, creating a boxy car-like shape capped by a small turret mounting a Madsen 20mm (0.78in) cannon and coaxial 7.92mm (0.31in) machine gun. Other machine guns were located just beneath the turret and facing backwards out of the rear of the hull. A powerful Scania-Vabis engine gave the Landsverk 180 a respectable top road speed of 80km/h (50mph), but the vehicle was soon obsolete in the context of modern World War II armour.

Country of origin:	Sweden
Crew:	5
Weight:	7000kg (15,400lb)
Dimensions:	Length: 5.87m (19.26ft); width: 2.5m (8.2ft); height: 2.33m (7.64ft)
Range:	290km (180 miles)
Armour:	8.5mm (0.33in)
Armament:	1 x 37mm (1.46in) cannon; 3 x 7.92mm (0.31in) MG
Powerplant:	1 x Scania-Vabis 6-cylinder diesel, developing 80hp (60kW)
Performance:	Maximum road speed: 80km/h (50mph)

Grenadier

The MOWAG Grenadier was an armoured car/armoured personnel carrier from the late 1960s and early 1970s which demonstrated multi-tasking in military vehicles. As an APC, it could carry eight personnel plus the driver, protecting them from small-arms fire. Even bullet-proof tyres could be fitted. It was fully amphibious, powered by a three-blade propeller. Extensive weapons fittings made it a purposeful combat vehicle. Options included a turret-mounted 20mm (0.78in) cannon, 80mm (3.15in) multiple rocket launchers, various anti-tank weapons and remote-control 7.62mm (0.3in) machine guns. The Grenadier series was effectively replaced by MOWAG's Piranha series of armoured cars in the 1980s.

Country of origin:	Switzerland
Crew:	1 + 8
Weight:	6100kg (13,450lb)
Dimensions:	Length: 4.84m (15.88ft); width: 2.3m (7.54ft); height: 2.12m (6.96ft)
Range:	550km (340 miles)
Armour:	Not disclosed
Armament:	Various (see text)
Powerplant:	1 x MOWAG 8-cylinder petrol, developing 202hp (150kW) at 3900rpm
Performance:	Maximum road speed: 100km/h (62mph)

Little Willie

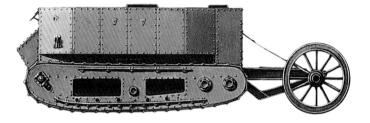

Little Willie can lay claim to being the progenitor of all armoured fighting vehicles. In 1915, two British Army officers, Colonel Ernest Swinton and Colonel Maurice Hankey, convinced Winston Churchill, then First Lord of the Admiralty, that petrol-driven tractors armoured with steel plates could cross enemy trenches while remaining impervious to small-arms fire. Little Willie appeared in prototype form in September 1915, but its performance was disappointing. Its Daimler six-cylinder engine could only power the 17.7-ton vehicle at 3.2km/h (2mph) on rough ground. It was also unable to traverse significant trenches, but nonetheless, Little Willie began the race for armoured development.

Country of origin:	United Kingdom
Crew:	3
Weight:	18,300kg (40,400lb)
Dimensions:	Length: 8.07m (26.48ft); width: 3.47m (11.38ft); height: 3.2m (11ft)
Range:	Not available
Armour:	(Mild steel) 6mm (0.23in)
Armament:	None
Powerplant:	1 x Daimler 6-cylinder petrol, developing 105hp (78.29kW) at 100rpm
Performance:	Maximum road speed: 3.2km/h (2mph)

Armoured Combat Vehicles

FV 721 Fox

The FV 721 Fox entered service with the British Army in 1973, having undergone development since 1965 as the replacement for the Ferret armoured car. Armament received a major upgrade from the Ferret's machine guns. The 30mm (1.18in) Rarden cannon was introduced, which when loaded with Armour-Piercing Discarding-Sabot Tracer (APDST) rounds can destroy light armoured vehicles at 1000m (3300ft) and even penetrate weaker armour points of MBTs. The Fox is a quick vehicle with a road speed of 104km/h (65mph) and can be made fully amphibious by fitting an external float screen. The wheels then power and steer the vehicle through the water.

Country of origin:	United Kingdom
Crew:	3
Weight:	6120kg (13,500lb)
Dimensions:	Length (gun included): 5.08m (16.67ft); width: 2.13m (6.99ft); height: 1.98m (6.5ft)
Range:	434km (270 miles)
Armour:	Aluminium (details classified)
Armament:	1 x 30mm (1.18in) Rarden cannon; 1 x coaxial 7.62mm (0.3in) MG; 2 x 4 smoke grenade launchers
Powerplant:	1 x Jaguar XK 4.2-litre 6-cylinder petrol, developing 190hp (142kW)
Performance:	Maximum speed: 104km/h (65mph); fording: 1m (3.3ft)/amphibious; gradient: 46 percent; vertical obstacle: 0.5m (1.6ft); trench: 1.22m (4ft)

Warrior MICV

The Warrior MICV is the British Army's premier combat reconnaissance vehicle. It was originally known as the MCV-80. This was developed in the mid-1970s and entered into service in 1986, when it was retitled 'Warrior'. Its main strengths are combat effectiveness and versatility. The 30mm (1.18in) Rarden cannon is its standard combat armament, but optional fittings include 90mm (3.54in) cannon, TRIGAT ATGW launchers, and, for future export models, 81mm (3.19in) mortar and even a 105mm (4.13in) gun. Non-combat versions include recovery and repair vehicles, artillery observation vehicles and communication vehicles. Eight infantry soldiers can be carried in the rear of the hull.

Country of origin:	United Kingdom
Crew:	2 + 8
Weight:	24,000kg (52,900lb)
Dimensions:	Length: 6.34m (20.8ft); width: 3.03m (9.94ft); height: 2.74m (8.99ft)
Range:	500km (310 miles)
Armour:	Aluminium (details classified)
Armament:	1 x 30mm (1.18in) Rarden cannon; 1 x coaxial 7.62mm (0.3in) chain gun; 2 x 4 smoke grenade launchers
Powerplant:	1 x Perkins CV-8 8-cylinder diesel, developing 550hp (410kW)
Performance:	Maximum road speed: 75km/h (45mph); fording: 1.3m (4.3ft); gradient: 60 percent; vertical obstacle: 0.75m (2.46ft); trench: 2.5m (8.2ft)

Dragoon

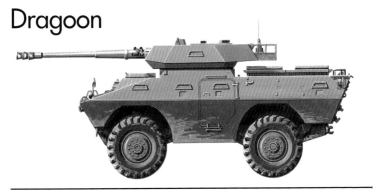

The Dragoon Armoured Fighting Vehicle is a fast 4x4 vehicle armed with a turret mounted 90mm (3.54in) KEnerga gun and coaxial 7.62mm (0.3in) machine gun. Wheels are recessed for travel over rough terrain and the steel hull is designed for fully amphibious operations. Since 1984, when production was taken over by the merger-created AV Technology Corporation, variants have emerged including an 81mm (3.19in) Armoured Mortar Carrier, a turretless APC carrying six infantry, a TOW ATGW launcher and an ambulance. Turret armament can be altered to 40mm (1.57in) cannon or 12.7mm (0.5in) machine gun. The Dragoon is in service with security forces in the US, Thailand, Turkey and various Latin American countries.

Country of origin:	United States
Crew:	3 + 6
Weight:	12,700kg (28,000lb)
Dimensions:	Length: 5.89m (19.3ft); width: 2.44m (8ft); height: 2.13m (6.98ft)
Range:	1045km (650 miles)
Armour:	Steel (details classified)
Armament:	1 x 90mm (3.54in) KEnerga gun; 1 x coaxial 7.62mm (0.3in) MG
Powerplant:	1 x Detroit 6V-53T 6-cylinder turbo diesel, developing 300hp (223kW) at 2800rpm
Performance:	Maximum road speed: 116km/h (72mph); fording: amphibious; gradient: 60 percent; vertical obstacle: 0.6m (2ft)

Gillois PA

The Gillois PA was named after the French General, J. Gillois. In the mid-1950s, Gillois began work on developing various amphibious bridging and ferry systems with the German engineering company, EWK. The result was the Gillois-EWK. The title 'Gillois PA' refers to 'Pont Amphibian', the Gillois' specific bridging configuration. The Gillois vehicle has a large inflatable flotation chamber on each side. Each chamber has nine watertight sections to prevent flooding if part of the chamber is damaged. In bridging operations, the PA transports an 8 x 4m (26.25 x 12ft) bridge slab which is swivelled through 90 degrees to connect with other bridge units to form a floating highway.

Country of origin:	France
Crew:	4
Weight:	26,915kg (59,425lb)
Dimensions:	Length: 11.86m (38.91ft); width: 3.2m (10.49ft); height: 3.99m (13.09ft)
Range:	780km (480 miles)
Armour:	Not applicable
Armament:	None
Powerplant:	1 x Deutz V12 diesel, developing 220hp (164kW)
Performance:	Maximum road speed: 64km/h (40mph); maximum water speed: 12km/h (7mph)

Schwimmwagen Type 166

The Schwimmwagen Type 166 was an amphibious light vehicle developed by Volkswagen in the early 1940s. It was meant to provide German infantry and airborne units with an amphibious version of the excellent Kübelwagen. A bulbous flotation body was added to the Kübelwagen and a chain-driven propeller (which had to be lowered prior to entering the water) situated at the rear of the hull. The front wheels acted as the rudder. With its maximum load of four men, the Schwimmwagen had an on-water speed of 11km/h (7mph). Of the 14,625 Schwimmwagens produced during WWII, most ended up serving on the Eastern Front, though small numbers went to North Africa.

Country of origin:	Germany
Crew:	1 + 3
Weight:	910kg (2007lb)
Dimensions:	Length: 3.82m (12.53ft); width: 1.48m (4.86ft); height: 1.61m (5.28ft)
Range:	520km (320 miles)
Armour:	Not applicable
Armament:	None
Powerplant:	1 x VW 4-cylinder petrol, developing 25hp (19kW)
Performance:	Maximum road speed: 80km/h (50mph); maximum water speed: 11km/h (7mph)

M2 and M3

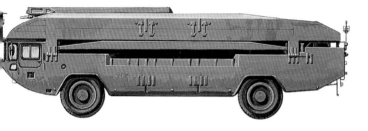

The EWK M2 vehicle entered production in 1968 and improved greatly on EWK's earlier Gillois design for the French Army. Aluminium side pontoons replaced Gillois' inflatable versions, and actually functioned as part of the floating-bridge structure. The M2's water-drive gave a slightly better amphibious speed than that of the Gillois and also made it more stable in heavy currents. Over 350 M2s were produced and still serve today, but in 1996 the more advanced M3 came onto the market. Eight M3s operated by 24 soldiers can build a bridge 100m (330ft) long in only 15 minutes, 50 percent faster than was possible with the M2. Both the M2 and M3 have enjoyed excellent export sales.

Country of origin:	Germany
Crew:	3
Weight:	25,300kg (55,800lb)
Dimensions:	Length: 12.82m (42.06ft); width: 3.35m (10.99ft); height: 3.93m (12.89ft)
Range:	725km (450 miles)
Armour:	Not applicable
Armament:	None
Powerplant:	2 x Deutz BF8 LC513 8-cylinder diesel, developing 362hp (270kW)
Performance:	Maximum road speed: 80km/h (50mph); maximum water speed: 13km/h (8mph)

Arisgator

Purpose-designed amphibious vehicles are very expensive to make. The Italian company Aris developed a far cheaper alternative by fitting a flotation kit to the US M113A2 armoured personnel carrier. (Though the M113 is itself amphibious, its performance in the water is generally poor.) The flotation kit has front and rear sections. At the front, a bow-shaped bolt-on section gives buoyancy and improves handling in turbulent waters. Two tail sections contain the propeller units. The only other modifications to the original M113 vehicle are redirected air intakes and exhaust pipes and better sealing around joints and hatches. The Arisgator is still in the trial and development stage, though orders with the Italian forces are likely.

Country of origin:	Italy
Crew:	2 + 11
Weight:	c.12,000kg (26,500lb)
Dimensions:	Length: 6.87m (22.54ft); width: 2.95m (9.68ft); height: 2.05m (6.73ft)
Range:	550km (340 miles)
Armour:	38mm (1.49in)
Armament:	1 x 12.7mm (0.5in) Browning M2 HB MG
Powerplant:	1 x Detroit 6V-53N 6-cylinder diesel, developing 215hp (160kW) at 2800rpm
Performance:	Maximum road speed: 68km/h (42mph)

K-61

The K-61 was a popular amphibious transporter developed shortly after World War II and exported widely throughout the Eastern Bloc and communist-allied Middle Eastern countries. It is little more than an amphibious chassis mounted with a spacious all-steel cargo/troop area. On-water propulsion is provided by two propellers at the rear of the hull, and amphibious speed is 10km/h (6mph). The great advantage of the K-61 is its carrying capacity. Up to 60 fully armed troops or 5000kg (11,000lb) of cargo can be transported on water, though only 3000kg (6600lb) of cargo on land. The K-61 has also been used as an amphibious weapons platform for mortars, AA guns and howitzers.

Country of origin:	Russia/Soviet Union
Crew:	2
Weight:	14,550kg (32,083lb)
Dimensions:	Length: 9.15m (30ft); width: 3.15m (10.33ft); height: 2.15m (7.05ft)
Range:	260km (160 miles)
Armour:	Not available
Armament:	Various (see text)
Powerplant:	1 x YaAZ M204VKr 4-cylinder diesel, developing 135hp (101kW)
Performance:	Maximum road speed: 36km/h (22mph); maximum water speed: 10km/h (6mph); gradient: 40 percent; vertical obstacle: 0.65m (2.13ft)

Amphibious Vehicles

BAV-485

The BAV-485 was inspired by the US DUKW amphibious vehicle used by Soviet troops during World War II under the Lend-Lease agreement. The chassis was based on that of the ZIL-151 6x6 truck, later the ZIL-157, and the body lines were modelled directly on the DUKW. In most senses, however, the BAV-485 was an improvement on the US vehicle. It had a drop-down tailgate at the rear of the cargo compartment, and could carry 25 fully equipped troops or 2500kg (5500lb) of cargo. A later model, the BAV-485A, even had a central tyre-pressure regulation system installed (though some DUKWs also had a similar system). In all models, amphibious propulsion came from a single propeller at the rear of the hull.

Country of origin:	Russia/Soviet Union
Crew:	2
Weight:	9650kg (21,278lb)
Dimensions:	Length: 9.54m (31.29ft); width: 2.5m (8.2ft); height: 2.66m (8.73ft)
Range:	530km (330 miles)
Armour:	Not applicable
Armament:	1 x 12.7mm (0.5in) DShKM MG (optional)
Powerplant:	1 x ZIL-123 6-cylinder petrol, developing 110hp (82kW)
Performance:	Maximum road speed: 60km/h (37mph); maximum water speed: 10km/h (6mph); gradient: 60 percent; vertical obstacle: 0.4m (1.3ft)

GAZ-46 MAV

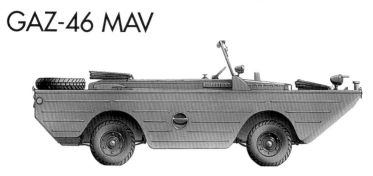

The GAZ-46 imitated the Ford GPA 4x4 amphibious jeep. For troop carrying, three soldiers sat on the rear bench seat, while the driver and commander had individual seats in the front. A fold-down windscreen provided some protection against water spray during amphibious operations. No armament was mounted on the vehicle. Though it was used almost entirely for reconnaissance duties, cargo transportation to a weight of 500kg (1100lb) was possible. The chassis came from the GAZ-67B 4x4 light vehicle and later the GAZ-69. A single three-blade propeller was mounted under the rear of the hull and driven off the engine, and a trim vane had to be fitted prior to entering the water.

Country of origin:	Russia/Soviet Union
Crew:	1 + 4
Weight:	2480kg (5470lb)
Dimensions:	Length: 5.06m (16.6ft); width: 1.74m (5.7ft); height: 2.04m (6.69ft)
Range:	500km (310 miles)
Armour:	Not available
Armament:	None
Powerplant:	1 x M-20 4-cylinder petrol, developing 55hp (41kW)
Performance:	Maximum road speed: 90km/h (56mph); maximum water speed: 9km/h (5.5mph); gradient: 60 percent

Amphibious Vehicles

GT-S

During World War II, experiments with oversnow/amphibious cars and personnel carriers were mostly unsuccessful. The GT-S was the first fully amphibious 'oversnow' vehicle of the post-war era and had the genuine ability to move from deep snow to water without any preparation. As with all oversnow vehicles, its tracks were very wide – 300mm (11.81in) – and ground pressure was only 0.24kg/sq cm (3.4lb/sq in). The wide tracks also propelled it in the water to speeds of 4km/h (2.5mph). The GT-S was a tough and reliable vehicle. It could carry 11 soldiers or 1000kg (2200lb) of cargo. A later variant, the GT-SM, was simply a bigger vehicle and had six road wheels instead of the GT-S' five.

Country of origin:	Russia/Soviet Union
Crew:	1 + 11
Weight:	4600kg (10,100lb)
Dimensions:	Length: 4.93m (16.17ft); width: 2.4m (7.87ft); height: 1.96m (6.43ft)
Range:	400km (250miles)
Armour:	Not available
Armament:	None
Powerplant:	1 x GAZ-61 6-cylinder petrol, developing 85hp (63kW)
Performance:	Maximum road speed: 35km/h (22mph); maximum water speed: 4km/h (2.5mph); gradient: 60 percent; vertical obstacle: 0.6m (2ft)

Pegaso VAP 3550/1

The Pegaso VAP 3550/1 was developed for use by the Spanish marines, but also serves marine forces in Egypt and Mexico. It was designed to be launched offshore from a Landing Ship Tank (LST) craft and transport men and equipment to the landing beachhead. The hull is separated into watertight compartments to reduce the danger of sinking if part of the hull is holed. Eighteen troops or 3000kg (6600lb) of cargo are transported in the front of the vehicle. A hydraulic crane is fitted at the rear for off-loading cargo and a 4500kg (9900lb) winch is set in the front bows. Two waterjets provide amphibious propulsion and two bilge pumps keep the craft free from leaks.

Country of origin:	Spain
Crew:	3 + 18
Weight:	12,500kg (27,550lb)
Dimensions:	Length: 8.85m (29.04ft); width: 2.5m (8.2ft); height: 2.5m (8.2ft)
Range:	800km (500 miles)
Armour:	(Steel) 6mm (0.24in)
Armament:	1 x 7.62mm (0.3in) MG (export versions only)
Powerplant:	1 x Pegaso 9135/5 6-cylinder turbo diesel, developing 190hp (142kW)
Performance:	Maximum road speed: 87km/h (54mph); maximum water speed: 10km/h (6mph); gradient: 60 percent

Vickers-Carden-Loyd Type 31

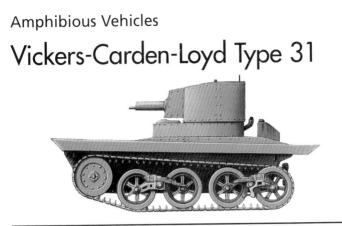

The Vickers-Carden-Loyd amphibious vehicle was the brainchild of J.V. Carden and V. Loyd, employees of the British Vickers works. During the late 1920s, they designed a series of light tanks for the British Army, one of which became the Vickers-Carden-Loyd Type 31 – the world's first operational amphibious tank. The Type 31 was basically a Vickers four-ton light tank fitted with a pontoon-shaped watertight hull. The vehicle floated by virtue of buoyant mudguards. Power came from a propeller at the rear of the hull which gave a top speed of 10km/h (6mph). Directional control was provided by a rudder. The Type 31 sold only on the export market, particularly to the Far East, and it inspired other nations to build their own.

Country of origin:	United Kingdom
Crew:	2
Weight:	3100kg (6800lb)
Dimensions:	Length: 3.96m (12.99ft); width: 2.08m (6.82ft); height: 1.83m (6ft)
Range:	260km (160 miles)
Armour:	(Steel) 9mm (0.35in) maximum
Armament:	1 x 7.7mm (0.31in) MG
Powerplant:	1 x Meadows 6-cylinder petrol, developing 56hp (42kW)
Performance:	Maximum road speed: 64km/h (39mph); maximum water speed: 10km/h (6mph)

Ford GPA

The Ford General Purpose Amphibious (GPA) had its origins in a National Defense Research Committee (NDRC) project in 1941 which sought to develop an amphibious 0.25-ton amphibious vehicle. A collaborative effort by the Marmon-Herrington Company, the boat builders Sparkman & Stephens and the Ford Motor Company resulted in the Ford GPA, an amphibious version of the Willys Jeep. The GPA did not achieve the Jeep's status. Production had been rushed to meet the needs of US invasion forces in North Africa and Italy, and only 12,778 out of the 50,000 ordered were built. It was too small to be a useful seagoing craft, and most went to the Russians under the Lend-Lease agreement.

Country of origin:	United States
Crew:	1 +3
Weight:	1647kg (3632lb)
Dimensions:	Length: 4.62m (15.16ft); width: 1.63m (5.35ft); height: 1.73m (5.68ft)
Range:	Not available
Armour:	None
Armament:	None
Powerplant:	1 x GPA-6005 4-cylinder petrol, developing 54hp (40kW)
Performance:	Maximum road speed: 105km/h (65mph); maximum water speed: 8km/h (5mph)

LVT-3

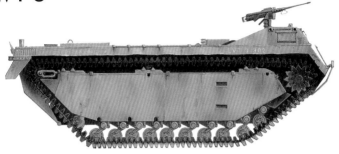

The LVT-3 was introduced at the tail end of World War II. A good design, however, ensured that it was used heavily by the US Marine Corps and Navy in the immediate post-war era. It was a spacious vehicle which could carry 30 infantry or 14,000kg (30,900lb) of cargo. The space was achieved by locating the two Cadillac engine units, bilge pumps, transmissions and fume extractors in two side sponsons. An additional advantage was that a rear loading ramp could be fitted (earlier LVTs were loaded/unloaded over the side of the hull). The LVT-3 was armed with one 12.7mm (0.5in) and two 7.62mm (0.3in) machine guns. Armoured panels were available for additional protection.

Country of origin:	United States
Crew:	3 + 30
Weight:	17,050kg (37,595lb)
Dimensions:	Length: 7.33m (24.05ft); width: 3.23m (10.59ft); height: 3.38m (11.09ft)
Range:	Road: 241km (150 miles); water: 121km (75 miles)
Armour:	None (see text)
Armament:	1 x 12.7mm (0.5in) MG; 2 x 7.62mm (0.3in) MGs
Powerplant:	2 x Cadillac petrol, developing 220hp (164kW)
Performance:	Maximum road speed: 27km/h (17mph); maximum water speed: 10km/h (6mph)

LVTP-5

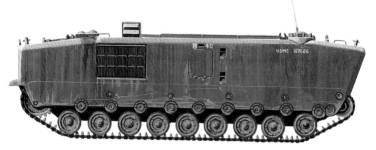

The Landing Vehicle, Tracked, Personnel, Mark 5 (LVTP-5) made a number of departures from previous LVT designs. It had an inverted V-shaped bow to improve its hydrodynamics, and the bow was lowered to allow troop or vehicle entry/exit (roof hatches provided other routes of access). Up to 34 fully equipped infantry could be transported inside, and were protected by the large hull constructed with 6mm (0.24in) armour plate. The LVTP-5 was propelled through the water by its tracks, and could maintain water speeds of 11km/h (7mph). Its driver sat in a cupola on top of the forward hull. The LVTP-5 was costly to maintain and prone to mechanical failure, and it was replaced in the 1970s by the LVTP-7.

Country of origin:	United States
Crew:	3 + 34
Weight:	37,422kg (82,516lb)
Dimensions:	Length: 9.04m (29.66ft); width: 3.57m (11.71ft); height: 2.91m (9.55ft)
Range:	306km (190 miles)
Armour:	(Steel) 6mm (0.24in)
Armament:	1 x 7.62mm (0.3in) MG
Powerplant:	1 x Continental 12-cylinder petrol, developing 810hp (604kW) at 2400rpm
Performance:	Maximum road speed: 48km/h (30mph); maximum water speed: 11km/h (7mph)

Amphibious Vehicles

AAAVR7A1

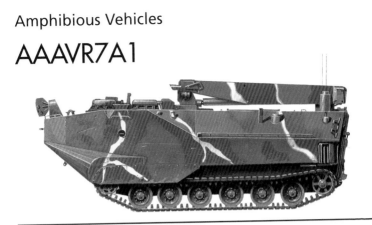

The Armoured Amphibian Assault Vehicle Recovery 7A1 (AAAVR7A1) emerged from the FMC Corporation as a prototype in 1979, and entered production in 1983. Its main role is recovering damaged vehicles or making engineering repairs on or from amphibious landing zones. It can also carry 21 combat-equipped troops or 4500kg (10,000lb) of cargo. For recovery operations, it uses a hydraulic crane with a 2700kg (6000lb) breaking strength and a crane winch with a 10,400kg (23,000lb) capacity. Also stored on board are a Miller Maxtron 300 welder, a portable generator and an air compressor. The AAAVR7A1 has either a 12.7mm (0.5in) Browning M2 HB or a 7.62mm (0.3in) M60 fitted for defence.

Country of origin:	United States
Crew:	5
Weight:	23,601kg (52,040lb)
Dimensions:	Length: 7.94m (26ft); width: 3.27m (10.73ft); height: 3.26m (10.7ft)
Range:	480km (300 miles)
Armour:	Not available
Armament:	1 x 12.7mm (0.5in) Browning M2 HB or 7.62mm (0.3in) M60
Powerplant:	1 x Cummins VT400 8-cylinder multi-fuel, developing 399hp (298kW)
Performance:	Maximum road speed: 72km/h (45mph); maximum water speed: 13km/h (8mph)

AAAV

The Advanced Amphibious Assault Vehicle (AAAV) represents the pinnacle of amphibious-vehicle technology. It is due to come into production in 2006, its primary client being the US Marine Corps. The AAAV is entirely self-deploying. Seventeen combat-ready Marines can be carried across water at 47km/h (30mph), propelled by high-power waterjets. A hydraulic trim vane is lowered when entering the water. On land, the AAAV will travel at 72km/h (45mph), fast enough to keep up with main battle tanks. It has full NBC systems and computerized fire control and its armour is resistant to 12.7mm (0.5in) machine-gun fire. Armament consists of a Bushmaster II 30mm (1.18in) cannon firing high-explosive or armour-piercing rounds.

Country of origin:	United States
Crew:	3 + 17
Weight:	33,525kg (73,922lb)
Dimensions:	Length: 9.01m (29.56ft); width: 3.66m (12ft); height: 3.19m (10.47ft)
Range:	480km (300 miles)
Armour:	Details classified
Armament:	1 x Bushmaster II 30mm (1.18in) cannon; 1 x 7.62mm (0.3in) MG
Powerplant:	1 x MTU MT883 12-cylinder multi-fuel, developing 2702hp (2015kW)
Performance:	Maximum road speed: 72km/h (45mph); maximum water speed: 47km/h (30mph); gradient: 60 percent; vertical obstacle: 0.9m (3ft); trench: 2.4m (8ft)

Saurer 4K 4FA-G1

The basic Saurer 4K 4FA armoured personnel carrier entered production in 196
and began a long line of variants. In its standard form, it was a steel-armoured
APC with a two-plus-eight personnel capacity and a single 12.7mm (0.5in) Browni
M2 HB machine gun mounted on a forward cupola. Little sophistication was prese
– the 4K 4FA could not conduct amphibious operations and had no night-vision
systems. The variants of the 4K 4FA ranged from the minor to the major. The 4K 3
G1 had a 230hp (172kW) engine as opposed to the 250hp (186kW) engine of the 4
By contrast, variants existed with Oerlikon 20mm (0.78in) cannon turrets and eve
81mm (3.19in) Oerlikon-Bührle multiple rocket launchers.

Country of origin:	Austria
Crew:	2 + 8
Weight:	12,200kg (26,900lb)
Dimensions:	Length: 5.35m (17.55ft); width: 2.5m (8.2ft); height: 1.65m (5.41ft)
Range:	370km (230 miles)
Armour:	(Steel) 20mm (0.78in) maximum
Armament:	1 x 12.7mm (0.5in) MG
Powerplant:	1 Saurer 4FA 6-cylinder turbo diesel, developing 250hp (186kW) at 2400rpm
Performance:	Maximum road speed: 65km/h (40mph); fording: 1m (3.3ft); gradient: 75 percent; vertical obstacle: 0.8m (2.6ft); trench: 2.2m (7.2ft)

obra

he Cobra armoured personnel carrier was a Belgian-developed machine.
ntroduced in the mid-1980s, it was doomed to commercial failure, despite being
nd vehicle in design and operation. It had a nine-man carrying capacity, a steel
oured body, and two main weapons: a 7.62mm (0.3in) GPMG and a roof-
nted Browning M2 HB 12.7mm (0.5in) machine gun. It was fully amphibious
out need for modification and had a speed over water of 10km/h (6.2mph),
ered by waterjet units located at the rear. Possibly its most distinctive feature
its drive system: a turbo engine powering an electric generator which in turn
e both wheels and waterjets.

untry of origin:	Belgium
ew:	3 + 9
eight:	8500kg (18,700lb)
nensions:	Length: 4.52m (14.83ft); width: 2.75m (9.02ft); height: 2.32m (7.61ft)
nge:	600km (370 miles)
mour:	Steel (details classified)
mament:	1 x 7.62mm (0.3in) GPMG; 1 x Browning M2 HB 12.7mm (0.5in) MG
werplant:	1 x Cummins VT-190 6-cylinder turbo diesel, developing 190hp (141kW) at 3300rpm
formance:	Maximum road speed: 75km/h (46mph); fording: amphibious

Ram/Kangaroo

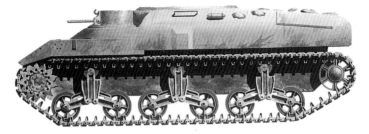

The Ram/Kangaroo was an expedient vehicle used to transport Canadian soldiers into action in Europe in late 1944. The vehicle was essentially a turretless Canadian Ram tank, which was developed in 1942 and 1943 but was quickly rendered obsolete by the introduction of the US Sherman tank. By mid-1944, 500 Rams were in storage in England, and these were converted into armoured personnel carriers. The turret was removed, benches were fixed in the interior alongside ammunition racks and a standard infantry No.19 wireless set was fitted. Ram/Kangaroos were light and mobile vehicles, and joined the ranks of several similar Allied tank conversions.

Country of origin:	Canada/United Kingdom
Crew:	2 + 8
Weight:	29,000kg (63,900lb)
Dimensions:	Length: 5.79m (19ft); width: 2.78m (9.12ft); height: 2.47m (8.1ft)
Range:	230km (140 miles)
Armour:	88mm (3.46in) maximum
Armament:	1 x 7.62mm (0.3in) MG
Powerplant:	1 x Continental R-975 9-cylinder diesel, developing 399hp (298kW)
Performance:	Maximum road speed: 40km/h (25mph); vertical obstacle: 0.6m (2ft); trench: 2.26m (7.41ft)

Wasp Mk IIC

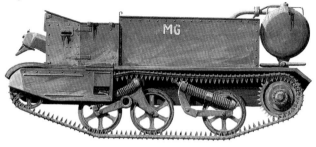

The Wasp was a flamethrower vehicle developed in the United Kingdom in the early 1940s. It was basically a Universal Carrier vehicle fitted with a flame-throwing device. Two fuel tanks and nitrogen pressure cylinders were fitted into the rear of the hull. The driver and co-driver sat in the front, a flamethrower nozzle sticking out of the front armoured wall. Aiming the flamethrower was a crude process of simply pointing the vehicle at the target, which could be engaged at about 100m (330ft). The Wasp Mk IIC was a Canadian variant. It added an extra crew member, the space acquired by reducing fuel capacity and relocating some fuel to a tank behind the hull.

Country of origin:	Canada/United Kingdom
Crew:	3
Weight:	3850kg (8500lb)
Dimensions:	Length: 3.65m (11.97ft); width: 2.03m (6.66ft); height: 1.58m (5.18ft)
Range:	180km (110 miles)
Armour:	(Steel) 10mm (0.39in) maximum
Armament:	1 x flamethrower; 1 x 7.7mm (0.303in) MG
Powerplant:	1 x Ford 9-cylinder petrol, developing 59hp (44kW)
Performance:	Maximum road speed: 48km/h (29mph)

YW 531

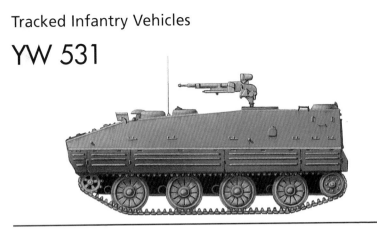

The YW 531 armoured personnel carrier was developed in the late 1960s for the Chinese Army and exported to military forces in Vietnam, Angola, Tanzania and Iraq throughout the 1970s. It was capable of holding 13 troops in the rear of the vehicle, with a two-man crew of driver and commander. The engine was located behind the commander, who sat on the right of the hull at the front and viewed the battlefield through a hatch or a 360-degree rotatable periscope which was integral to the hatch. Driver vision was provided by two periscopes. Like most communist APCs, the YW 531 was fully amphibious, the Chinese vehicle requiring a trim board to be fitted to the front of the hull before entering the water.

Country of origin:	China
Crew:	2 + 13
Weight:	12,500kg (27,600lb)
Dimensions:	Length: 5.74m (18.83ft); width: 2.99m (9.8ft); height: 2.11m (6.92ft)
Range:	425km (260 miles)
Armour:	Not available
Armament:	1 x 12.7mm (0.5in) MG
Powerplant:	1 x Deutz Type 6150L 6-cylinder diesel, developing 257hp (192kW)
Performance:	Maximum road speed: 50km/h (31mph); fording: amphibious; vertical obstacle: 0.6m (2ft); trench: 2m (6.6ft)

YW 703

The YW 703 is actually a version of the Norinco YW 531H armoured personnel carrier, China's main APC type. A 25mm (0.98in) cannon separates the YW 703 from all the other YW 531H derivatives, of which there are many. Other combat versions include the Type 85, armed with a 120mm (4.72in) or 82mm (3.23in) mortar, and a 122mm (4.8in) self-propelled howitzer version. Non-combat variants include the Type 85 command-post vehicle, an armoured recovery vehicle, and an ambulance. The YW 531H can be confused with the YW 534, though the former does not have the bank of four smoke grenade launchers set on either side of the turret.

Country of origin:	China
Crew:	3 + 7
Weight:	15,400kg (31,000lb)
Dimensions:	Length: 6.15m (20.18ft); width: 3.13m (10.27ft); height: 1.88m (6.17ft)
Range:	500km (310 miles)
Armour:	Steel (details classified)
Armament:	1 x 25mm (0.98in) cannon
Powerplant:	1 x Deutz Type BF8L413F 8-cylinder diesel, developing 320hp (239kW)
Performance:	Maximum road speed: 65km/h (40mph); fording: amphibious; vertical obstacle: 0.6m (2ft); trench: 2.2m (7.2ft)

OT-62

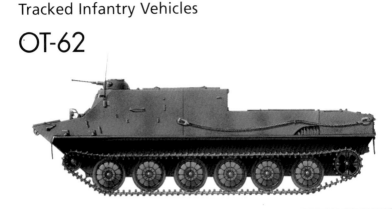

Soviet armoured personnel carriers were widely distributed throughout Europe and the Middle East during the 1960s and 1970s, often through export but also through licensed production or simple copy. The OT-62 was the Czech version of the Russian BTR-50PK. It entered service with the Czech military in 1964 and with the Polish Army in 1966 as a variant called TOPAS. Like the BTR-50PK, the OT-62 has an all-welded armoured hull with slightly less carrying capacity (18 as opposed to 20 passengers) but more powerful engines. Two waterjets at the rear of the vehicle provide propulsion during amphibious use. The Polish TOPAS version was designed for vehicular recovery operations.

Country of origin:	Czechoslovakia
Crew:	3 + 18
Weight:	15,100kg (33,300lb)
Dimensions:	Length: 7m (22.97ft); width: 3.22m (10.56ft); height: 2.72m (8.92ft)
Range:	460km (290 miles)
Armour:	14mm (0.55in) maximum
Armament:	1 x 7.62mm (0.3in) PKY MG and various other configurations
Powerplant:	1 x PV6 6-cylinder turbo diesel, developing 300hp (224kW) at 1200rpm
Performance:	Maximum road speed: 60km/h (37mph); fording: amphibious; gradient: 70 percent; vertical obstacle: 1.1m (3.6ft); trench: 2.8m (9.2ft)

AMX VCI

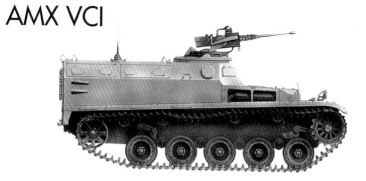

The AMX VCI (Véhicule de Combat d'Infanterie) went into production in 1957 to meet a French Army requirement to replace the cancelled Hotchkiss TT6 and TT9 armoured personnel carriers. As the name suggests, the vehicle is constructed around the modified chassis of the AMX-13 light tank. It carried three crew and 10 soldiers, the latter sitting back to back in a bisected internal compartment at the rear, accessible by double doors. Standard armament is a 12.7mm (0.5in) M2 HB machine gun pintle-mounted on the roof. Updated AMX VCIs have NBC and night-vision systems. The AMX VCI was developed into a large number of variants, ranging from TOW-armed anti-tank vehicles to the RATAC radar-carrier vehicle.

Country of origin:	France
Crew:	3 + 10
Weight:	15,000kg (33,100lb)
Dimensions:	Length: 5.7m (18.7ft); width: 2.67m (8.76ft); height: 2.41m (7.9ft)
Range:	350km (220 miles)
Armour:	(Steel) 30mm (1.18in) maximum
Armament:	1 x 12.7mm (0.5in) M2 HB MG
Powerplant:	1 x SOFAM 8Gxb 8-cylinder petrol, developing 250hp (186kW) at 3200rpm
Performance:	Maximum road speed: 60km/h (37mph); fording: 1m (3.3ft); gradient: 60 percent; vertical obstacle: 1m (3.3ft); trench: 1.6m (5.3ft)

AMX VTT/TB

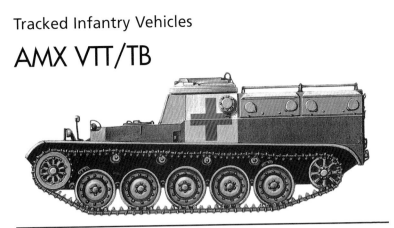

The chassis of the AMX-13 light tank yielded a bewildering number of variants. Most prolific were the series of vehicles based upon the AMX VCI mechanized infantry combat vehicle, developed from the late 1950s onwards. The standard VCI was converted into, amongst other vehicles, an 81mm (3.19in) mortar vehicle, a battery command post, an ENTAC missile launcher, a Roland SAM vehicle, a TOW anti-tank missile vehicle, a combat engineer vehicle and an ambulance vehicle – this being the AMX VTT/TB. The VTT/TB was more of a battlefield rescue vehicle than an ambulance, as it had no facilities for advanced medical care. It could carry four sitting and three stretchered patients as well as two orderlies and the two-man crew.

Country of origin:	France
Crew:	2 + 9
Weight:	14,300kg (31,500lb)
Dimensions:	Length: 5.7m (18.7ft); width: 2.67m (8.76ft); height: 1.92m (6.29ft)
Range:	350km (220 miles)
Armour:	(Steel) 30mm (1.18in) maximum
Armament:	None
Powerplant:	1 x SOFAM 8Gxb 8-cylinder petrol, developing 250hp (186kW) at 3200rpm
Performance:	Maximum road speed: 60km/h (37mph); fording: 1m (3.3ft); gradient: 60 percent; vertical obstacle: 1m (3.3ft); trench: 1.6m (5.3ft)

SPz lang HS30

The HS30 was destined to be blighted by technical problems throughout its active life. Consequently, only 2176 vehicles were built (out of a projected 4450) between 1958 and 1962. In the early 1970s, remaining HS30s were replaced with Marder mechanized infantry combat vehicles. The HS30 was a basic armoured personnel carrier which could carry five soldiers and a three-man crew inside an all-welded steel hull. It was not amphibious, neither did it have an NBC option, both serious deficits in the Cold War era. It was, however, well armed. A turret-mounted 20mm (0.78in) Hispano HS820 was the primary weapon, but ATGWs and M40A1 106mm (4.17in) recoilless rifles were further options.

Country of origin:	Germany
Crew:	3 + 5
Weight:	14,600kg (32,200lb)
Dimensions:	Length: 5.56m (18.24ft); width: 2.25m (7.38ft); height: 1.85m (6.07ft)
Range:	270km (170 miles)
Armour:	(Steel) 30mm (1.18in) maximum
Armament:	1 x 20mm (0.78in) Hispano HS820 cannon and other options
Powerplant:	1 x Rolls-Royce 8-cylinder petrol, developing 235hp (175kW) at 3800rpm
Performance:	Maximum road speed: 51km/h (32mph); fording: 0.7m (2.3ft); gradient: 60 percent; vertical obstacle: 0.6m (2ft); trench: 1.6m (5.3ft)

Tracked Infantry Vehicles

M113A1G

The M113A1G is a German version of the US M113 armoured personnel carrier, a variant of which is a mortar-carrier. The troop compartment is converted to hold a 120mm (4.72in) mortar, reducing total personnel capacity to five. The mortar is fired directly out of an open space in the rear of the hull roof, and can hit targets 6200m (20,300ft) away. A 7.62mm (0.3in) machine gun provides a local defensive capability. The on-board store of mortar ammunition is 60 shells while the machine gun has 2400 rounds of 7.62mm (0.3in) ammunition. The Federal German Armed Forces have produced over 4000 M113A1G vehicles in other variants which include radar vehicles, ambulances and ATGW carriers.

Country of origin:	Germany
Crew:	5
Weight:	12,800kg (28,200lb)
Dimensions:	Length: 4.86m (15.94ft); width: 2.68m (8.79ft); height: 1.85m (6.07ft)
Range:	480km (300 miles)
Armour:	35mm (1.38in) maximum
Armament:	1 x 120mm (4.72in) mortar; 1 x 7.62mm (0.3in) MG
Powerplant:	1 x Detroit 6V-53N 6-cylinder diesel, developing 212hp (158kW) at 2800rpm
Performance:	Maximum road speed: 68km/h (42mph); fording: amphibious; gradient: 60 percent; vertical obstacle: 0.6m (2ft); trench: 1.68m (5.51ft)

M113 Zelda

The US M113 entered into production in 1954 to fulfil a US Army order for air-transportable armoured vehicles, and used aluminium armour to keep weight low. Since then, over 70,000 have been made and service continues in over 35 countries despite US production ceasing in 1992. The M113 is an armoured hull mounted on a tracked suspension capable of transporting 11 soldiers with the protection of 38mm (1.49in) of armour. It is fully amphibious. Hundreds of variants have been produced, from missile launchers to engineer vehicles. The Israeli Zelda is a standard M113 but with additional side and floor armour to protect against rocket-propelled grenades and mine detonations respectively.

Country of origin:	Israel
Crew:	2 + 11
Weight:	12,500kg (27,600lb)
Dimensions:	Length: 5.23m (17.16ft); width: 3.08m (10.1ft); height: 1.85m (6.07ft
Range:	480km (300 miles)
Armour:	(Aluminium) 38mm (1.49in)
Armament:	Various MG configurations
Powerplant:	1 x Detroit Diesel 6V-53T 6-cylinder diesel, developing 212hp (158kW) at 2800rpm
Performance:	Maximum road speed: 61km/h (38mph); fording: amphibious; gradient: 60 percent; vertical obstacle: 0.6m (2ft); trench: 1.68m (5.51ft)

Tracked Infantry Vehicles

SU-60

The SU-60 was Japan's first post-war tracked armoured personnel carrier. It entered service with the Japanese Ground Self Defence Force in 1960 and was eventually replaced by the Type 73 in the early 1970s. A general US M113 appearance belies a different crew configuration. The driver and bow machine-gunner sat at the front of the vehicle on the right and left respectively, with the commander between them. The final crew member sat just behind and to the right of the commander, and would operate the 12.7mm (0.5in) roof-mounted machine gun. Variants of the SU-60 include two mortar carriers, an NBC detection vehicle, an anti-tank vehicle and a bulldozer.

Country of origin:	Japan
Crew:	4 + 6
Weight:	11,800kg (26,000lb)
Dimensions:	Length: 4.85m (15.91ft); width: 2.4m (7.87ft); height: 1.7m (5.58ft)
Range:	300km (190 miles)
Armour:	Steel (details classified)
Armament:	1 x 12.7mm (0.5in) Browning M2 HB MG
Powerplant:	1 x Mitsubishi 8 HA 21 WT 8-cylinder diesel, developing 220hp (164kW) at 2400rpm
Performance:	Maximum road speed: 45km/h (28mph); fording: 1m (3.3ft); gradient: 60 percent; vertical obstacle: 0.6m (2ft); trench: 1.82m (5.97ft)

Type 73

Like the US M113, the Type 73 has an aluminium-armoured hull, a choice made after Komatsu's steel-armoured prototype was rejected in favour of Mitsubishi's aluminium contribution. Unlike the US vehicle, the Type 73 is not amphibious unless an optional swim-kit is fitted. However, NBC and night-vision equipment is standard. Production and service began in 1973, and 225 of the vehicles have entered use with the Japanese Ground Self Defence Force. To date, the Type 73 has only been produced in one variant, a command post vehicle, although components from the Type 73 are used in the Type 75 ground wind-measuring system and Type 75 130mm (5.12in) rocket launcher.

Country of origin:	Japan
Crew:	3 + 9
Weight:	13,300kg (29,300lb)
Dimensions:	Length: 5.8m (19ft); width: 2.8m (9.2ft); height: 2.2m (7.2ft)
Range:	300km (190 miles)
Armour:	Aluminium (details classified)
Armament:	1 x 12.7mm (0.5in) MG; 1 x 7.62mm (0.3in) MG
Powerplant:	1 x Mitsubishi 4ZF V4 diesel, developing 300hp (202kW) at 2200rpm
Performance:	Maximum road speed: 70km/h (43mph); fording: amphibious with swim-kit; gradient: 60 percent; vertical obstacle: 0.7m (2.3ft); trench: 2m (5.6ft)

Tracked Infantry Vehicles

BTR-50

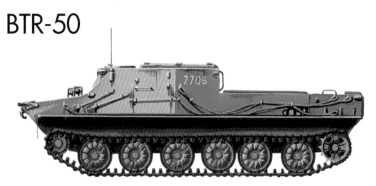

Between 1957 and the early 1970s, the BTR-50 served as the standard Soviet armoured personnel carrier before it was superseded by the BMP-1. It was a lightly armed (1 x 7.62mm/0.3in machine gun) APC with a large carrying capacity of 20 personnel. The low-profile hull meant that the occupants entered and exited over the vehicle's side rather than through hatches and doors. A later version, the BTR-50K, had an enclosed armoured roof and roof hatches for access. The chassis of the vehicle was basically that of the PT-76 light tank and its engine was a modified version of that used in the T-54 main battle tank. Waterjets powered the vehicle when in amphibious mode.

Country of origin:	Russia/Soviet Union
Crew:	2 + 20
Weight:	14,200kg (31,300lb)
Dimensions:	Length: 7.03m (23.06ft); width: 3.14m (10.3ft); height: 2.07m (6.79ft)
Range:	400km (250 miles)
Armour:	(Steel) 10mm (0.39in)
Armament:	1 x 7.62mm (0.3in) MG
Powerplant:	1 x Model V6 6-cylinder diesel, developing 240hp (179kW) at 1800rpm
Performance:	Maximum road speed: 44km/h (27mph); fording: amphibious; gradient: 70 percent; vertical obstacle: 1.1m (3.6ft); trench: 2.8m (9.2ft)

MT-LB

The MT-LB was a multi-purpose vehicle which entered service in 1974. It was designed to replace the 30-year-old AT-P armoured artillery tractors, but went on to fulfil a multitude of roles. Configurations included: artillery tractor, repair vehicle, engineer vehicle, mobile command and control centre, ambulance, Gopher SAM system and standard armoured personnel carrier. The basic vehicle was fully amphibious and had the option of swapping its 350mm (13.78in) wide tracks for 565mm (22.24in) versions to reduce its ground pressure in snowy or muddy conditions. As an APC it could carry 11 personnel, a rear hatch being the only access for crew and passengers.

Country of origin:	Russia/Soviet Union
Crew:	2 + 11
Weight:	14,900kg (32,900lb)
Dimensions:	Length: 7.47m (24.5ft); width: 2.85m (9.35ft); height: 2.42m (7.94ft)
Range:	525km (330 miles)
Armour:	(Steel) 3–10mm (0.11–0.39in)
Armament:	1 x 12.7mm (0.5in) MG; or 1 x 7.62mm (0.3in) MG
Powerplant:	1 x YaMZ-238N 8-cylinder diesel, developing 220hp (164kW) at 2400rpm
Performance:	Maximum road speed: 62km/h (39mph); fording: amphibious; gradient: 60 percent; vertical obstacle: 0.6m (2ft); trench: 2.41m (7.9ft)

Tracked Infantry Vehicles

KIFV K-200

The Korean Infantry Fighting Vehicle K-200 is the first of a series of South Korean fighting vehicles developed by the Dae Woo Industries company. Borrowing from the US AIFV, it has become a powerful and reliable armoured personnel carrier. It can carry nine infantry and its three-man crew into battle at speeds of 74km/h (46mph). In amphibious mode, it achieves 7km/h (4mph) on water, propelled by its tracks. Standard armament is usually two machine guns: a 12.7mm (0.5in) and a 7.62mm (0.3in) weapon. However, optional armament configurations include 20mm (0.78in) Vulcan cannon and two mortar carriers – 81mm (3.19in) and 106mm (4.17in). An NBC reconnaissance variant has recently been developed.

Country of origin:	South Korea
Crew:	3 + 9
Weight:	12,900kg (28,400lb)
Dimensions:	Length: 5.48m (19.15ft); width: 2.84m (9.32ft); height: 2.51m (8.23ft)
Range:	480km (300 miles)
Armour:	Aluminium and steel (details classified)
Armament:	1 x 12.7mm (0.5in) MG; 1 x 7.62mm (0.3in) MG
Powerplant:	1 x MAN D-284T V8 diesel, developing 280hp (208kW) at 2300rpm
Performance:	Maximum road speed: 74km/h (46mph); fording: amphibious; gradient: 60 percent; vertical obstacle: 0.64m (2.1ft); trench: 1.68m (5.51ft)

Carden-Loyd Mk VI

Carden-Loyd tankettes were an unsuccessful inter-war experiment in providing unarmoured mobile machine-gun carriers for pairs of infantrymen. The first tankette was produced in 1925, a small tracked vehicle big enough for one man only, subsequently topped with a flimsy shield and a Hotchkiss machine gun to form the Carden-Loyd Mk I. Several variations were then produced, focusing mainly on experiments with track and suspension configurations. In 1926, a two-man version was produced which became the Vickers machine-gun-armed Carden-Loyd Mk IV in 1928. Two more versions emerged and achieved some sales abroad, but the vehicles were tactically impractical and had no future past the mid-1930s.

Country of origin:	United Kingdom
Crew:	2
Weight:	1600kg (3500lb)
Dimensions:	Length: 2.47m (8.1ft); width: 1.7m (5.58ft); height: 1.22m (4ft)
Range:	160km (100 miles)
Armour:	9mm (0.35in) maximum
Armament:	1 x 7.7mm (0.303in) Vickers MG
Powerplant:	1 x Ford T 4-cylinder petrol, developing 40hp (30kW)
Performance:	Maximum road speed: 45km/h (28mph)

Bren Gun Carrier

The Bren Carrier was more correctly known as the Universal (Bren Gun) Carrier Produced between 1934 and 1960, it was used to transport a two-man Bren gun team, though initially it was designed as a gun tractor for a Vickers machine gun an a four-man crew. It was the advent of the Bren gun in 1936 which put an end to its gun tractor days. In effect, the Carrier was little more than an armoured metal box. The engine was placed in the centre of the vehicle next to the driver and gunner – the noise was apparently deafening. Despite their crudity, the Carriers were much used, and around 10 could be found in each infantry battalion. Various experiment models abounded, including versions mounting 25-pounder (87.6mm/3.45in) guns.

Country of origin:	United Kingdom
Crew:	2
Weight:	4000kg (8800lb)
Dimensions:	Length: 3.65m (11.97ft); width: 2.11m (6.92ft); height: 1.57m (5.15ft)
Range:	250km (150 miles)
Armour:	10mm (0.39in) maximum
Armament:	1 x 7.62mm (0.3in) Bren MG
Powerplant:	1 x Ford V8 petrol, developing 85hp (63kW) at 3500rpm
Performance:	Maximum road speed: 48km/h (30mph)

FV433 Stormer

The Stormer is another British vehicle to use the Alvis Scorpion hull as its foundation. Development of the Stormer ran through the 1970s and production self began in 1981. It is a fairly standard armoured personnel carrier, carrying three crew and eight infantry with a good road speed of 80km/h (50mph). It has sold well in export, particularly to Indonesia, Malaysia and Oman. The Stormer's main credit is its versatility. The basic vehicle can be fitted with lots of optional equipment and weaponry, including NBC systems, a flotation screen, night-vision instruments and guns ranging from 12.7mm (0.5in) machine guns to 90mm (3.54in) cannon and Starstreak missiles.

Country of origin:	United Kingdom
Crew:	3 + 8
Weight:	12,700kg (28,000lb)
Dimensions:	Length: 5.33m (17.49ft); width: 2.4m (7.87ft); height: 2.27m (7.45ft)
Range:	650km (400 miles)
Armour:	Aluminium (details classified)
Armament:	Various
Powerplant:	1 x Perkins T6/3544 6-cylinder turbo diesel, developing 250hp (186kW) at 2600rpm
Performance:	Maximum road speed: 80km/h (50mph); fording: amphibious; gradient: 60 percent; vertical obstacle: 0.6m (2ft); trench: 1.75m (5.74ft)

Tracked Infantry Vehicles

M75

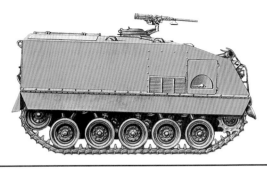

The International Harvester M75 was an initial US attempt to replace the wartime M3 half-track and produce a modern armoured personnel carrier. Its design was flawed in that it relied on expensive tank components for its production, especially the running gear, engine and transmission. Mainly for reasons of cost, only 1729 were produced between 1951 and 1954. The M75 looked towards the M113 in design concept. It featured a steel armoured box with a sloped glacis front big enough for two crew and 10 soldiers. Twin doors at the rear of the hull provided entry and exit. Armament consisted of one 12.7mm (0.5in) Browning M2 HB machine gun mounted on the roof.

Country of origin:	United States
Crew:	2 + 10
Weight:	18,828kg (41,516lb)
Dimensions:	Length: 5.19m (17.03ft); width: 2.84m (9.32ft); height: 2.77m (9.09ft)
Range:	185km (115 miles)
Armour:	(Steel) 15.9mm (0.63in)
Armament:	1 x 12.7mm (0.5in) Browning M2 HB
Powerplant:	1 x Continental AO-895-4 6-cylinder petrol, developing 295hp (220kW) at 2660rpm
Performance:	Maximum road speed: 71km/h (44mph); fording: 1.22m (4ft); gradient: 60 percent; vertical obstacle: 0.46m (1.5ft); trench: 1.68m (5.51ft)

M59

The M59 was in production between 1954 and 1959, before being phased out in favour of the M113 armoured personnel carrier. It was a basic tracked APC with an all-welded steel hull, a two-man crew, and carrying capacity for 10 soldiers. In theory, it was amphibious, propulsion coming from its tracks when in the water. However, experience showed that even mildly choppy water could destabilize its float characteristics. The commander of an M59 had a dedicated viewing cupola. Initially this had a 360-degree traverse, but later it was replaced with a fixed cupola fitted with four periscopes. The M59 spawned only one production variant, the M84 107mm (4.21in) mortar carrier.

Country of origin:	United States
Crew:	2 + 10
Weight:	19,323kg (38,197lb)
Dimensions:	Length: 5.61m (18.4ft); width: 3.26m (10.7ft); height: 2.27m (7.45ft)
Range:	164km (102 miles)
Armour:	(Steel) 16mm (0.63in)
Armament:	1 x 12.7mm (0.5in) Browning M2 HB MG
Powerplant:	1 x General Motors Model 302 6-cylinder petrol, developing 127hp (95kW) at 3350rpm
Performance:	Maximum road speed: 51km/h (32mph); fording: amphibious; gradient: 60 percent; vertical obstacle: 0.46m (1.5ft); trench: 1.68m (5.51ft)

M114A1E1

The M114 was a command and reconnaissance derivative of the M113 armoured personnel carrier and served in the US Army from 1964 to 1982. It was a simple aluminium armoured hull on a tracked chassis, though unlike in the M113, the crew compartment was given over to communications equipment. Armament was a central feature of the vehicle. At first, M114s were armed with manually operated machine guns, but by the late 1960s the commander had a remote-controlled 12.7mm (0.5in) or even a 20mm (0.78in) Hispano-Suiza cannon fitted to a cupola in front of his hatch. The M114 was phased out from the late 1970s after disappointing off-road performance during the Vietnam war.

Country of origin:	United States
Crew:	3 or 4
Weight:	6930kg (15,280lb)
Dimensions:	Length: 4.46m (14.63ft); width: 2.33m (7.64ft); height: 2.16m (7.09ft)
Range:	440km (270 miles)
Armour:	(Aluminium) 37mm (1.46in)
Armament:	1 x 12.7mm (0.5in) MG or 1 x 20mm (0.78in) Hispano-Suiza cannon; 1 x 7.62mm (0.3in) MG
Powerplant:	1 x Chevrolet 283-V8 8-cylinder petrol, developing 160hp (119kW)
Performance:	Maximum road speed: 58km/h (36mph); fording: amphibious; gradient: 60 percent; vertical obstacle: 0.5m (1.6ft); trench: 1.5m (4.9ft)

M-60P

The M60P appears to look to the West and the US M113 for its inspiration rather than to the East and Soviet armoured personnel carriers. Like subsequent Yugoslav APCs, however, it is a medley of various foreign parts and design elements. The Soviet SU-76 self-propelled gun chassis provides the basis for the suspension, an Austrian Steyr-type engine gives the power, and Western APCs, such as the US M59 and British FV432, contribute to overall design. An M60PB anti-tank variant was later produced. This featured two 82mm (3.23in) recoilless rifles, though by the mid-1970s these were ineffective against modern main battle tank armour. The M60P only operated in Yugoslavia, and is still in service today.

Country of origin:	Yugoslavia
Crew:	3 + 10
Weight:	11,000kg (24,300lb)
Dimensions:	Length: 5.02m (16.47ft); width: 2.77m (9.09ft); height: 2.77m (9.09ft)
Range:	400km (250 miles)
Armour:	(Steel) 25mm (0.98in)
Armament:	1 x 12.7mm (0.5in) MG; 1 x 7.62mm (0.3in) MG
Powerplant:	1 x FAMOS 6-cylinder diesel, developing 140hp (104kW)
Performance:	Maximum road speed: 45km/h (28mph); fording: 1.25m (4.1ft); gradient: 60 percent; vertical obstacle: 0.6m (2ft); trench: 2m (6.6ft)

M-80 MICV

Though indebted to Soviet armoured personnel carrier design, the M-80 Mechanised Infantry Combat Vehicle (MICV) is essentially a Yugoslav design. It is an amphibious APC with an all-welded steel armour hull, with NBC protection and night-vision devices fitted as standard. Its most distinctive feature is the configuration of turret armament. As well as two Yugoslav copies of the Soviet Sagger ATGW, the turret mounts a 30mm (1.18in) cannon and a 7.62mm (0.3in) machine gun. Both these weapons are set in turret slits to allow anti-aircraft engagement at an elevation of 75 degrees. Consequently, the M-80 is able to engage low-flying aircraft at ranges of up to 1500m (4900ft).

Country of origin:	Yugoslavia
Crew:	3 + 7
Weight:	13,700kg (30,200lb)
Dimensions:	Length: 6.4m (20.99ft); width: 2.59m (8.49ft); height: 2.3m (7.55ft)
Range:	500km (310 miles)
Armour:	(Steel) 30mm (1.18in)
Armament:	2 x Yugoslav Sagger ATGWs; 1 x 30mm (1.18in) cannon; 1 x 7.62mm (0.3in) MG
Powerplant:	1 x HS-115-2 8-cylinder turbo diesel, developing 260hp (194kW)
Performance:	Maximum road speed: 60km/h (37mph); fording: amphibious; gradient: 60 percent; vertical obstacle: 0.8m (2.6ft); trench: 2.2m (7.2ft)

EE-3 Jararaca

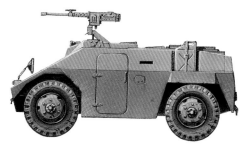

The EE-3 Jararaca was produced by the now-dissolved ENGESA company. It is basically a diminutive 4x4 scout car only 4.12m (13.52ft) in length and 1.56m (5.12ft) in height. Its small size and light weight give it excellent manoeuvrability and speed, qualities it can maintain over rough ground using a central tyre-pressure regulation system. All tyres are of run-flat type. The hull is constructed from double-layer steel armour plate. Inside is a three-man crew with the driver positioned centrally over the front glacis plate. Three periscopes provide him with hatch-down visibility. The EE-3 accepts various armament configurations ranging from the standard 12.7mm (0.5in) Browning machine gun to a MILAN ATGW.

Country of origin:	Brazil
Crew:	3
Weight:	5500kg (12,100lb)
Dimensions:	Length: 4.12m (13.52ft); width: 2.13m (6.99ft); height: 1.56m (5.12ft)
Range:	750km (470 miles)
Armour:	Double-layer steel (details classified)
Armament:	1 x 12.7mm (0.5in) Browning M2 HB as standard
Powerplant:	1 x Mercedes-Benz OM 314A 4-cylinder turbo diesel, developing 120hp (89kW) at 2800rpm
Performance:	Maximum road speed: 100km/h (60mph); fording: 0.6m (2ft); gradient: 60 percent; vertical obstacle: 0.4m (1.3ft); trench: 0.4m (1.3ft)

Wheeled Infantry Vehicles

LAV-25

The Light Armoured Vehicle 25 (LAV-25) is in most ways a copy of the Swiss MOWAG Piranha, one of the world's most successful armoured personnel carriers. Built by General Motors of Canada, it is an 8x8 armoured vehicle with capacity for three crew and six passengers, the latter sitting back to back in the hull rear. Like the Piranha, the LAV-25 has evolved into a large number of variants, including maintenance and recovery vehicles, ATGW carriers, Mobile Electronic Warfare Support System and even an Assault Gun Vehicle armed with a 105mm (4.13in) cannon. The standard turret is usually fitted with a 25mm (0.98in) M242 chain gun and a 7.62mm (0.3in) coaxial machine gun.

Country of origin:	Canada
Crew:	3 + 6
Weight:	12,882kg (28,405lb)
Dimensions:	Length: 6.39m (20.96ft); width: 2.5m (8.2ft); height: 2.56m (8.39ft)
Range:	668km (414 miles)
Armour:	Classified
Armament:	1 x 25mm (0.98in) M242 chain gun; 1 x 7.62mm (0.3in) coaxial MG; various other options available (see text)
Powerplant:	1 x Detroit Diesel 6-cylinder diesel, developing 275hp (205kW)
Performance:	Maximum road speed: 100km/h (60mph); fording: amphibious; gradient: 60 percent; vertical obstacle: 0.5m (1.6ft); trench: 2.06m (6.76ft)

VTP-1 Orca

The VTP-1 Orca ('Killer Whale') was developed by Industrias Cardoen SA in the early 1980s to fulfil its own brief for a multi-purpose armoured vehicle. With a carrying capacity of 16 fully armed men and a total length of 7.84m (25.72ft), the Orca stands as possibly the largest 6x6 armoured personnel carrier in the world. It has an all-welded steel hull with armour of 6 to 12mm (0.24–0.47in). Multiple mounts for machine guns are set around the top of the hull over the troop compartment. Even with its great size, the Orca can maintain a high road speed of 120km/h (75mph), and its 6x6 configuration also gives good cross-country mobility and performance.

Country of origin:	Chile
Crew:	2 + 16
Weight:	18,000kg (39,700lb)
Dimensions:	Length: 7.84m (25.72ft); width: 2.5m (8.2ft); height: 2.5m (8.2ft)
Range:	1000km (620 miles)
Armour:	6–12mm (0.24–0.47in)
Armament:	Multiple MGs
Powerplant:	1 x General Motors 6V-53T 6-cylinder diesel, developing 260hp (194kW) at 2400rpm
Performance:	Maximum road speed: 120km/h (75mph); gradient: 60 percent

Wheeled Infantry Vehicles

Fahd

The Fahd is a large armoured personnel carrier able to carry 10 fully armed soldiers as well as the two-man crew. Though an Egyptian vehicle, it was designed in Germany and actually uses a Mercedes-Benz truck chassis. The armoured hull provides the usual APC protection against small-arms fire and shell splinters, and steel shutters close over the windows when in combat. A standard Fahd is completely unarmed but there are many options for roof-mounted machine guns, cannons and ATGW launchers. A variant has even been produced fitted with the 30mm (1.18in) cannon turret from the Russian BMP-2. Firing ports are provided on both sides of the troop compartment.

Country of origin:	Egypt
Crew:	2 + 10
Weight:	10,900kg (24,000lb)
Dimensions:	Length: 6m (19.68ft); width: 2.45m (8.04ft); height: 2.1m (6.89ft)
Range:	800km (500 miles)
Armour:	Steel (details classified)
Armament:	None as standard (see text)
Powerplant:	1 x Mercedes-Benz OM-352 A 6-cylinder turbo diesel, developing 168hp (125kW) at 2800rpm
Performance:	Maximum road speed: 90km/h (56mph); fording: 0.7m (2.29ft); gradient: 70 percent; vertical obstacle: 0.5m (1.6ft); trench: 0.9m (2.9ft)

Patria XA-180

The Patria XA-180 is a 6x6 armoured personnel carrier used mainly by Scandinavian military forces and the Republic of Ireland. It was developed in the early 1980s and entered service in 1983 with the Finnish Army. Its bow-like front testifies to a fully amphibious capability, something essential in the wet climes of northern Europe, though a trim vane has to be fitted prior to amphibious operations. The hull is all-welded steel armour with double doors in the hull rear providing entry and exit for up to 10 soldiers. Standard armament on the XA-180 is a roof-mounted machine gun, but variants include an ATGW carrier and an air-defence version fitted with the Crotale New Generation SAM system.

Country of origin:	Finland
Crew:	2 + 10
Weight:	15,000kg (33,100lb)
Dimensions:	Length: 7.35m (24.11ft); width: 2.89m (9.48ft); height: 2.47m (8.1ft)
Range:	800km (500 miles)
Armour:	Steel (details classified)
Armament:	1 x 7.62mm (0.3in) or 12.7mm (0.5in) MG
Powerplant:	1 x Valmet 6-cylinder turbo diesel, developing 236hp (175kW)
Performance:	Maximum road speed: 105km/h (65mph); fording: amphibious; gradient: 70 percent; vertical obstacle: 0.6m (2ft); trench: 1m (3.3ft)

M201 VLTT

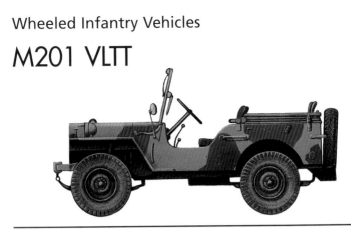

With the end of World War II, France found itself with an urgent need to restock its store of military vehicles. Through a mixture of war surplus, the Lend-Lease agreement with the US and battle-recovered vehicles, the French government was able to gather some 22,000 Willys MB or Ford GPW Jeeps. These were either repaired, restored or used for spare parts at the ERGM vehicle plant at La Maltournée near Paris. The vehicles which emerged were known as VLTT (Voiture Légère Tous Terrains). Like the originals, these 4x4 jeeps had a 100km/h (62mph) top speed, good off-road handling and came fitted with a collapsible soft top.

Country of origin:	France
Crew:	1 + 3
Weight:	1520kg (3352lb)
Dimensions:	Length: 3.36m (11.02ft); width: 1.58m (5.18ft); height: 1.77m (5.81ft)
Range:	348km (216 miles)
Armour:	Not applicable
Armament:	None
Powerplant:	1 x 4-cylinder diesel, developing 61hp (46kW)
Performance:	Maximum road speed: 100km/h (62mph)

anhard M3

he Panhard M3 remains one of the world's most successful armoured personnel
carriers, if only for its massive export sales to over 35 countries with particular
centrations in Africa and the Middle East. There is little exceptional about the
and consequently it is ideal for transforming into local variants. It is a 4x4
oured vehicle which can carry 10 men as well as a two-man crew, and negotiate
gh terrain with confidence. Access and exit are through two side and two rear
rs. It is fully amphibious, and can maintain 4km/h (2.5mph) in water, propelled
ts wheels. The many M3 variants include engineer vehicles, anti-aircraft
icles, an ambulance and radar versions.

ountry of origin:	France
rew:	2 + 10
Veight:	6100kg (13,450lb)
imensions:	Length: 4.45m (14.59ft); width: 2.55m (8.37ft); height: 2m (6.56ft)
ange:	600km (370 miles)
rmour:	12mm (0.47in) maximum
rmament:	Various
owerplant:	1 x Panhard M4 HD 4-cylinder petrol, developing 90hp (67kW)
erformance:	Maximum road speed: 90km/h (56mph); fording: amphibious; gradient: 60 percent; vertical obstacle: 0.3m (1ft); trench: 0.8m (2.6ft)

VXB-170

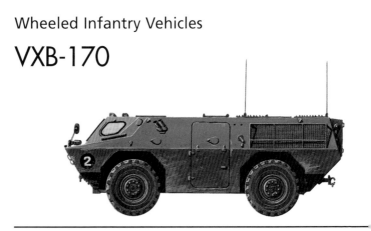

The VXB-170 was a 4x4 armoured personnel carrier developed by the French military truck manufacturer Berliet in the mid-1960s. It went into production 1973. It mainly went into service with the French gendarmerie, who found it a useful multi-purpose armoured vehicle ideally suited for security use. The VXB-1 is a 4x4 fully amphibious APC with a carrying capacity of 12 or 13 soldiers. Windows are bullet-proofed and can be opened to provide firing-ports if necessa Four roof hatches and three side doors provide multiple entry and exit routes. A optional feature was a 4500kg (9900lb) capacity winch which could be installed i the front of the hull.

Country of origin:	France
Crew:	12
Weight:	12,700kg (28,000lb)
Dimensions:	Length: 5.99m (19.65ft); width: 2.5m (8.2ft); height: 2.05m (6.73ft)
Range:	750km (470 miles)
Armour:	7mm (0.28in)
Armament:	1 x 7.62mm (0.3in) MG
Powerplant:	1 x Berliet V800M 8-cylinder diesel, developing 170hp (127kW)
Performance:	Maximum road speed: 85km/h (53mph); fording: amphibious; gradient: 60 percent

nhard VCR

e VCR is another fine addition to Panhard's range of military vehicles. It comes
1 6x6 or 4x4 configurations. The 6x6 version can raise its centre tyres when on
s or hard surfaces to reduce tyre wear and improve fuel efficiency. When off-
, the central tyres are then lowered to improve traction and mobility. All VCRs
ully amphibious. They are propelled by their wheels in the water, though the
TT version has two waterjets, one either side of the hull. Like all Panhard
cles, the VCR has numerous variants. As well as SAM, ATGW, command post,
ulance and repair vehicle variants, the VCR can be fitted with NBC protection
night-vision devices.

untry of origin:	France
ew:	3 + 9
eight:	7000kg (15,400lb)
mensions:	Length: 4.57m (14.99ft); width: 2.49m (8.17ft); height: 2.03m (6.66ft)
nge:	800km (500 miles)
mour:	(Steel) 12mm (0.47in)
mament:	1 x 7.62mm (0.3in) MG
werplant:	1 x Peugeot PRV 6-cylinder petrol, developing 145hp (108kW) at 5500rpm
rformance:	Maximum road speed: 100km/h (62mph); fording: amphibious; gradient: 60 percent; vertical obstacle: 0.8m (2.6ft); trench: 1.1m (3.6ft)

Auverland A3

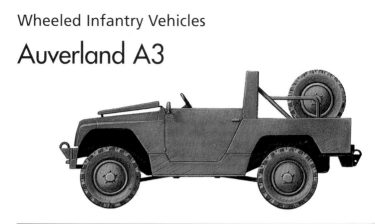

The Auverland A3 is a 4x4 light vehicle in extensive use with the French Army gendarmerie and air force. It was developed from the SAMO 4x4 vehicle after Auverland took over the SAMO concern in the mid-1980s. Little known outside Europe, it remains one of the most competent off-road military vehicles available today. It has a top road speed of 115km/h (71mph) and it has excellent traction in rough or muddy terrain. Two basic versions are available: the A3 standard vehicle and the A3L with a lengthened wheelbase. Both versions come with soft- or hard-options. A3 vehicles are unarmed on delivery, but a weapons post is provided behind the front seats to mount a machine gun, usually an AAT-52 or an FN MAG.

Country of origin:	France
Crew:	1 + 3
Weight:	1710kg (3771lb)
Dimensions:	Length: 3.85m (12.63ft); width: 1.54m (5.05ft); height: 1.7m (5.58ft)
Range:	800km (500 miles)
Armour:	Not available
Armament:	None
Powerplant:	1 x Peugeot XUD-9A 4-cylinder turbo diesel, developing 93hp (69kW)
Performance:	Maximum road speed: 115km/h (71mph)

Borgward B2000

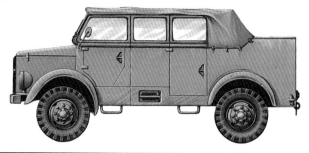

The Borgward B2000 was one of the first military vehicles to enter service with the West German Federal Armed Forces created in 1955. Borgward already had a name for itself as the producer of cars and trucks for private use, and in that year it rose to the challenge of producing a 0.75-ton light military vehicle capable of transporting a squad of eight soldiers and all relevant equipment. The first prototype had four-wheel drive and an open driving cab with a hinged windscreen. This became designated the B2000. Unlike many other personnel carriers, the B2000 had a windowed superstructure. Between 1955 and 1961, 5672 vehicles were produced.

Country of origin:	Germany
Crew:	1 + 8
Weight:	3050kg (6725lb)
Dimensions:	Length: 7.5m (24.6ft); width: 5.28m (17.32ft); height: 2.15m (7.05ft)
Range:	470km (290 miles)
Armour:	Not applicable
Armament:	None
Powerplant:	1 x Borgward 6-cylinder diesel, developing 80hp (60kW)
Performance:	Maximum road speed: 94km/h (58mph)

VW 181

The Volkswagen 181 was an updated version of the World War II-era Type 82 Kübelwagen, built to fill a gap in the Bundeswehr's vehicle range while they waited for production of the French, West German and Italian Europa Jeep. Volkswagen relied heavily on commercial technology for the Type 181. It was rear-wheel drive and could carry loads of up to 400kg (880lb). When the Europa Jeep project was cancelled in 1976, the Type 181 received an upgrade. It became a 4x4 vehicle with a 500kg (1100lb) cargo capacity and was renamed the Type 183 'Iltis'. Production of the Type 181 ran into the 1980s and thousands are still in service around the world today.

Country of origin:	Germany
Crew:	2 + 3
Weight:	1350kg (2980lb)
Dimensions:	Length: 3.78m (12.4ft); width: 1.64m (5.38ft); height: 1.62m (5.31ft)
Range:	320km (200 miles)
Armour:	Not applicable
Armament:	None
Powerplant:	1 x VW 4-cylinder petrol, developing 44hp (32.5kW)
Performance:	Maximum road speed: 110km/h (68mph)

Faun Kraka 640

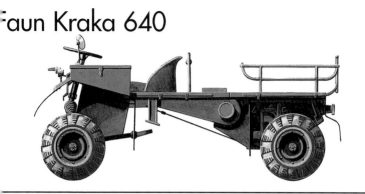

The Faun Kraka 640 began its development life in the early 1960s. It was designed by Union AG (a Faun-Werke subsidiary) as a multi-purpose general utility vehicle capable of operating in standard European off-road conditions. The very small dimensions of the vehicle, plus the fact it could be folded down for air transit, meant that most orders (around 860 vehicles) went to the Bundeswehr paratroop forces. It is an extremely simple vehicle, powered by a two-cylinder BMW engine which chain-drives the wheels. With a cargo capacity of 0.75 tons, the Kraka has hosted several large weapons platforms, including 20mm (0.78in) AA cannon and MILAN ATGW systems.

Country of origin:	Germany
Crew:	2 + 6
Weight:	1610kg (3550lb)
Dimensions:	Length: 2.78m (9.12ft); width: 1.51m (4.95ft); height: 1.28m (4.19ft)
Range:	Not available
Armour:	None
Armament:	None as standard (see text)
Powerplant:	1 x BMW 427 2-cylinder petrol, developing 25hp (19kW)
Performance:	Maximum road speed: 55km/h (34mph); gradient: 50 percent

Wheeled Infantry Vehicles

TM 90

The TM 90 was one in a series of security vehicles/armoured personnel carriers produced by Thyssen in the 1970s. It was particularly designed for police use in anti-terrorist and riot-control contexts. The chassis was an all-wheel-drive Daimler-Benz model. On top of this was an armoured superstructure with specially angled joints and panels to deflect blows from hand-held weapons. Bullet-proof windows were fitted, and to accommodate the police market, a siren, blue light and a loudspeaker were also standard. The basic vehicle was unarmed, though a machine gun could be mounted next to the roof hatch. Because of better-suited vehicles in the marketplace, the TM 90 achieved few domestic or export sales.

Country of origin:	Germany
Crew:	4
Weight:	4200kg (9300lb)
Dimensions:	Length: 4.4m (14.44ft); width: 2.05m (6.73ft); height: 1.85m (6.07ft)
Range:	600km (370 miles)
Armour:	Not available
Armament:	None
Powerplant:	1 x 6-cylinder diesel, developing 134hp (100kW)
Performance:	Maximum road speed: 110km/h (68mph)

TM 125

In spite of its small appearance, the TM 125 can carry 12 personnel, the passengers sitting five abreast down each side of the hull. The hull features a total of six firing ports, while vision for driver and commander is provided by two windows. Armoured shutters can be closed over the windows if necessary. Operational durability is enhanced by using run-flat tyres – even with all tyres totally deflated the TM 125 can maintain 40km/h (25mph) for distances up to 80km (50 miles). TM 125s come with a variety of armament options, including Rheinmetall 20mm (0.78in) cannon and TOW ATGWs. The vehicle is also fully amphibious, powered by two propellers mounted at the rear of the hull and steered by the front wheels.

Country of origin:	Germany
Crew:	2 + 10
Weight:	7600kg (16,800lb)
Dimensions:	Length: 5.54m (18.18ft); width: 2.46m (8.07ft); height: 2.01m (6.59ft)
Range:	700km (430 miles)
Armour:	Not available
Armament:	Optional
Powerplant:	1 x Daimler-Benz OM 352 4-cylinder turbo diesel, developing 125hp (93kW)
Performance:	Maximum road speed: 85km/h (53mph); fording: amphibious; gradient: 80 percent; vertical obstacle: 0.55m (1.8ft)

TPz-1 Fuchs

The Transportpanzer 1 Fuchs is still in production and nearly 1000 have been delivered to the German Army alone. Export versions are used in the UK, Israel, the Netherlands, the US and several other countries. Built by Henschel Wehrtechnik, this vehicle was selected from a long series of prototype German armoured personnel carriers developed throughout the 1960s and 1970s. It is a fully amphibious 6x6 vehicle with space for carrying 10 soldiers in a rear troop compartment. In water, it can attain speeds of 10.5km/h (6.5mph) using twin propellers set beneath the rear of the hull. Numerous variants exist, such as an NBC reconnaissance vehicle, an EOD vehicle and a RASIT radar carrier.

Country of origin:	Germany
Crew:	2 + 10
Weight:	18,300kg (40,350lb)
Dimensions:	Length: 6.76m (22.18ft); width: 2.98m (9.78ft); height: 2.3m (7.55ft)
Range:	800km (500 miles)
Armour:	Steel (details classified)
Armament:	1 x 7.62mm (0.3in) MG
Powerplant:	1 x Mercedes-Benz OM402A 8-cylinder diesel, developing 320hp (239kW) at 2500rpm
Performance:	Maximum road speed: 105km/h (65mph); fording: amphibious; gradient: 70 percent; trench: 1.6m (5.3ft)

Condor

The Condor armoured personnel carrier was developed as a replacement for the UR-416 APC. Since it entered production in 1981, it has achieved good export sales, particularly in Malaysia. Two crew pilot the vehicle, the driver sitting at the front of the vehicle behind bullet-proof windows (shuttered in action), and the commander sitting behind him under a forward hatch cover in the roof. Twelve infantry occupy seats in the rear compartment. The hull is of all-welded steel armour. Armament fittings vary. They include 7.62mm (0.3in) and 12.7mm (0.5in) machine guns, 20mm (0.78in) cannon and ATGW systems. The Condor is fully amphibious, though a trim vane needs to be fitted before entering the water.

Country of origin:	Germany
Crew:	2 + 12
Weight:	12,400kg (27,300lb)
Dimensions:	Length: 6.13m (20.11ft); width: 2.47m (8.1ft); height: 2.18m (7.15ft)
Range:	900km (560 miles)
Armour:	Steel (details classified)
Armament:	Varied (see text)
Powerplant:	1 x Daimler-Benz OM 352A 6-cylinder supercharged diesel, developing 168hp (125kW)
Performance:	Maximum road speed: 100km/h (62mph); fording: amphibious; gradient: 60 percent; vertical obstacle: 0.55m (1.8ft)

ATF 2 Dingo

The ATF 2 Dingo is one of the more recent additions to German military vehicle ranks. Its carrying capacity is only four soldiers, apart from the one-man crew, but the occupants are well protected by the mine deflector system in the hull. This diverts the force of both anti-personnel and anti-tank mine explosions away from the troop and operator compartments. Air conditioning, onboard intercom, a rear driving camera, and NBC protection make the Dingo a particularly user-friendly vehicle to operate in hostile areas. Its chassis is that of the Unimog U1550L, which provides the Dingo with excellent off-road mobility. The Dingo has entered service with the German Army.

Country of origin:	Germany
Crew:	1 + 4
Weight:	8800kg (19,400lb)
Dimensions:	Length: 5.23m (17.16ft); width: 2.31m (7.58ft); height: 2.38m (7.8ft)
Range:	700km (430 miles)
Armour:	Not available
Armament:	1 x 7.62mm (0.3in) MG
Powerplant:	1 x Mercedes-Benz OM 366LA 6-cylinder turbo diesel, developing 237hp (177kW)
Performance:	Maximum road speed: 106km/h (66mph)

GTK/MRAV

The Gepanzerten Transportkraftfahrzeug/Multi-Role Armoured Vehicle (GTK/MRAV) is a joint German/United Kingdom/Netherlands project to develop a versatile next-generation armoured personnel carrier. The 6x6 base vehicle is the operator compartment and chassis. Onto this permanent base fit different interchangeable mission modules – such as a command-and-control module and a field-ambulance module – to form the rear compartment. The modules can be changed in less than one hour. Consequently, the GTK/MRAV can be many different vehicles within the remit of a single operation. The base vehicle is made of steel armour and the hull is shaped to deflect mine explosions.

Country of origin:	Germany/United Kingdom/Netherlands
Crew:	Up to 10 men, depending on module
Weight:	26,500kg (58,400lb)
Dimensions:	Length: 7.23m (23.72ft); width: 2.99m (9.8ft); height: 2.37m (7.78ft)
Range:	1050km (625 miles)
Armour:	Classified
Armament:	Various depending on module
Powerplant:	1 x MTU 8-cylinder diesel, developing 710hp (530kW)
Performance:	Maximum road speed: 103km/h (64mph)

Wheeled Infantry Vehicles

FUG

The FUG is an amphibious scout car based upon the Soviet BRDM-1. Amphibious power is provided by two waterjets set in the rear of the hull, and the only preparation required for entering the water is to erect a trim vane at the front of the vehicle. The FUG is in most ways a simple vehicle. Its hull is made of all-welded steel armour plate and its only armament is a single 7.62mm (0.3in) SGMB machine gun. Three more modern features are central tyre-pressure regulation, infrared headlights and NBC options. The FUG is mainly in service today with former Eastern Bloc nations such as Hungary, the Czech Republic, Poland and Romania.

Country of origin:	Hungary
Crew:	2 + 4
Weight:	7000kg (15,400lb)
Dimensions:	Length: 5.79m (18.99ft); width: 2.5m (8.2ft); height: 1.91m (6.23ft)
Range:	600km (370 miles)
Armour:	(Steel) 10mm (0.39in)
Armament:	1 x 7.62mm (0.3in) SGMB MG
Powerplant:	1 x Csepel D.414.44 4-cylinder diesel, developing 100hp (75kW)
Performance:	Maximum road speed: 87km/h (54mph); fording: amphibious; gradient: 32 percent; vertical obstacle: 0.4m (1.3ft)

RBY Mk1

The RBY Mk1 is a light reconnaissance vehicle first manufactured by Israel Aircraft Industries in the mid-1970s. Though the hull is all-welded steel with 8mm (0.31in) armour, there is no top cover for the crew compartment. Also, the front windscreen can be folded flat for unimpaired visibility. These features increase the RBY's vulnerability to small-arms and shell fire, but reduce the chances of occupant heat exhaustion in the hot Middle Eastern climate. A variety of machine guns and cannon, even a 106mm (4.17in) recoilless rifle, can be fitted to the rim of the hull. The RBY Mk1's bonnet and bumpers are made of fibre glass designed to disintegrate harmlessly if the vehicle strikes a mine.

Country of origin:	Israel
Crew:	2 + 6
Weight:	3600kg (7900lb)
Dimensions:	Length: 5.02m (16.47ft); width: 2.03m (6.66ft); height: 1.66m (5.45ft)
Range:	550km (340 miles)
Armour:	(Steel) 8mm (0.31in)
Armament:	Various MGs and cannons
Powerplant:	1 x Chrysler 6-cylinder petrol, developing 120hp (89kW)
Performance:	Maximum road speed: 100km/h (62mph); fording: 0.4m (1.3ft); gradient: 60 percent

RAM V-2L

The RAM V-2L is one variant amongst many in a series of light vehicles built by RAMTA Structures and Systems, a subsidiary of Israel Aircraft Industries. The first of the RAM family was the V-1, a 4x4 light armoured fighting vehicle which held two crew, seven passengers, and was armed with 7.62mm (0.3in) machine guns and 106mm (4.17in) recoilless rifles. The key distinction between the RAM V-1 and the subsequent V-2 is that the former has an open-top hull, whereas the latter is fully enclosed. Both the V-2 and V-1 split into many sub-variants, including versions fitted with TOW ATGW launchers and 20mm (0.78in) cannon anti-aircraft turrets.

Country of origin:	Israel
Crew:	2 + 7 or 8
Weight:	5750kg (12,700lb)
Dimensions:	Length: 5.52m (18.11ft); width: 2.03m (6.66ft); height: 1.72m (5.64ft)
Range:	800km (500 miles)
Armour:	(Steel) 8mm (0.31in)
Armament:	1 x 12.7mm (0.5in) MG; 2 x 7.62mm (0.3in) MG
Powerplant:	1 x Deutz 6-cylinder diesel, developing 132hp (98kW)
Performance:	Maximum road speed: 96km/h (60mph); fording: 1m (3.3ft); gradient: 64 percent; vertical obstacle: 0.8m (2.6ft)

at Campagnola 1107 AD

e Fiat Campagnola entered service with the Italian Army in 1951, and was
ased closely on the US Willys jeep. It featured four-wheel drive, an open
ture, and a 1901cc petrol engine. This basic vehicle became the foundation of
equent improved versions. The Campagnola A (1955), Campagnola B (1960) and
pagnola C (1968) had modified engines in either diesel or petrol formats. In
, the Campagnola 1107 AD was introduced. It was fitted with an 80hp (60kW)
cc engine and all wheels had independent suspension systems. With good
lling and a top speed of 120km/h (75mph) the Campagnola became a popular
cle not only with the Italian military, but also in sports endurance driving.

untry of origin:	Italy
ew:	1 + 5
eight:	2420kg (5336lb)
mensions:	Length: 3.77m (12.37ft); width: 1.58m (5.64ft); height: 1.9m (6.23ft)
nge:	400km (250 miles)
mour:	Not applicable
mament:	None
werplant:	1 x Fiat 4-cylinder petrol, developing 80hp (60kW)
rformance:	Maximum road speed: 120km/h (75mph)

Fiat OTO Melara Type 6614

The Type 6614 is a typical modern armoured personnel carrier. It entered production in 1979 with Fiat and Otobreda, and is still used today in countr as divergent as South Korea, Argentina and Tunisia. It has an armoured hull 6–? (0.24–0.31in) thick, enough to protect it from small-arms fire and shell splinters Firing ports are located in the doors and along the hull, and each has its own vi block situated just above. These allow the 10 soldiers and one crew member to out heavy fire from inside the vehicle if necessary. Outside there is a roof hatch mounted 12.7mm (0.5in) machine gun. Specialist equipment includes wheel-arc fire extinguishers and night-vision equipment.

Country of origin:	Italy
Crew:	1 + 10
Weight:	8500kg (18,700lb)
Dimensions:	Length: 5.86m (19.23ft); width: 2.5m (8.2ft); height: 1.78m (5.84f
Range:	700km (430 miles)
Armour:	(Steel) 6–8mm (0.24–0.31in)
Armament:	1 x 12.7mm (0.5in) MG
Powerplant:	1 x Fiat 8062.24 6-cylinder turbo diesel, developing 160hp (119k\
Performance:	Maximum road speed: 100km/h (62mph); fording: amphibious; gradient: 60 percent; vertical obstacle: 0.4m (1.3ft)

SA Guardian

e ASA Guardian is used mainly in security and police work, particularly
r counter-terrorist and riot-control operations. It was developed by stretching
heelbase of the Fiat Campagnola light vehicle, upgrading to a more powerful
e and adding sturdier armour plate. The vehicle is resistant to small-arms
nd even tyres and windows are bullet-proof. No weapon is fitted as standard,
ere is the option to mount a machine gun on the rim of the hatch in the
e of the roof. In addition, both driver and front-seat passenger have firing
in the doors. The Guardian is used throughout Italy and also in various Middle
rn countries.

ntry of origin:	Italy
v:	6
ght:	2730kg (6019lb)
ensions:	Length: 3.68m (12.07ft); width: 1.75m (5.74ft); height: 2.12m (6.96ft)
ge:	380km (240 miles)
our:	Not available
ament:	None (see text)
erplant:	1 x Mercedes-Benz, Fiat or Rover 4-cylinder petrol, developing 80hp (60kW)
ormance:	Maximum road speed: 120km/h (75mph)

IVECO 40-10 WM

In basic form, the IVECO 40-10 WM is a 4x4 truck based on the Fiat Daily commercial vehicle, though it has been strengthened for military use. The rear section of the vehicle defines its role. Apart from a basic open cargo area format, the vehicle can take various box bodies, including a command-and-control centre, field ambulance, an engineering unit, a vehicle refuelling system and a police secure unit. Alternatively, a 106mm (4.17in) recoilless rifle, various heavy machine gun configurations, and ATGW launchers can be mounted on the flat bed. The 40-10 WM is in service in Italy, Canada, Pakistan and Belgium. A key advantage of the vehicle is that it is air-transportable within a C-130 Hercules aircraft.

Country of origin:	Italy
Crew:	1 + 2
Weight:	4400kg (9700lb)
Dimensions:	Length: 4.9m (16.08ft); width: 2m (6.56ft); height: 2.38m (7.8ft)
Range:	500km (310 miles)
Armour:	Not available
Armament:	Various (see text)
Powerplant:	1 x Type 8142 4-cylinder diesel, developing 103hp (77kW)
Performance:	Maximum road speed: 100km/h (62mph)

Chaimite V-200

The BRAVIA Chaimite armoured personnel carrier was a Portuguese-licensed version of the US Cadillac Gage Commando V-150 armoured car. It is a 4x4 vehicle with the usual amphibious capabilities and a steel armoured hull. Carrying capacity is nine soldiers. The V-200 is one of nine versions of the Chaimite available, each distinguished usually by its armament. The V-200 is armed simply with twin turret-mounted 7.62mm (0.3in) machine guns. Subsequent versions go up in denominations of 100. The V-400, for example, is fitted with a 90mm (3.54in) cannon, whereas the V-700 is armed with ATGW systems. Recently, 6x6 and 8x8 prototype versions of the Chaimite have been produced.

Country of origin:	Portugal
Crew:	2 + 9
Weight:	7300kg (16,100lb)
Dimensions:	Length: 5.6m (18.37ft); width: 2.26m (7.41ft); height: 2.26m (7.41ft)
Range:	950km (590 miles)
Armour:	(Steel) 7.94mm (0.31in) maximum
Armament:	2 x 7.62mm (0.3in) MGs
Powerplant:	1 x M75 V8 petrol, developing 210hp (157kW)
Performance:	Maximum road speed: 110km/h (68mph); fording: amphibious; gradient: 65 percent; vertical obstacle: 0.9m (2.9ft)

Bravia Commando Mk III

The Commando Mk III is an armoured personnel carrier ideally suited to urban security use. It is manufactured by Bravia, based in Lisbon, Portugal, and was originally developed for the Portuguese National Guard. The chassis is actually that of a truck, the 4x4 Bravia Gazela, with a hull superstructure of armoured steel plate. With a thickness of between 6.35mm (0.25in) and 7.94mm (0.31in), the armour is sufficiently thick to stop low-powered small-arms fire and hand-thrown missiles. Windows can be covered with armoured shutters in action. A turret surmounting the hull carries a 12.7mm (0.5in) MG and a 7.62mm (0.3in) coaxial machine gun. The vehicle can also mount a 60mm (2.36in) grenade launcher pod.

Country of origin:	Portugal
Crew:	3 + 5
Weight:	4855kg (10,700lb)
Dimensions:	Length: 4.97m (16.31ft); width: 1.93m (6.33ft); height: 2.05m (6.73ft)
Range:	800km (500 miles)
Armour:	(Steel) 7.94mm (0.31in) maximum
Armament:	1 x 12.7mm (0.5in) MG; 1x 7.62mm (0.3in) coaxial MG
Powerplant:	1 x Perkins 4-cylinder diesel, developing 81hp (60kW) at 2800rpm
Performance:	Maximum road speed: 90km/h (56mph); gradient: 70 percent

BA-20

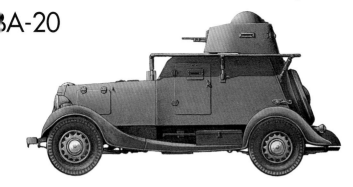

The BA-20 was a Russian scout/command vehicle which replaced the FAI-M light armoured car. Its truck ancestry is visually clear, and it used the chassis of the GAZ-M1 truck with a superstructure of armoured steel plate. This plate had a thickness of 4–6mm (0.16–0.24in), enough to protect against small-arms fire. The BA-20 had a small turret with a 7.62mm (0.3in) DT machine gun and slightly sloping armoured plates to enhance missile deflection. Two basic versions were produced: the BA-20 with a clothes-line aerial, and the later BA-20M which had a whip aerial. A major upgrade in 1939 using the 6x4 GAZ-21 truck chassis was abandoned before production began.

Country of origin:	Russia/Soviet Union
Crew:	2
Weight:	2340kg (5160lb)
Dimensions:	Length: 4.1m (13.5ft); width: 1.8m (5.9ft); height: 2.3m (7.6ft)
Range:	350km (220 miles)
Armour:	(Steel) 4–6mm (0.16–0.24in)
Armament:	1 x 7.62mm (0.3in) MG
Powerplant:	1 x GAZ-M1 4-cylinder petrol, developing 50hp (37kW)
Performance:	Maximum road speed: 90km/h (56mph)

Wheeled Infantry Vehicles

BA-64

With the onset of the German–Soviet war in 1941, the Red Army discovered that most of its armoured cars were inadequately armoured and outclassed by German vehicles. The BA-64 was an attempt to remedy these problems. Its armoured plates were angled steeply to increase bullet and missile deflection, the suspension was strengthened over previous vehicles to improve off-road durability and it had bullet-proof tyres and bullet-proof glass in the driver's observation visor. Most significantly, it had four-wheel drive which enabled it to climb 30-degree slopes. Armament remained light – a single 7.62mm (0.3in) Degtyarev machine gun mounted in the turret.

Country of origin:	Russia/Soviet Union
Crew:	2
Weight:	2360kg (5200lb)
Dimensions:	Length: 3.67m (12.04ft); width: 1.52m (4.99ft); height: 1.88m (6.17ft)
Range:	560km (350 miles)
Armour:	(Steel) 4–15mm (0.16–0.59in)
Armament:	1 x 7.62mm (0.3in) MG
Powerplant:	1 x GAZ-MM 4-cylinder petrol, developing 54hp (40kW)
Performance:	Maximum road speed: 80km/h (50mph)

GAZ-67B

The GAZ-67A was a Soviet vehicle but one heavily influenced by the 20,000 US Jeeps imported into the USSR from 1942. Its was produced by the Gorkiy Avtomobil Zavod (GAZ – Gorky Automobile Factory) and was based around the Bantam Jeep in its shape, 4x4 configuration, and its Soviet Ford M1 four-cylinder petrol engine. The GAZ-67A was a crude vehicle with inadequate acceleration, but it was rugged and dependable. The GAZ-67B had a longer wheelbase than the GAZ-67A, and the two models stayed in production until 1953. Post-war service included French Indochina and Korea, and the vehicles still crop up in civilian hands, even today.

Country of origin:	Russia/Soviet Union
Crew:	4
Weight:	1320kg (2910lb)
Dimensions:	Length: 3.35m (10.99ft); width: 1.69m (5.54ft); height: 1.7m (5.57ft)
Range:	750km (470 miles)
Armour:	Not applicable
Armament:	Not applicable
Powerplant:	1 x GAZ M1 4-cylinder petrol, developing 54hp (40kW)
Performance:	Maximum road speed: 90km/h (56mph)

BRDM-2

The BRDM-2, also called the BTR-40-P2, was introduced into service in the mid 1960s. Like its predecessor the BRDM-1, the BRDM-2 was an amphibious reconnaissance vehicle but with several significant modifications. Chief amongst these was a new engine, the GAZ-41 V8, which could develop 140hp (104kW) of power instead of the BRDM-1's 90hp (67kW). The greater power was combined with an increased range of 750km (465 miles) as opposed to 500km (310 miles). Armament was also increased on the BRDM-2. One 14.5mm (0.57in) KPVT machine gun was mounted on the turret along with a coaxial 7.62mm (0.3in) machine gun, and a Sagger ATGW launcher could be fitted as an option.

Country of origin:	Russia/Soviet Union
Crew:	5
Weight:	7000kg (15,435lb)
Dimensions:	Length: 5.7m (18.7ft); width: 2.35m (7.71ft); height: 2.3m (7.6ft)
Range:	750km (465 miles)
Armour:	(Steel) 10mm (0.39in) maximum
Armament:	1 x 14.5mm (0.5in) or 7.62mm (0.3in) MG
Powerplant:	1 x GAZ-41 V8 petrol, developing 140hp (104kW)
Performance:	Maximum road speed: 100km/h (62mph); fording: amphibious; gradient: 60 percent; vertical obstacle: 0.4m (1.31ft); trench: 1.25m (4.1ft)

BRDM-2 with SA-9

The success of the BRDM-2 design resulted in a rash of variants amongst Soviet forces, particularly in the role of guided-missile launcher. In 1972 the BRDM was issued with its standard turret removed and replaced by an SA-9 Gaskin SAM system. The unit consists of four launcher tubes mounted on a dedicated turret, each holding an SA-9 Gaskin infrared-seeker missile with an engagement altitude of around 4000m (13,123ft). In the early 1980s the vehicle acquired a Gun Dish radar on the front of the turret to give the SAM system all-weather capability, something it previously lacked. Two ATGW variants of the BRDM-2 were also launched in 1973 and 1977, mounting Swatter-B and Spandrel command-to-line-of-sight missiles.

Country of origin:	Russia/Soviet Union
Crew:	4
Weight:	7000kg (15,435lb)
Dimensions:	Length: 5.75m (18.86ft); width: 2.35m (7.71ft); height: 2.31m (7.58ft)
Range:	750km (465 miles)
Armour:	(Steel) 10mm (0.39in) maximum
Armament:	4 x SA-9 Gaskin SAMs
Powerplant:	1 x GAZ-41 V8 petrol, developing 140hp (104kW)
Performance:	Maximum road speed: 100km/h (62mph); fording: amphibious; gradient: 60 percent; vertical obstacle: 0.4m (1.3ft); trench: 1.25m (4.1ft)

BTR-70

The BTR-70 is essentially an improved BTR-60. Its hull is slightly longer than that of the BTR-60, and it features triangular access doors to the troop compartment on both sides, set between the second and third axles. Two roof hatches provide additional access. The troop compartment holds nine infantrymen sitting back to back along a central bench. Three firing ports and a vision block are on each side of the compartment. The two-man crew sit towards the front of the vehicle, and each has three forward and one side-facing periscope. Armament is confined to the small forward turret, and consists of one 14.5mm (0.57in) KPVT machine gun with a coaxial 7.62mm (0.3in) machine gun.

Country of origin:	Russia/Soviet Union
Crew:	2 + 9
Weight:	11,500kg (25,400lb)
Dimensions:	Length: 7.53m (24.7ft); width: 2.8m (9.19ft); height: 2.23m (7.32ft)
Range:	600km (370 miles)
Armour:	Steel (details classified)
Armament:	1 x 14.5mm (0.57in) KPVT MG; 1 x coaxial PKT 7.62mm (0.3in) MG
Powerplant:	1 x ZMZ-4905 8-cylinder petrol, developing 240hp (179kW) at 2100rpm
Performance:	Maximum road speed: 80km/h (50mph); fording: amphibious; gradient: 60 percent; vertical obstacle: 0.7m (2.3ft); trench: 2.7m (8.9ft)

UAZ-469B

The UAZ-469B is a light 4x4 utility vehicle developed in the late 1960s at the Ul'yanovsk Motor Vehicle Plant. In many ways it is a basic civilian-type off-road vehicle. A payload of 600kg (1300lb) can be carried (though only if a maximum of two men are on board) and a similar weight can be towed. The standard vehicle has a soft top and a folding windscreen. A hard-top version is available for more heavyweight logistical duties. There is also an ambulance version, the UAZ-469G, with space for four stretcher-carried patients. Today the UAZ-469B is the primary light vehicle in the Russian Federation with export destinations including Afghanistan, Cuba, Egypt, Iran, Poland and Syria.

Country of origin:	Russia/Soviet Union
Crew:	1 + 8
Weight:	2290kg (5050lb)
Dimensions:	Length: 4.03m (13.22ft); width: 1.79m (5.87ft); height: 2.02m (6.63ft)
Range:	620km (385 miles)
Armour:	Not applicable
Armament:	None
Powerplant:	1 x ZMZ-451 4-cylinder petrol, developing 75hp (56kW)
Performance:	Maximum road speed: 100km/h (62mph); fording: 0.8m (2.6ft); gradient: 62 percent

Al-Faris AF-40-8-1

The Al-Faris AF-40-8-1 is a conventionally designed 8x8 armoured personnel carrier. There are actually two versions of the vehicle on the market: the AF-40-8-1, the APC version, and the AF-40-8-2, an armoured reconnaissance vehicle. Both have the same steel hull and basic features, but the latter is usually more heavily armed. The Al-Faris has many armament options ranging from TOW ATGWs and 106mm (4.17in) recoilless rifles to turrets fitted with 120mm (4.72in) heavy mortars and 25mm (0.98in) cannon. An ingenious feature of the Al Faris is its adjustable suspension, which can be used to alter ground clearance from 150mm (5.91in) to 600mm (23.62in).

Country of origin:	Saudi Arabia
Crew:	1 + 11
Weight:	19,500kg (43,000lb)
Dimensions:	Length: 7.9m (25.92ft); width: 2.94m (9.65ft); height: 2.36m (7.74ft)
Range:	800km (500 miles)
Armour:	Steel (details classified)
Armament:	Various (see text)
Powerplant:	1 x Deutz BF 10L513 10-cylinder diesel, developing 400hp (298kW)
Performance:	Maximum road speed: 90km/h (55mph); fording: amphibious; gradient: 80 percent; vertical obstacle: 1.52m (4.99ft); trench: 2.5m (8.2ft)

Tatrapan

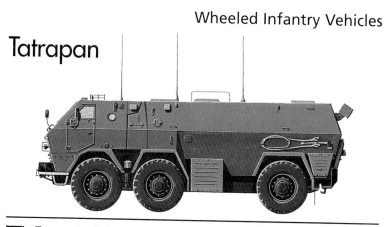

The Tatrapan is a 6x6 armoured personnel vehicle designed around the chassis of the TATRA T-815 VP 21 265 truck. It is one of the larger vehicles on the APC market, 8.46m (27.76ft) long and able to carry 11 fully equipped soldiers as well as the two-man crew. The armoured body is of all-welded steel construction. For entry and exit to and from the troop compartment there is one hatch each side between the second and third wheels, two hatches in the roof, and a hatch at the hull rear. The side and rear hatches are all fitted with firing ports. An NBC system is fitted as standard to the Tatrapan. Apart from use with the Czech and Slovakian armed forces, the Tatrapan is used by several Middle Eastern countries.

Country of origin:	Slovakia
Crew:	2 + 11
Weight:	20,600kg (45,400lb)
Dimensions:	Length: 8.46m (27.76ft); width: 2.5m (8.2ft); height: 2.75m (9.02ft)
Range:	850km (530 miles)
Armour:	Steel (details classified)
Armament:	1 x 12.7mm (0.5in) MG; 1 x 7.62mm (0.3in) MG
Powerplant:	1 x Tatra T3-930-51 12-cylinder diesel, developing 355hp (265kW)
Performance:	Maximum road speed: 70km/h (43mph); gradient: 60 percent

Casspir

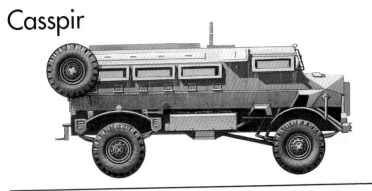

After more than 20 years of service, the Casspir remains one of South Africa's most dependable armoured personnel carriers. It is instantly recognizable by its high ground clearance of 0.41m (1.35ft) at the axles. This is part of the Casspir's defence against anti-tank mines. Also, the belly of the hull is V-shaped to deflect any explosive forces away from the troop compartment. To suit the rough South African terrain the Casspir has a long-range fuel tank for an 850km (530 mile) maximum range. It also contains a drinking water tank. Since its introduction, the Casspir has been heavily used for security and riot control work. Consequently all windows have protective shutters and rubber bullet and CS gas launchers can be fitted.

Country of origin:	South Africa
Crew:	2 + 10
Weight:	12,580kg (27,700lb)
Dimensions:	Length: 6.87m (22.54ft); width: 2.5m (8.2ft); height: 2.85m (9.35ft)
Range:	850km (530 miles)
Armour:	Steel (details classified)
Armament:	1–3 x 7.62mm (0.3in) MGs
Powerplant:	1 x ADE-325T 6-cylinder diesel, developing 170hp (127kW) at 2800rpm
Performance:	Maximum road speed: 90km/h (56mph); fording: 1m (3.3ft); gradient: 65 percent; vertical obstacle: 0.5m (1.6ft); trench: 1.06m (3.48ft)

MR-600

he BMR-600 infantry fighting vehicle was developed for the Spanish Army
during the 1970s, and has gone on to see export service in Egypt, Saudi Arabia
Peru. In many ways it is a conventional armoured personnel carrier. It is fully
hibious with two waterjets providing propulsion from the rear of the hull.
tweight aluminium armour provides protection from small-arms fire and shell
ters for the two crew members and 11 other occupants. A cupola on the roof
ides a weapon mount. In the Spanish Army, a 12.7mm (0.5in) Browning M2 HB
ted as standard, though a 20mm (0.78in) cannon is optional. Other combat
ions of the BMR-600 include ATGW launcher and 81mm (3.19in) mortar carrier.

untry of origin:	Spain
ew:	2 + 11
eight:	14,000kg (30,900lb)
mensions:	Length: 6.15m (20.18ft); width: 2.5m (8.2ft); height: 2m (6.6ft)
nge:	1000km (620 miles)
mour:	(Aluminium) 38mm (1.49in) estimated
mament:	1 x 12.7mm (0.5in) Browning M2 HB
werplant:	1 x Pegaso 9157/8 6-cylinder diesel, developing 310hp (231kW) at 2200rpm
rformance:	Maximum road speed: 103km/h (64mph); fording: amphibious; gradient: 60 percent; vertical obstacle: 0.6m (2ft); trench: 1.35m (4.43ft)

Wheeled Infantry Vehicles

BLR

The Santa Barbara BLR armoured personnel carrier is an internal security vehicle in service with the Spanish Marines and Guardia Civil, as well as security forces in Ecuador. It is a 4x4 vehicle with a steel armoured hull, bullet-proof windows and security-minded extras such as bullet-proof tyres and autom fire-extinguishers for the engine and wheels. There is no standard armament b cupola mount is available for various machine-gun and cannon configurations. available is a 90mm (3.54in) cannon in a dedicated turret. In addition, smoke- a gas-grenade launchers can be fitted. Unlike many APCs, the BLR is not amphibi which indicates its security rather than military role.

Country of origin:	Spain
Crew:	1 + 12
Weight:	12,000kg (26,500lb)
Dimensions:	Length: 5.65m (18.54ft); width: 2.5m (8.2ft); height: 1.99m (6.53f
Range:	570km (350 miles)
Armour:	(Steel) 8mm (0.31in)
Armament:	See text
Powerplant:	1 x Pegaso 9220 6-cylinder diesel, developing 210hp (157kW)
Performance:	Maximum road speed: 93km/h (58mph); fording: 1.1m (3.3ft); gradient: 60 percent

RO VAMTAC

e URO VAMTAC (Vehículo de Alta Movilidad Táctico – Vehicle of High Tactical
obility) is one of the new generation of modular vehicles. Different modular
artments can be fitted to the rear of the vehicle to change its role. Current
les include ATGW carrier, SAM system, ambulance (pictured here), command-
ontrol centre and infantry shelter. It is powered by a Steyr M16-TCA diesel
h generates 119hp (89kW) and a maximum road speed of 130km/h (81mph). Its
ng depth is 0.75m (2.46ft) without preparation, but with a snorkel fitted this
ases to 1.5m (4.9ft). The VAMTAC is intended to become the Spanish Army's
ard light vehicle, though an expensive price tag may reduce sales.

ntry of origin:	Spain
w:	1
ght:	5000kg (11,000lb)
ensions:	Length: 4.85m (15.91ft); width: 2.19m (7.18ft); height: 1.89m (6.2ft)
ge:	600km (370 miles)
our:	Not available
ament:	Depends on module (see text)
erplant:	1 x Steyr M16-TCA 6-cylinder turbo diesel, developing 119hp (89kW)
ormance:	Maximum road speed: 130km/h (81mph); fording: 1.5m (4.9ft) with snorkel

Sonderwagen SWI

The Geschützer Sonderwagen SWI was part of the MOWAG MR 8-01 series of armoured personnel carriers developed in the 1950s. It was specifically made for the Federal German Border Police as a security APC. Its armed counterpart was the SW2, which featured a 20mm (0.78in) cannon mounted on the turret. Both vehicles had two sets of three smoke grenade launchers. The ba vehicle had an all-welded steel hull with the engine located in the rear. It could carry three to five personnel including the crew. Because it was mainly intende for urban duties, the SW1 was not amphibious and did not have NBC fittings or night-vision systems.

Country of origin:	Switzerland
Crew:	3–5
Weight:	8200kg (18,100lb)
Dimensions:	Length: 5.31m (17.42ft); width: 2.25m (7.38ft); height: 1.88m (6.17ft)
Range:	400km (250 miles)
Armour:	Steel
Armament:	None
Powerplant:	1 x Chrysler R 318-233 4-cylinder petrol, developing 161hp (120kV
Performance:	Maximum road speed: 80km/h (50mph); fording: 1.1m (3.6ft); gradient: 60 percent

Roland

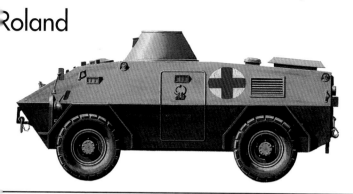

The Roland is a MOWAG vehicle with over 30 years of service with armies worldwide. Generally, it has been used in security and police roles, but it can be converted to many other duties such as armoured personnel carrier, ambulance and command-and-control vehicle. It has three crew and a capacity to carry three other passengers in the troop compartment. Entry and exit are by two doors mounted in the sides of the hull. Once inside, the occupants are protected from small-arms fire up to 7.62mm (0.3in) in calibre. Defence is provided by a single 7.62mm (0.3in) or 12.7mm (0.5in) machine gun, pintle-mounted on the roof. Each door is also fitted with a firing port.

Country of origin:	Switzerland
Crew:	3 + 3
Weight:	4700kg (10,400lb)
Dimensions:	Length: 4.44m (14.57ft); width: 2.01m (6.59ft); height: 2.03m (6.66ft)
Range:	550km (340 miles)
Armour:	(Steel) 8mm (0.31in)
Armament:	1 x 7.62mm (0.3in) or 12.7mm (0.5in) MG
Powerplant:	1 x Chrysler 8-cylinder petrol, developing 202hp (151kW)
Performance:	Maximum road speed: 110km/h (68mph); fording: 1m (3.3ft); gradient: 60 percent

Wheeled Infantry Vehicles

MOWAG Spy

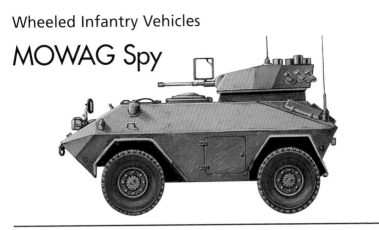

The MOWAG Spy is a 4x4 version of the excellent Piranha series of vehicles. It has a basic armoured personnel carrier shape, though the sides of the hull are angled steeply to deflect both small-arms fire and the force of mine explosions, aided by a ground clearance of 0.5m (1.64ft). Armament is located in a small turret at the rear of the vehicle. Standard fitment is a 12.7mm (0.5in) Browning M2 HB with a coaxial 7.62mm (0.3in) general-purpose machine gun. The latter can be mounted in a pair to provide extra firepower and dispense with the Browning. Other options include a 20mm (0.78in) Oerlikon GAS-AOA cannon. All weapons are remotely operated from inside the crew compartment.

Country of origin:	Switzerland
Crew:	3
Weight:	7500kg (16,500lb)
Dimensions:	Length: 4.52m (14.83ft); width: 2.5m (8.2ft); height: 1.66m (5.45ft)
Range:	700km (430 miles)
Armour:	Details classified
Armament:	1 x 12.7mm (0.5in) MG; 1 x 7.62mm (0.3in) coaxial MG
Powerplant:	1 x Detroit or Cummins 8-cylinder petrol, developing 216hp (161kW) at 2800rpm
Performance:	Maximum road speed: 110km/h (68mph); fording: amphibious; gradient: 70 percent

Shorland SB401

The Shorland SB401 armoured personnel carrier is recognizably derived from the standard British Army Land Rover. Its chassis is the Land Rover's long-wheelbase version (2.77m/9.09ft), and most of its components are from the standard Land Rover vehicle. However, the addition of a heavy armour-plated body meant that the chassis had to be strengthened. Powering this heavy vehicle requires a Rover V8 engine developing 91hp (68kW) at 3500rpm. The armour plate gives protection against high-velocity 7.62mm (0.3in) rifle and machine-gun rounds at above 25m (82ft) range. A glass-fibre interior floor reduces the risk of shrapnel wounds from explosives thrown under the vehicle.

Country of origin:	United Kingdom
Crew:	2 + 6
Weight:	3545kg (7800lb)
Dimensions:	Length: 4.29m (14.07ft); width: 1.78m (5.84ft); height: 2.16m (7.09ft)
Range:	368km (229 miles)
Armour:	Not available
Armament:	None
Powerplant:	1 x Rover V8 petrol, developing 91hp (68kW) at 3500rpm
Performance:	Maximum road speed: 104km/h (65mph); vertical obstacle: 0.23m (0.75ft)

Sandringham 6

The Sandringham 6 is an armoured personnel carrier based on the long-wheelbase Land Rover but in 6x6 configuration. Despite its soft-skinned appearance, the Sandringham 6 is heavily clad in an all-welded steel armour body, resistant to most small-arms fire and shell splinters. The two-man crew are seated behind transparent armour screens, which are equal in strength to the metal armour. Armoured shutters can also be dropped over these windows. Six firing ports are provided around the vehicle – four in the hull and two in the rear doors – and a 7.62mm (0.3in) machine gun can be fitted onto a cupola on the roof. This is aimed by periscope. For riot-control duties, a gas-grenade launcher can replace this gun.

Country of origin:	United Kingdom
Crew:	2 + 8
Weight:	3700kg (8200lb)
Dimensions:	Length: 4.44m (14.57ft); width: 1.69m (5.54ft); height: 2.08m (6.82ft)
Range:	300km (190 miles)
Armour:	Not available
Armament:	Optional (see text)
Powerplant:	1 x Rover V8 petrol, developing 91hp (68kW) at 3500rpm
Performance:	Maximum road speed: 95km/h (59mph)

Supacat ATMP

The Supacat All-Terrain Mobile Platform (ATMP) has been in service with the British Army since 1984, and has proved to be a versatile workhorse. Its purpose is to provide logistical mobility to infantry units. With a 6x6 configuration and a weight of only 2520kg (5600lb), it can move over the roughest terrain. It is also amphibious. The latest versions feature the Ackerman steering system; steering is performed by the front wheels when on the road, but the driver can switch to skid steering when going cross-country, locking the wheels on one side of the vehicle when turning corners. The Supacat is air-portable by Chinook helicopter and it can pull loads of 3.2 tons, 1.5 tons more than a Land Rover.

Country of origin:	United Kingdom
Crew:	1 + 5
Weight:	2520kg (5560lb)
Dimensions:	Length: 3.15m (10.33ft); width: 2m (6.6ft); height: 1.89m (6.2ft)
Range:	600km (370 miles)
Armour:	(Aluminium) 5mm (0.19in)
Armament:	1 x 7.62mm (0.3in) MG optional
Powerplant:	1 x VW-Audi ADE 1900 4-cylinder turbo diesel, developing 54hp (40kW)
Performance:	Maximum road speed: 48km/h (30mph); fording: amphibious; gradient: 45 percent

Valkyr

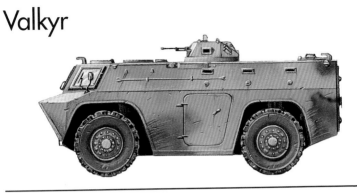

The Valkyr was originally a licensed-built Belgian vehicle, the BDX, which was based on an Irish armoured personnel carrier prototype called the Timoney. In the late 1980s, the British Vickers firm collaborated with the BDX manufacturers, Beherman-Demoen, and produced a UK version called the Valkyr. The Valkyr transports two crew and 10 fully armed infantry. It is amphibious, with propulsion usually provided by its wheels, though two rear-mounted waterjets are optional. The basic Valkyr is armed with a single machine gun, but the armoured fighting vehicle has a large turret featuring a 90mm (3.54in) cannon or a 60mm (2.36in) gun-mortar. A MILAN ATGW system can also be fitted.

Country of origin:	United Kingdom
Crew:	2 + 10
Weight:	11,500kg (25,400lb)
Dimensions:	Length: 5.6m (18.37ft); width: 2.5m (8.2ft); height: 2.27m (7.45ft)
Range:	700km (430 miles)
Armour:	Not available
Armament:	1 x 7.62mm (0.3in) MG
Powerplant:	1 x Detroit Diesel 4-53T V8 diesel, developing 300hp (224kW) at 2800rpm
Performance:	Maximum road speed: 100km/h (62mph); fording: amphibious; gradient: 60 percent; vertical obstacle: 0.45m (1.48ft)

FS100 Simba

Alvis, the company responsible for the production of the Simba, defines the vehicle as 'a 4x4 wheeled armoured personnel carrier, primarily used in internal security and counter-insurgency roles'. The Simba is characteristic of a climate in which peacekeeping and anti-terrorism duties occupy much of the military timetable. It comes in several variants. An armoured personnel version can transport eight fully armed soldiers, and is armed with a single turret-mounted machine gun. The armoured infantry fighting vehicle version has a 20 or 25mm (0.78 or 0.98in) cannon. Other variants include ATGW vehicles and 81mm (3.19in) mortar carriers. Only the Philippines have bought the Simba, choosing the APC.

Country of origin:	United Kingdom
Crew:	2 + 8
Weight:	10,000kg (22,100lb)
Dimensions:	Length: 5.35m (17.55ft); width: 2.5m (8.2ft); height: 2.59m (8.49ft)
Range:	660km (410 miles)
Armour:	(Steel) 8mm (0.31in) estimated maximum
Armament:	Various (see text)
Powerplant:	1 x Perkins 210Ti 8-cylinder diesel, developing 210hp (157kW) at 2500rpm
Performance:	Maximum road speed: 100km/h (62mph); fording: 1m (3.3ft); gradient: 60 percent; vertical obstacle: 0.45m (1.48ft)

Scout

The Cadillac Gage Commando Scout, to give it its proper title, has a boat-like appearance which belies the fact that it is not amphibious (its maximum fording depth is 1.17m/3.84ft). Its name suggests a reconnaissance role, which is its primary duty, but it can also perform anti-tank and command post missions with different fitments. Turret options include a TOW ATGW launcher, a combination of a 40mm (1.58in) grenade launcher and a 12.7mm (0.5in) machine gun, or a twin machine gun. Its light weight and aerodynamic shape give the Scout an operating range of 1290km (800 miles), greater than most reconnaissance vehicles. It also has run-flat tyres as standard.

Country of origin:	United States
Crew:	2–3
Weight:	7240kg (15,960lb)
Dimensions:	Length: 5m (16.4ft); width: 2.05m (6.73ft); height: 2.16m (7.09ft)
Range:	1290km (800 miles)
Armour:	Steel (details classified)
Armament:	1 x 7.62mm (0.3in) MG
Powerplant:	1 x Cummins V6 diesel, developing 155hp (115kW) at 3300rpm
Performance:	Maximum road speed: 96km/h (60mph); fording: 1.17m (3.84ft); gradient: 60 percent; vertical obstacle: 0.6m (2ft)

4KH7FA SB20 Greif ARV

The Greif ARV was developed from the chassis of the Jadgpanzer SK105 Light Tank/Tank Destroyer. This was developed by Sauer-Werke in the mid-1960s and featured a heavily armoured steel hull capable of stopping 20mm (0.78in) cannon ammunition across its frontal sections. Greif ARV production began in 1976 and combined the SK105's mobility and armour protection with a new superstructure designed for engineering processes. It has a hydraulic crane with a 6500kg (14,300lb) lift capacity and a frontal winch which can pull a 20,000kg (44,100lb) load. The winch has 100m (328ft) of cable. Other engineering equipment such as welding gear is stored internally.

Country of origin:	Austria
Crew:	4
Weight:	19,800kg (43,700lb)
Dimensions:	Length: 6.7m (21.98ft); width: 2.5m (8.2ft); height: 2.3m (7.55ft)
Range:	625km (390 miles)
Armour:	(Steel) 25mm (0.98in) maximum
Armament:	1 x 12.7mm (0.5in) MG
Powerplant:	1 x Steyr 7FA 6-cylinder turbo diesel, developing 320hp (239kW) at 1900rpm
Performance:	Maximum road speed: 67km/h (42mph); fording: 1m (3.3ft); gradient: 75 percent; vertical obstacle: 0.8m (2.6ft); trench: 2.41m (7.91ft)

SIBMAS ARV

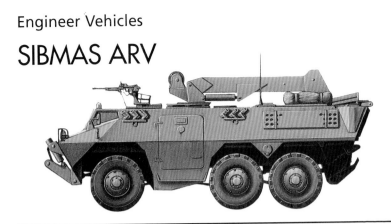

The basis of the SIBMAS Armoured Recovery Vehicle is the SIBMAS APC developed in the mid-1970s by B.N. Constructions Ferroviaires et Métalliques. This capacious vehicle could carry 16 passengers and was also converted to various anti-tank configurations. An ARV variant was produced in the early 1980s to fulfil an order from the Malaysian military. It added a winch, crane and rear spades to the APC. The winch can pull 20,000kg (44,100lb) and the crane has a lift capacity of 10,500kg (23,150lb). Stabilizing spades are fitted at the front and rear of the hull. Twenty-four of the ARVs have been produced, mainly for the Malaysian market.

Country of origin:	Belgium
Crew:	5
Weight:	16,500kg (36,400lb)
Dimensions:	Length: 7.63m (25.03ft); width: 2.54m (8.33ft); height: 3.2m (10.49ft)
Range:	800km (500 miles)
Armour:	Not disclosed
Armament:	1 x 7.62mm (0.3in) MG
Powerplant:	1 x MAN D2566 MK 6-cylinder turbo diesel, developing 320hp (239kW) at 1900rpm
Performance:	Maximum road speed: 100km/h (62mph); fording: amphibious; gradient: 70 percent; vertical obstacle: 0.6m (2ft); trench: 1.5m (4.9ft)

Pionierpanzer 1

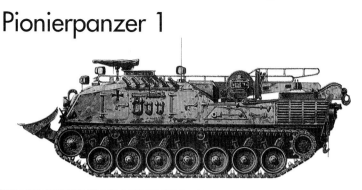

The Pionierpanzer 1 is an Armoured Engineer Vehicle (AEV) variant of the Leopard 1 MBT family. Produced by MaK it relies on the same chassis and powerplant as the Leopard's Armoured Recovery Vehicle variant, though instead of the ARV's spare powerplant the Pionierpanzer is fitted with a spiral earth-boring device. The earth-borer is capable of drilling a hole up to 2m (6.6ft) deep and 700mm (27.56in) wide. For major engineering work, the Pionierpanzer 1 has a large dozer blade at the front with optional scarifiers for lifting road surfaces. Significant quantities of explosives can also be stored inside the hull for use in demolition work.

Country of origin:	Germany
Crew:	4
Weight:	40,800kg (90,000lb)
Dimensions:	Length: 7.98m (26.18ft); width (with dozer blade): 3.75m (12.3ft); height: 2.69m (8.83ft)
Range:	800km (500 miles)
Armour:	40mm (1.57in) maximum
Armament:	1 x 7.62mm (0.3in) MG; 1 x 7.62mm (0.3in) anti-aircraft MG
Powerplant:	1 x MTU MB838 10-cylinder multi-fuel, developing 830hp (619kW)
Performance:	Maximum road speed: 65km/h (40mph); fording: 2.1m (6.9ft); gradient: 60 percent; vertical obstacle: 1.15m (3.77ft); trench: 3m (9.8ft)

Skorpion

The Skorpion is an automated and self-propelled minelaying system. Its uses the standard chassis of the US M548 tracked cargo-carrying vehicle, but mounts a rack of mine dispensers. Each dispenser unit consists of five tubes, each tube holding 20 mines, and there are six units in total. The mines can be anti-personnel or anti-tank, though the vehicle is typically used to dispense AT-2 anti-tank mines. They are ejected to either side of the rear of the vehicle from the dispensers. The mines can be fitted with delay fuses to activate the mine only once the minelaying team have retreated. In five minutes, the Skorpion can sow a minefield 1500x50m (4900 x 160ft).

Country of origin:	Germany
Crew:	2
Weight:	12,000kg (26,500lb)
Dimensions:	Length: 5.85m (19.19ft); width: 2.87m (9.42ft); height: 3.17m (10.4ft)
Range:	600km (370 miles)
Armour:	Not applicable
Armament:	1 x minelaying system; 1 x 7.62mm (0.3in) MG
Powerplant:	1 x Detroit Diesel 6V-53N 6-cylinder petrol, developing 202hp (151kW)
Performance:	Maximum road speed: 40km/h (25mph)

MAN/Krupp Leguan

The MAN/Krupp Leguan bridge-laying vehicle entered production in 1988, and brought together the vehicle expertise of MAN and the engineering know-how of Krupp. Unlike many military bridge layers, the Leguan is based upon a truck rather than an MBT. The chassis is that of a standard MAN-ÖAF 36.422 VFAE 8x8 heavy truck. Its cab, however, is slung lower to accommodate the 26m (85.3ft) 50-ton folding bridge which occupies the rear cargo area. The bridge can be deployed and recovered in only eight minutes, and with a 60-ton weight capacity it can handle most MBT and heavy goods traffic. The vehicle is mainly in use with the armed forces of Norway and Singapore.

Country of origin:	Germany
Crew:	2
Weight:	35,600kg (78,500lb)
Dimensions:	Length: 15.3m (50.19ft); width: 4.01m (13.16ft); height: 4m (13.12ft)
Range:	600km (370 miles)
Armour:	Not applicable
Armament:	None
Powerplant:	1 x MAN D 2866LD/422 diesel, developing 412hp (307kW)
Performance:	Maximum road speed: 72km/h (45mph)

Pionierpanzer Dachs 2

The Pionierpanzer Dachs 2 is the update of the earlier Pionierpanzer 1. The Dachs 2 has a digging bucket at the end of its telescopic arm rather than the spiral drill fitted on its predecessor. Though developed and primarily used in Germany, the Dachs 2 has exported well, and is currently in service with Belgium, the Netherlands, Italy and Canada. Its chassis is that of the Leopard 1 MBT. During transit, the telescopic arm is laid down along the right-hand side of the hull. At the front, a dozer blade acts as a minesweeping shield. The Dachs 2 has several specialist features. Its digger can be operated by remote control, and it has onboard tools for splitting concrete and steel girders.

Country of origin:	Germany
Crew:	3
Weight:	43,000kg (94,800lb)
Dimensions:	Length: 9.01m (29.56ft); width: 3.25m (10.66ft); height: 2.57m (8.43ft)
Range:	650km (400 miles)
Armour:	Not available
Armament:	1 x 7.62mm (0.3in) MG
Powerplant:	1 x MTU MB838 CaM5000 10-cylinder diesel, developing 818hp (610kW)
Performance:	Maximum road speed: 62km/h (39mph)

FSB 2000

The FSB 2000 is a folding float-bridge system deployed from the back of a 6x6 or 8x8 truck, in this case an 8x8 MAN mil gl A1. The truck itself is a popular vehicle with a six-cylinder turbo diesel and a payload of around seven tons. To deploy the bridge, the vehicle positions itself close to a riverbank and slides the hinged bridge sections down a ramp into the water on rollers. Several sections can be interconnected and a 100m (328ft) bridge can be constructed in under an hour. Independent sections can be towed by tug boats to make an amphibious crossing. The FSB system has exported widely, and versions are currently in use with the US Army.

Country of origin:	Germany
Crew:	1 + 2
Weight:	(bridge system) 4800kg (10,600lb)
Dimensions:	(bridge system) Length: 6.7m (21.98ft); width: (folded) 3.03m (9.94ft); height: 1.27m (4.17ft)
Range:	Not applicable
Armour:	Not applicable
Armament:	None
Powerplant:	1 x MAN diesel, developing 248hp (185kW)
Performance:	Maximum road speed: 90km/h (56mph); fording: 1.2m (3.9ft)

MAN FSG

The MAN FSG is an ingenious temporary road-surface layer produced as a joint development for the French Army and the German Federal Armed Forces. It is designed to lay an aluminium road surface 50m (160ft) long and 4.2m (13.8ft) wide over muddy, snow-covered or eroded terrain. One of its main applications is to create a solid drive surface on riverbanks during fording operations. In the German Army, the road system is laid in flat hinged sections from the back of an all-wheel-drive SX90 truck, whereas in the French Army, a Renault 6x6 TRM 10000 is used. In both cases, the two-man crew are able to either lay or retract the road surface in 10 to 20 minutes.

Country of origin:	Germany
Crew:	2
Weight:	27,500kg (60,600lb)
Dimensions:	Length: 11.45m (37.58ft); width: 2.99m (9.81ft); height: 3.52m (11.55ft)
Range:	800km (500 miles)
Armour:	Not applicable
Armament:	None
Powerplant:	1 x 8-cylinder diesel, developing 355hp (265kW)
Performance:	Maximum road speed: 80km/h (50mph)

Bergepanzer 3 Buffalo ARV

The Bergepanzer 3 (BPz 3) was produced between 1992 and 1997 and is currently in service with both German and Dutch armed forces. It is based on the chassis of the Leopard 2 MBT. The chassis choice was necessitated by the introduction of the Leopard 2 itself, which placed demands on ARVs not met by any existing vehicle. Yet the Buffalo can accomplish more than just vehicle rescue. It is capable of major earthworks using its forward dozer blade, and its crane can hoist objects weighing up to 35 tons. Welding and cutting gear are standard on board equipment. The BPz 3 has replaced the US M88 ARV amongst Leopard 2 armoured units in Germany.

Country of origin:	Germany
Crew:	3
Weight:	54,300kg (120,000lb)
Dimensions:	Length: 9.07m (29.76ft); width: 3.54m (11.61ft); height: 2.73m (8.96ft)
Range:	650km (400 miles)
Armour:	Not available
Armament:	1 x 7.62mm (0.3in) MG
Powerplant:	1 x MTU MB873 Ka-501 12-cylinder turbo diesel, developing 1500hp (1119kW)
Performance:	Maximum road speed: 68km/h (42mph)

Keiler Mine-Clearing System

The Keiler Mine-Clearing System began production in 1996 under the Rheinmetall Landsysteme GmbH company. The system uses an M-48 cast-steel armoured hull. A carrier arm extends from the front with 24 mine-clearing flails (known, from their shape, as 'elephant's feet'). With the flails in motion, the Keiler can clear a track through a minefield up to 250mm (9.84in) deep, 4.7m (15.4ft) wide and 120m (400ft) long in less than 10 minutes. The mines are either detonated by the flails or wrenched from the ground and flung aside. The Keiler's 100 percent clearance rate has placed it in heavy demand with UN and NATO mine-clearance units operating in war zones.

Country of origin:	Germany
Crew:	2
Weight:	5300kg (11,687lb)
Dimensions:	Length (clearance arm retracted): 7.83m (25.69ft); width: 3.76m (12.34ft); height: 3.75m (12.3ft)
Range:	350km (220 miles)
Armour:	Not available
Armament:	Not available
Powerplant:	1 x MTU MB871 Ka-501 8-cylinder diesel, developing 1086hp (810kW)
Performance:	Maximum road speed: 50km/h (31mph)

Faun ATF 70-4

Faun has made a successful business of supplying military logistical vehicles, in particular a family of mobile lifting machines. The ATF 70-4 is an All-Terrain Mobile Crane system, its 8x8 drive giving it excellent cross-country mobility. Its telescopic lifting arm has a weight capacity of 70 tons and when fully extended, has a total reach of 40.5m (133ft). The lifting gear has its own separate motor to ensure maximum traction, and the vehicle itself develops enough power to negotiate 73 percent gradients. The ATF 70-4 has hydropneumatic suspension with levelling adjustment which allows it to maintain a solid lifting base during recovery operations.

Country of origin:	Germany
Crew:	2
Weight:	48,000kg (105,800lb)
Dimensions:	Length (with crane): 12.87m (42.22ft); width: 2.75m (9.02ft); height: 3.73m (12.24ft)
Range:	400km (250 miles)
Armour:	Not applicable
Armament:	Not applicable
Powerplant:	1 x Mercedes-Benz 8-cylinder diesel, developing 375hp (280kW)
Performance:	Maximum road speed: 78km/h (48mph)

SMT-1

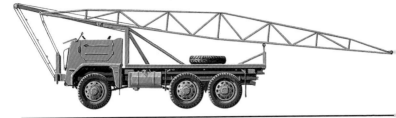

The SMT-1 is a portable bridge system introduced into the Polish armed forces in the mid-1970s. Total length of the bridge is 11m (36ft). When deployed, it is supported on trestles which can be adjusted to give the bridge surface a 3.5m (11.5ft) ground clearance. The bridge is mounted on a heavily modified Star 66 two-ton 6x6 truck. Its cab has no roof, which allows the truck to safely deploy and retract the bridge as it is pulled over the front of the vehicle by winch cables, though it has the drawback of not providing much weather protection for the crew. Once in place, the bridge can safely support 40 tons of traffic at any one moment, though the bridge itself only weighs 2.3 tons.

Country of origin:	Poland
Crew:	3
Weight:	9600kg (21,200lb)
Dimensions:	Length: 11.97m (39.27ft); width: 3.3m (10.82ft); height: 3.15m (10.33ft)
Range:	500km (310 miles)
Armour:	Not applicable
Armament:	None
Powerplant:	1 x S-47 6-cylinder petrol, developing 103hp (77kW)
Performance:	Maximum road speed: 50km/h (31mph)

MDK-2M

The MDK-2M is a powerful ditch-digging machine introduced into Soviet forces in 1965. Its tracked chassis belongs to the AT-T heavy artillery tractor, but fitted with a hydraulically operated dozer blade at the front and a rotary-head circular ditching machine at the rear. Using eight cutting heads, the ditcher can move an average of 400 to 500 cubic metres (14,100 to 17,700 cubic feet) of soil each hour, and in a single pass can cut a trench 3.5m (11.5ft) wide by 1.7m (5.6ft) deep. The excavated soil is channelled away from the trench down a tube while the dozer blade cuts out the shape of the floor and walls. The MDK-2M is operated by only two crew members.

Country of origin:	Russia/Soviet Union
Crew:	2
Weight:	28,000kg (61,700lb)
Dimensions:	Length: 8m (26.25ft); width: 3.4m (11.15ft); height: 3.95m (12.96ft)
Range:	500km (310 miles)
Armour:	Not applicable
Armament:	Not applicable
Powerplant:	1 x Model V-401 12-cylinder diesel, developing 414hp (309kW)
Performance:	Maximum road speed: 35km/h (22mph)

Engineer Vehicles

Ural-375E KET-L

The Ural-375E KET-L is a recovery vehicle based on a modified Ural-375D truck chassis. It is equipped with two main winches. A rear winch is capable of pulling 15 tons, and the frontal winch can pull five tons. The KET-L is also fitted with a jib crane which has a 2.4m (7.9ft) reach and a lift capacity of 1.5 tons. The crane is used for towing other vehicles, as the KET-L has no dedicated towing hook. Cross-country, the KET-L can tow vehicles up to five tons, though on-road, the tow weight is 10 tons. During recovery operations, vehicles up to 13.5 tons can be retrieved by the static vehicle without using its anchor plate. Tools carried include oxyacetylene cutters and two sections of timber to place beneath the wheels in muddy operations.

Country of origin:	Russia/Soviet Union
Crew:	1 + 2
Weight:	12,400kg (27,300lb)
Dimensions:	Length: 8.25m (27.07ft); width: 2.69m (8.83ft); height: 2.68m (8.79ft)
Range:	570km (350 miles)
Armour:	Not applicable
Armament:	None
Powerplant:	1 x ZIL-375 8-cylinder petrol, developing 180hp (134kW)
Performance:	Maximum road speed: 75km/h (47mph)

BREM-1

The BREM-1 entered production in 1984, and utilized the chassis of the T72 MBT to create a powerful battlefield recovery and engineering vehicle. At the hull front is a hydraulically powered bulldozer blade which doubles as a frontal stabilizer when the BREM-1 is using its crane. The crane itself can lift 12 tons of weight, while the BREM's winch has a pull capacity of 25 tons or 100 tons (101 tonnes) with special adaptation. An auxiliary winch is also fitted. As a recovery vehicle, the only armament is one 12.7mm (0.5in) NSVT heavy machine gun. In Russian forces, the BREM-1 is steadily being replaced by the more modern BREM-80U, which is developed from the T-80 MBT.

Country of origin:	Russia/Soviet Union
Crew:	3
Weight:	41,000kg (90,400lb)
Dimensions:	Length: 7.98m (26.18ft); width: 3.46m (11.35ft); height: 2.43m (7.97ft)
Range:	700km (450 miles)
Armour:	Not available
Armament:	1 x 12.7mm (0.5in) NSVT MG
Powerplant:	1 x 12-cylinder diesel, developing 839hp (626kW)
Performance:	Maximum road speed: 60km/h (37mph)

BgBv 82

The Bärgnings Bandvagn (BgBv 82) is a versatile ARV developed in the late 1960s and produced entirely in 1973, when the total production of 24 vehicles was completed. It is still in service today, and is unusual since it was an original design rather than one adapted from an existing vehicle. The hull is all-welded steel, and its three-man crew sit at the front of the vehicle in an armoured cab topped with a 20mm (0.78in) cannon. Two-thirds of the hull is open, and mounts a HM 20 winch and a Hiab-Foco 9000 lifting crane. The former can pull 20,000kg (44,100lb), while the crane can lift 5500kg (12,100lb).The BgBv 82 is also fully amphibious to suit Sweden's wet terrain.

Country of origin:	Sweden
Crew:	4
Weight:	26,300kg (58,000lb)
Dimensions:	Length: 7.2m (23.62ft); width: 3.2m (10.49ft); height: 2.45m (8.04ft)
Range:	480km (300 miles)
Armour:	Classified
Armament:	1 x 20mm (0.78in) cannon; 6 x smoke dischargers
Powerplant:	1 x Volvo-Penta THD-100C 6-cylinder turbo diesel, developing 310hp (231kW) at 2200rpm
Performance:	Maximum road speed: 56km/h (35mph); fording: amphibious; gradient: 60 percent; vertical obstacle: 0.6m (2ft); trench: 2.5m (8.2ft)

Entpannungspanzer 65

The Entpannungspanzer 65 (Entp. Pz. 65) is constructed using the chassis of the Swiss Pz.68 MBT, the turretless superstructure designed for engineering and ARV work. Its main recovery tool is an A-frame winch system which can lift up to 15,000kg (33,100lb). The pulling weight of the 120m (394ft) main winch is 25,000kg (55,100lb), though this rises to 75 tons if block and tackle are used. A 240m (787ft) auxiliary winch can draw light weights of up to 500kg (1100lb). Welding equipment and an air compressor are stored internally. Because of its MBT derivation, the Entp. Pz. 65 retains armour over the frontal section of the crew compartment up to 60mm (2.36in) in depth.

Country of origin:	Switzerland
Crew:	5
Weight:	38,000kg (83,800lb)
Dimensions:	Length: 7.6m (24.93ft); width: 3.06m (10.04ft); height: 3.25m (10.66ft)
Range:	300km (190 miles)
Armour:	(Steel) 60mm (2.36in) maximum
Armament:	1 x 7.5mm (0.28in) MG; 8 x smoke dischargers
Powerplant:	1 x MTU MB 837 8-cylinder diesel, developing 704hp (525kW) at 2200rpm
Performance:	Maximum road speed: 55km/h (34mph); fording: 1.2m (3.9ft); gradient: 70 percent; vertical obstacle: 0.75m (2.46ft); trench: 2.6m (8.5ft)

Churchill ARC

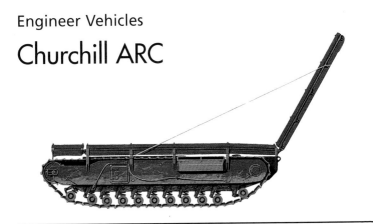

The Churchill Armoured Ramp Carrier (ARC) was developed by the British 79th Armoured Division as an obstacle-bridging vehicle. Production began in 1943. The vehicle consisted of a turretless Churchill tank with two timbered trackways, one set above each track, and extendable ramps leading off both ends of the trackways. When facing an obstacle the ARC would drive as close to it as possible before extending the ramps to breach the gap. Once in place, the ramps could support the weight of any Allied tank. Alternatively, the ARC was sometimes driven right into a gap and the vehicle itself used as a bridge. The later Mk II ARC was identical to the Mk I apart from longer ramps.

Country of origin:	United Kingdom
Crew:	4
Weight:	38,400kg (84,700lb)
Dimensions:	Length: 7.44m (24.41ft); width: 2.43m (7.97ft); height: 2.13m (6.99ft)
Range:	144km (89 miles)
Armour:	(Steel) 88mm (3.46in) maximum
Armament:	None
Powerplant:	1 x Bedford 12-cylinder diesel, developing 350hp (261kW) at 2200rpm
Performance:	Maximum road speed: 20km/h (12mph)

Chieftain AVLB

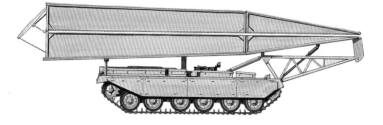

The Chieftain Armoured Vehicle Launched Bridge (AVLB) remains one of the British Army's main mobile bridge-laying systems. Some 37 are in service in the UK, while another 14 are in service with the Iranian Army. The AVLB is essentially a Chieftain MBT chassis mounted with one of two bridge types. The No.8 Class 60 bridge is 24m (78.7ft) long and 4.16m (13.65ft) wide. The No.9 bridge is 13.5m (44.3ft) long and the same width. Both bridges are transported on the AVLB in a hinged double section connected to the front of the hull. They are laid by a hydraulic system pulling them over the front of the vehicle, and can bridge gaps roughly 1.5m (4.9ft) shorter than their length.

Country of origin:	United Kingdom
Crew:	3
Weight:	53,300kg (117,500lb)
Dimensions:	Length: 13.74m (45.08ft); width: 4.16m (13.65ft); height: 3.92m (12.86ft)
Range:	400km (250 miles)
Armour:	Steel (details classified)
Armament:	2 x 7.62mm (0.3in) GPMG
Powerplant:	1 x Leyland L50 12-cylinder multi-fuel, developing 750hp (559kW) at 2100rpm
Performance:	Maximum road speed: 48km/h (30mph); fording: 1.07m (3.51ft); gradient: 60 percent; vertical obstacle: 0.91m (2.98ft)

FV106 Samson

The FV106 Samson Armoured Recovery Vehicle entered production in 1978 and further extended the Scorpion family of vehicles. Its chassis is directly borrowed from the Scorpion Combat Vehicle Reconnaissance (CVR), and its hull is that of the FV103 Spartan Armoured Personnel Carrier. As an ARV, the Samson is entirely unarmed. At the rear of the hull is a heavy-duty winch and two anchor spades which extend to the ground during lifting operations. Side racks contain timber for various field applications. The winch has 229m (751ft) of wire cable and a pull capacity of 12 tons, though the Samson requires a 4:1 snatch block to pull weights greater than itself. The winch is powered directly from the Samson's main engine.

Country of origin:	United Kingdom
Crew:	3
Weight:	8740kg (19,300lb)
Dimensions:	Length: 4.78m (15.68ft); width: 4.78m (15.68ft); height: 2.55m (8.37ft)
Range:	483km (300 miles)
Armour:	Classified
Armament:	1 x 7.62mm (0.3in) MG
Powerplant:	1 x Jaguar J60 N01 Mk100B 6-cylinder petrol, developing 195hp (145kW) at 4750rpm
Performance:	Maximum road speed: 55km/h (34mph); fording: 1.07m (3.51ft); gradient: 70 percent; vertical obstacle: 0.5m (1.6ft); trench: 2.06m (6.76ft)

Challenger ARRV

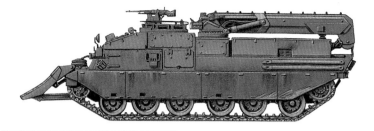

The Challenger Armoured Repair and Recovery Vehicle (ARRV) is, as its name suggests, based upon the Challenger MBT. Like the earlier Chieftain ARRV, the Challenger model uses two Rotzler winches and an Atlas crane. Pulling and lifting capacities are 68 tons for the main winch, 20 tons for the auxiliary winch, and 43 tons for the crane. The front dozer blade can be used as either a stabilizing blade or applied to earth-moving projects. In the latter role, the Challenger ARRV can move 229 cubic metres (8100 cubic feet) of earth an hour. The vehicle is also fitted with night-vision devices and armed with a 7.62mm (0.3in) FN MAG machine gun.

Country of origin:	United Kingdom
Crew:	3
Weight:	62,000kg (136,700lb)
Dimensions:	Length: 9.59m (31.46ft); width: 3.51m (11.52ft); height: 3m (9.84ft)
Range:	450km (280 miles)
Armour:	Chobham/steel (details classified)
Armament:	1 x 7.62mm (0.3in) FN MAG MG
Powerplant:	1 x Perkins CV12 TCA 1200 12-cylinder petrol, developing 1200hp (895kW) at 2300rpm
Performance:	Maximum road speed: 60km/h (37mph); fording: 1.07m (3.51ft); gradient: 58 percent; vertical obstacle: 0.9m (2.9ft); trench: 2.8m (9.2ft)

Engineer Vehicles

BAT-2

The BAT-2 is one of a large series of Ukrainian vehicles based upon the tracked chassis of the MT-T artillery tractor. It is a general engineer vehicle, but one ideally suited to earth-shifting or obstacle-clearing operations, using its large V-shaped hydraulically powered articulating dozer blade. A boom crane with a two-ton lifting capacity enables the BAT-2 to undertake vehicle recovery missions. The BAT-2 is also fitted with a ripping device, designed mainly for tearing up frost-hardened ground, a necessity in the harsh Ukrainian winters. The cab is fully armoured to protect the crew and features NBC systems for enhanced battlefield survivability.

Country of origin:	Ukraine
Crew:	2 + 8
Weight:	39,700kg (87,500lb)
Dimensions:	Length: 9.64m (31.63ft); width: 4.2m (13.78ft); height: 3.69m (12.11ft)
Range:	500km (310 miles)
Armour:	Not applicable
Armament:	None
Powerplant:	1 x V-64-4 12-cylinder multi-fuel diesel, developing 700hp (522kW)
Performance:	Maximum road speed: 60km/h (37mph); fording: 1.3m (4.3ft); vertical obstacle: 0.8m (2.6ft)

M32

Though developed in 1943 as a combat tank-recovery vehicle, the M32 remained in service in the United States and then abroad into the late 1950s. The hull and chassis are instantly recognizable as those of the M4 Sherman tank. The Sherman was converted into an M32 by removing the turret and replacing it with an A-frame crane and a winch with a 27,210kg (60,000lb) pull capacity. A single 12.7mm (0.5in) Browning M2 HB machine gun was also mounted on the superstructure for crew defence against infantry attack, though some could also be seen with 81mm (3.19in) mortars. Approximately 1500 M32s were produced during World War II.

Country of origin:	United States
Crew:	6
Weight:	28,000kg (61,700lb)
Dimensions:	Length: 5.93m (19.46ft); width: 2.68m (8.79ft); height: 2.74m (8.99ft)
Range:	300km (190 miles)
Armour:	(Steel) 76mm (2.99in)
Armament:	1 x 12.7mm (0.5in) Browning M2 HB machine gun; 1 x 81mm (3.19in) mortar
Powerplant:	1 x Continental R975-C1 9-cylinder petrol, developing 350hp (261kW) at 2400rpm
Performance:	Maximum speed: 40km/h (25mph); fording: 1.22m (4ft); gradient: 58 percent; vertical obstacle: 0.61m (2ft); trench: 1.88m (6.17ft)

Sherman T15E1

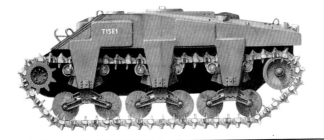

The attempt to mechanize mine clearance led to the production of a huge range of vehicles during World War II. US M4 Sherman tanks in particular were converted into several mine-clearing variants. First came the Mine Exploder T1E3. This utilized two large rollers extended to the front of the vehicle on side arms which detonated mines on contact. Many other versions later arrived, such as the Mine Resistant Vehicle T15E1. The basis of the T15E1 was simply a turretless M4 tank laden with extra body and belly armour. It was intended to detonate mines by driving over them, but the concept was as impractical as it sounds. No T15E1s were actually tested in combat.

Country of origin:	United States
Crew:	5
Weight:	33,200kg (73,200lb)
Dimensions:	Length: 5.9m (19.36ft); width: 2.75m (9.02ft); height: 2.04m (6.69ft)
Range:	270km (170 miles)
Armour:	Not applicable
Armament:	None
Powerplant:	2 x General Motors 6-cylinder petrol, developing 500hp (373kW)
Performance:	Maximum road speed: 29km/h (18mph)

M48 AVLB

The M48 Armoured Vehicle-Launched Bridge (AVLB) was a variant of the M48 MBT. Basically the chassis was exactly the same as that of the tank, but the turret was removed and replaced with a hydraulically operated scissor bridge. The bridge itself was 19.2m (63ft) long and 4.01m (13.16ft) wide. Laying the bridge took only three minutes, retracting it took between 10 and 30 minutes. The actual width of obstacle the bridge could span was 18.28m (59.97ft). The M48 was used extensively by the US Army but was also exported to several other countries. Earlier models were recognizable by two 12.7mm (0.5in) Browning machine guns, each mounted in a turret. Later models were unarmed.

Country of origin:	United States
Crew:	2
Weight:	55,205kg (121,727lb)
Dimensions:	Length: 11.28m (37ft); width: 4m (13.12ft); height: 3.9m (12.79ft)
Range:	500km (310 miles)
Armour:	120mm (4.72in) maximum
Armament:	None
Powerplant:	1 x Continental AVDS-1790-2A 12-cylinder diesel, developing 750hp (559kW) at 2400rpm
Performance:	Maximum road speed: 48km/h (30mph); fording: 1.22m (4ft); gradient: 60 percent; vertical obstacle: 0.9m (2.95ft); trench: 2.59m (8.5ft)

M88A1

Developed in the early 1960s, the M88 Armoured Recovery Vehicle was produced until 1964, with roughly 1000 vehicles entering service with the US Army and US Marine Corps. Its chief role was MBT recovery. It was equipped with an A-frame boom, two winches and a dozer blade. The boom could pull up to 25 tons when the dozer was set into the ground to stabilize the vehicle, and could lift just under eight tons. The two winches were located at the front of the hull, one capable of pulling 23,000kg (50,700lb) and the other 13,600kg (30,000lb). A Browning M2HB 12.7mm (0.5in) machine gun was mounted on top of the crew compartment for anti-aircraft use.

Country of origin:	United States
Crew:	4
Weight:	50,803kg (112,020lb)
Dimensions:	Length: 8.27m (27.13ft); width: 3.43m (11.25ft); height: 2.92m (9.58ft)
Range:	450km (280 miles)
Armour:	Not applicable
Armament:	1 x 12.7mm (0.5in) Browning M2HB MG
Powerplant:	1 x Continental AVDS-1790-2DR 12-cylinder diesel, developing 980hp (730kW) at 2800rpm
Performance:	Maximum road speed: 42km/h (26mph); fording: 1.63m (5.35ft); gradient: 60 percent; vertical obstacle: 1.06m (3.48ft); trench: 2.62m (8.59ft)

M578

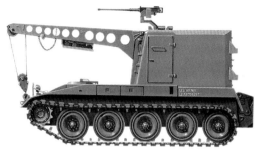

The M578 was developed specifically as a support vehicle for the M107 175mm (6.89in) and the M110 203mm (8in) self-propelled howitzers. A vehicle was required to assist with the frequent barrel changes required by these weapons, and the M578 filled the brief. The M578 was constructed using the same chassis and basic turret design as the howitzers themselves, the key differences being a hydraulically powered crane replacing the gun and a hydraulic stabilizing blade fitted to the rear hull. Despite the M107 and M110 now being out of service, the M578 continues in use as a Light Armoured Recovery Vehicle (LARV), and saw service in the Gulf War.

Country of origin:	United States
Crew:	3
Weight:	24,300kg (53,600lb)
Dimensions:	Length: 6.42m (21.06ft); width: 3.15m (10.33ft); height: 2.92m (9.58ft)
Range:	725km (450 miles)
Armour:	Not available
Armament:	1 x 12.7mm (0.5in) Browning M2 HB MG
Powerplant:	1 x General Motors 8V-71T 8-cylinder diesel, developing 405hp (302kW) at 2300rpm
Performance:	Maximum road speed: 55km/h (34mph); fording: 1.07m (3.51ft); gradient: 60 percent; vertical obstacle: 1.02m (3.35ft); trench: 2.36m (7.74ft)

M9 ACE

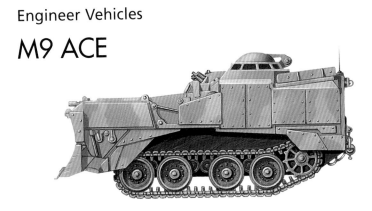

Though the M9's role is purely as an earthmover, it is one of a new generation of sophisticated engineer vehicles. Unusually for an earthmover, it is fully amphibious and propels itself through water at speeds of 4.8km/h (3mph) using its tracks. The crew sit in the rear of the vehicle and a large apron/dozer blade is located at the front. This is deployed by using hydraulic rotary actuators to lower the front of the vehicle. When driving, shock-absorbing accumulators in the chassis give a smooth ride over most terrains up to a maximum speed of 48km/h (30mph). The driver's position has chemical/biological protection and the vehicle is armoured against small-arms fire and shell splinters.

Country of origin:	United States
Crew:	3
Weight:	16,327kg (36,001lb)
Dimensions:	Length: 6.25m (20.51ft); width: 3.2m (10.5ft); height: 2.7m (8.86ft)
Range:	322km (200 miles)
Armour:	Not available
Armament:	None
Powerplant:	1 x Cummins V903C 8-cylinder diesel, developing 220hp (164kW)
Performance:	Maximum road speed: 48km/h (30mph)

Crotale

The Crotale was developed to fulfil a South African order for an advanced all-weather SAM system. Designated 'Cactus' in South Africa, the Crotale missile has sold well around the world and has recently been updated in the Crotale Next-Generation Air Defence Missile System. The original-format vehicle is a Hotchkiss-Brandt-designed 4x4 armoured hull, used for both the target-acquisition and firing vehicles. The firing vehicle mounts four R.440 missiles, each with a range of approximately 8500m (28,000ft) and a blast radius of 8m (26ft). The target-acquisition vehicle carries a Doppler pulse search and surveillance radar with an 18km (11-mile) acquisition range.

Country of origin:	France
Crew:	3
Weight:	(launcher vehicle) 27,300kg (60,200lb)
Dimensions:	Length: 6.22m (20.4ft); width: 2.65m (8.69ft); height (vehicle): 2.04m (6.69ft)
Range:	500km (310 miles)
Armour:	3–5mm (0.12–0.2in)
Armament:	4 x Matra R.440 SAM missiles
Powerplant:	1 x diesel generator and 4 x electric motors, developing 236hp (176kW)
Performance:	Maximum road speed: 70km/h (43mph); fording: 0.68m (2.23ft); gradient: 40 percent; vertical obstacle: 0.3m (1ft)

Shahine

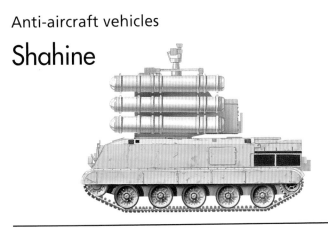

Unlike many mobile SAM systems, the Shahine is heavily armoured. Its firing and acquisition units are both mounted on an AMX-30 MBT chassis with armour 15–80mm (0.59–3.15in) thick. The traction and power of the AMX-30 chassis give the Shahine great versatility in deployment and excellent cross-country mobility. Target acquisition is performed by a separate vehicle mounting a pulse-Doppler surveillance radar and acquisition electronics. The launcher contains six Matra R.460 SAM missiles, each being guided by the command-control centre to its target. A reloading vehicle accompanies the Shahine unit, and can reload the entire system using an onboard crane.

Country of origin:	France
Crew:	3
Weight:	(launcher vehicle) 38,799kg (85,554lb)
Dimensions:	Length: 6.59m (21.62ft); width: 3.1m (10.17ft); height: 5.5m (18ft)
Range:	600km (370 miles)
Armour:	15–80mm (0.59–3.15in)
Armament:	6 x Matra R.460 SAM missiles
Powerplant:	1 x Hispano-Suiza HS110 12-cylinder multi-fuel, developing 690hp (515kW)
Performance:	Maximum road speed: 65km/h (40mph); fording: 1.3m (4.3ft); gradient: 60 percent; vertical obstacle: 0.93m (3.05ft)

Flakpanzer 38 (t)

The Flakpanzer 38 (t) was produced from the chassis of the Czech LT-38 tracked vehicle in 1943, though it did not enter service until 1944. By locating the engine in the front of the chassis, an armoured section could be constructed at the rear. This held a Flak 38 20mm (0.78in) cannon suitable for low-level air defence. The Flakpanzer 38 (t) was totally inadequate for its role, with limited mobility and firepower. Only 160 were made during WWII, and most of these were sent out to the Russian front where they were used in ground-assault roles in support of infantry units. The Flak 38 cannon proved particularly useful against soft-skinned vehicles.

Country of origin:	Germany
Crew:	5
Weight:	9800kg (21,600lb)
Dimensions:	Length: 4.61m (15.12ft); width: 2.13m (6.98ft); height: 2.25m (7.38ft)
Range:	210km (130 miles)
Armour:	10–50mm (0.39–1.96in)
Armament:	1 x Flak 38 20mm (0.78in) cannon
Powerplant:	1 x Praga AC 6-cylinder petrol, developing 147hp (110kW)
Performance:	Maximum road speed: 42km/h (26mph)

Anti-aircraft vehicles

Möbelwagen

The Flakpanzer IV Möbelwagen had a troubled pre-production stage. Its original configuration of four Flak 38 20mm (0.78in) cannon mounted on a PzKpfw IV chassis was produced by Krupp in early 1943. The cannon operators were protected by four hinged 20mm (0.78in) armour shields which could be lowered for 360-degree gun traverse. However, the design was not given official approval, and it took until 1944 before a new version was accepted, this time armed with a 37mm (1.46in) Flak 43 gun. Production began in April 1944, and about 240 were made by the end of the war. The Möbelwagen was technologically superseded by the Ostwind and Wirbelwind AAA systems.

Country of origin:	Germany
Crew:	5
Weight:	25,000kg (55,100lb)
Dimensions:	Length: 4.61m (15.12ft); width: 2.88m (9.44ft); height: 2.7m (8.86ft)
Range:	200km (125 miles)
Armour:	60mm (2.63in)
Armament:	4 x 20mm (0.78in) Flak 38 L/112.5 cannon (prototype); 1 x 37mm (1.46in) Flak 43 cannon (production model)
Powerplant:	1 x HL 120 Maybach 12-cylinder petrol, developing 268hp (200kW)
Performance:	Maximum road speed: 38km/h (24mph); fording: 1m (3.3ft); gradient: 60 percent; vertical obstacle: 0.6m (2ft); trench: 2.2m (7.2ft)

Wirbelwind

The Wirbelwind was an attempt to enhance the mobile firepower of frontline German units in the face of an increasing Allied air supremacy in 1944. Four 20mm (0.78in) Flak 38 L/112.5 cannon were set into a nine-sided armoured turret, which was then mounted on the chassis of battle-damaged Panzer IV tanks. While the Wirbelwind did prove effective against low-flying aircraft, its competitor, the Flakpanzer IV Ostwind, armed with a single 37mm (1.46in) Flak 43 L/89 cannon, proved to have superior knockdown power and replaced the Wirbelwind. Plans to upgrade the Wirbelwind were halted by the collapse of German industry towards the end of the war.

Country of origin:	Germany
Crew:	3
Weight:	22,000kg (48,510lb)
Dimensions:	Length: 5.92m (19.42ft); width: 2.9m (9.51ft); height: 2.7m (8.86ft)
Range:	200km (125 miles)
Armour:	60mm (2.63in)
Armament:	4 x 20mm (0.78in) Flak 38 L/112.5 cannon
Powerplant:	1 x HL 120 Maybach 12-cylinder petrol, developing 268hp (200kW)
Performance:	Maximum road speed: 38km/h (24mph); fording: 1m (3.3ft); gradient: 60 percent; vertical obstacle: 0.6m (2ft); trench: 2.2m (7.2ft)

Anti-aircraft vehicles

Flakpanzer 1 Gepard

The Gepard emerged in the late 1960s as an indigenous self-propelled anti-aircraft gun (SPAAG) for the West German Army, which had formerly used the US M42 40mm (1.57in) system. It entered service in 1976 and was subsequently bought by the Belgians and Dutch, as well as the Germans. The Gepard chassis is based on the Leopard 1 MBT with downgraded armour requirements, while the Contraves turret mounts twin 35mm (1.38in) Oerlikon KDA cannon and a retractable search radar. Fire-control is fully computerized with ground- or aerial-engagement options and, amongst latest models, a Siemens laser rangefinder. The Oereikon cannon have a cyclical rate of fire of 550rpm, in 20- or 40-round bursts.

Country of origin:	Germany
Crew:	4
Weight:	47,300kg (104,000lb)
Dimensions:	Length: 7.68m (25.19ft); width: 3.27m (10.72ft); height: 3.01m (9.87ft)
Range:	550km (340 miles)
Armour:	40mm (1.57in)
Armament:	2 x 35mm (1.38in) cannon; eight smoke dischargers
Powerplant:	1 x MTU MB 838 Ca M500 10-cylinder multi-fuel, developing 830hp (619kW)
Performance:	Maximum road speed: 64km/h (40.5mph); fording: 2.5m (8.2ft)

Roland

The Roland SAM system is a Franco-German production which began in the 1960s and involved France's Aérospatiale and West Germany's Messerschmitt-Bölkow-Blohm. Known collectively as Euromissile, the two companies developed the clear-weather (Roland 1) and all-weather (Roland 2) versions of the missile. The German Army's TELAR vehicle is the chassis of the Marder MICV (pictured here), while the French opted for the chassis of the AMX-30 MBT. Both versions carry two launch-ready missiles, one either side of the pulse-Doppler radar turret, with eight more stored. The radar system features an Identification Friend or Foe (IFF) assessment computer which on the Marder version can detect targets at up to 18km (11 miles).

Country of origin:	France/West Germany
Crew:	3
Weight:	34,800kg (76,7004lb)
Dimensions:	Length: 6.92m (22.7ft); width: 3.24m (10.63ft); height: 2.92m (9.58ft)
Range:	600km (370 miles)
Armour:	Steel (details classified)
Armament:	2 + 8 Roland SAM missiles
Powerplant:	1 x MTU mB 833Ea-500 6-cylinder diesel, developing 590hp (440kW)
Performance:	Maximum road speed: 60km/h (37mph); fording: 1.5m (4.9ft); gradient: 60 percent; vertical obstacle: 1m (3.3ft); trench: 2.5m (8.2ft)

Sidam 25

The OTOBREDA Sidam 25 entered production in 1989. It is basically four Oerlikon KBA 25mm (0.98in) automatic cannon turret-mounted on the ever-popular M113 APC. Using an optronic fire-control system, the weapon is highly accurate against low-flying aerial targets within its 2000m (6650ft) effective range. Rate of fire is 2400 rounds per minute and the turret takes 600 rounds when fully loaded, enough ammunition for around eight two-second bursts. Thirty armour-piercing rounds are also held in an internal magazine for use against ground targets. Using the almost ubiquitous M113 vehicle meant simple logistics and affordable spare parts.

Country of origin:	Italy
Crew:	3
Weight:	15,100kg (33,300lb)
Dimensions:	Length: 5.04m (16.54ft); width: 2.67m (8.76ft); height (without turret): 1.82m (5.97ft)
Range:	550km (342 miles)
Armour:	(Aluminium) – 38mm (1.49in)
Armament:	4 x 25mm (0.98in) Oerlikon KBA cannon
Powerplant:	1 x Detroit 6V-53T 6-cylinder diesel, developing 266hp (198kW)
Performance:	Maximum road speed: 69km/h (40mph); fording: amphibious; gradient: 60 percent; vertical obstacle: 0.61m (2ft); trench: 1.68m (5.51ft)

Type 87 AWSP

The Type 87 Automatic Western Self-Propelled (AWSP) was developed in the late 1970s as a replacement for the obsolete US M42 Duster AAA system, then in use with the Japanese military. Looking abroad for inspiration, Japanese engineers took the turret system of the German Gepard air-defence system and mounted it on the Type 74 MBT chassis. Testing was completed in 1987 from when Mitsubishi Heavy Industries started to produce the first of 180 AWSP vehicles. Like the Gepard, the Type 87 is armed with two 35mm (1.38in) Oerlikon KDA cannon, but with a much-improved fire-control system. The tower at the back of the turret mounts the acquisition and tracking radar.

Country of origin:	Japan
Crew:	3
Weight:	36,000kg (79,400lb)
Dimensions:	Length: 7.99m (26.21ft); width: 3.18 m (10.43ft); height: 4.4m (14.44ft)
Range:	500km (310 miles)
Armour:	Steel (details classified)
Armament:	2 x 35mm (1.38in) Oerlikon KDA cannon
Powerplant:	1 x 10F22WT 10-cylinder diesel, developing 718hp (536kW)
Performance:	Maximum road speed: 60km/h (37mph); fording: 1m (3.3ft); gradient: 60 percent; vertical obstacle: 1m (3.3ft); trench: 2.7m (8.9ft)

SA-4 Ganef

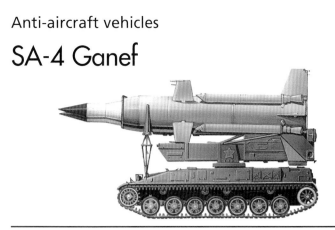

The SA-4 Ganef SAM system entered Soviet service in 1964. The launch vehicle (designated 2P24) is the tracked chassis of both the GMZ armoured minelayer and, later, the M1973 152mm (5.98in) self-propelled howitzer (though the latter vehicle used a shortened version of the SA-4 chassis). Each carrier is powered by a 12-cylinder diesel engine providing the 520hp (388kW) necessary to move the two Ganef missiles mounted above, each weighing 1800kg (4000lb). The missiles sit on a turntable mounting capable of 360-degree traverse and 45-degree elevation. NBC, air filtration and infrared night-vision devices are standard equipment on the 2P24 to enable operations in hazardous environments.

Country of origin:	Russian Federation/Soviet Union
Crew:	3–5
Weight:	30,000kg (66,150lb)
Dimensions:	Length (with missiles): 9.46m (31.03ft); width: 3.2m (10.5ft); height (with missiles): 4.47m (14.67ft)
Range:	450km (280 miles)
Armour:	15–20mm (0.59–0.78in)
Armament:	2 x SA-4 Ganef SAM missiles
Powerplant:	1 x V-59 12-cylinder diesel, developing 520hp (388kW)
Performance:	Maximum road speed: 45km/h (28mph)

SA-6 Gainful

The SA-6 Gainful was developed in the early 1960s and entered active service in 1967. It went on to be one of the most successful anti-aircraft weapons of the 20th century, exported worldwide and combat-proven by Egypt and Syria in the 1973 Yom Kippur war. Three SA-6 missiles are transported on the modified chassis of a ZSU-23-4, also used to form the ZSU-23-4 Shilka self-propelled anti-aircraft gun system. Both vehicles have radiation warning systems, NBC protection and fire-control equipment. The typical SA-6 battery consists of one 'Straight Flush' fire-control vehicle, four actual launcher vehicles and two ZIL-131 6x6 resupply trucks. SA-6 missiles are radar-guided and have a maximum range of 22,000m (72,200ft).

Country of origin:	Russian Federation/Soviet Union
Crew:	3
Weight:	14,000kg (30,900lb)
Dimensions:	Length: 7.39m (24.25ft); width: 3.18m (10.43ft); height: (with missiles) 3.45m (11.32ft)
Range:	260km (160 miles)
Armour:	15mm (0.59in)
Armament:	3 x SA-6 Gainful SAMs
Powerplant:	1 x model V-6R 6-cylinder diesel, developing 240hp (179kW)
Performance:	Maximum road speed: 44km/h (27mph); fording: 1m (3.3ft); gradient: 60 percent; vertical obstacle: 1.1m (3.6ft); trench: 2.8m (9.2ft)

SA-8 Gecko

The SA-8 Gecko was the first Soviet air-defence system to combine surveillance, target acquisition and missile launcher in one vehicle. It has proved to be a popular system, particularly in the Middle East, and in the Soviet Army it replaced the 57mm (2.24in) anti-aircraft gun. The Gecko's transportation is handled by the chassis of the ZIL-167 6x6 vehicle. This is fully amphibious, propulsion coming from two waterjets. It features an NBC-protected crew compartment and a central tyre-pressure regulation system. Two Gecko infrared- and active-seeker-guided missiles are mounted ready to fire, controlled by two tracking and two guidance radars. An updated version of the Gecko, the SA-8B, has six missiles in enclosed containers.

Country of origin:	Russian Federation/Soviet Union
Crew:	5
Weight:	17,499kg (38,587lb)
Dimensions:	Length: 9.14m (30ft); width: 2.8m (9.19ft); height (with radar lowered): 4.2m (13.92ft)
Range:	250km (155 miles)
Armour:	Not known
Armament:	6 x SA-8 Type 9M33 SAMs
Powerplant:	1 x 5D20 B-300 diesel with gas-turbine auxiliary drive, developing 299hp (223kW)
Performance:	Maximum road speed: 80km/h (50mph); fording: amphibious

SA-13 Gopher

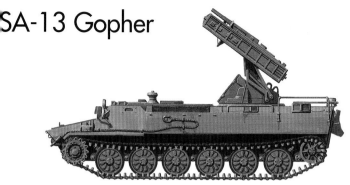

The ZRK-BD Strela 10 (NATO reporting name SA-13 Gopher) was introduced into Soviet forces in the late 1970s as a replacement for the SA-9 Gaskin. It onsists of four SA-13 infrared-guided missiles transported by a modified MT-LB Multipurpose Armoured Vehicle acting as a TELAR (Transporter Erector Launcher nd Radar). The MT-LB was chosen for its exceptional mobility and fully mphibious hull (power in the water comes from the MT-LB's wide tracks). Each ELAR vehicle usually carries eight missile reloads in a cargo compartment at the ear. SA-13 missiles have an effective range of 5000m (16,400ft) to an altitude of 500m (11,500ft).

Country of origin:	Russian Federation/Soviet Union
Crew:	3
Weight:	12,080kg (26,636lb)
Dimensions:	Length: 6.93m (22.74ft); width: 2.85m (9.35ft); height: 3.96m (13ft)
Range:	500km (310 miles)
Armour:	7–14mm (0.28–0.55in)
Armament:	4 + 4 9M37 SAM missiles
Powerplant:	1 x YaMZ-239V 8-cylinder diesel, developing 709hp (529kW)
Performance:	Maximum road speed: 61.5km/h (38mph); fording: amphibious; gradient: 60 percent; vertical obstacle: 0.7m (2.3ft); trench: 2.7m (8.9ft)

SA-10 Grumble

The S-300PMU1 (NATO reporting name SA-10 Grumble) is a cutting-edge air-defence system developed in the early 1970s, operational service beginning in 1980. The key advantage of the SA-10 is that it can acquire and engage multiple targets simultaneously across a very broad spectrum of altitude – 25m (82ft) to 30,000m (98,400ft). The four-missile erector-launcher is mounted on a 5P85SE2 or 5P85TE2 semi-trailer pulled by a MAZ-7910 8x8 tractor truck. Three missiles can be launched in one second, each for different targets. During deployment, the missile battery consists of an engagement control centre, a Doppler target-acquisition radar, a trailer-mounted FLAP LID radar system, and up to 12 erector launchers.

Country of origin:	Russian Federation/Soviet Union
Crew:	Unknown
Weight:	43,300kg (95,500lb)
Dimensions:	Length: 11.47m (37.63ft); width: 10.17m (33.36ft); height: 3.7m (12.14ft)
Range:	650km (400 miles)
Armour:	Classified
Armament:	4 x 5V55K SA-10 SAMs
Powerplant:	1 x D12A-525A 12-cylinder diesel, developing 517hp (386kW)
Performance:	Maximum road speed: 60km/h (37mph)

SA-11 Gadfly

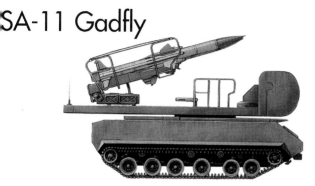

The 9K37M1 BUK-1 SAM system (NATO reporting name SA-11 Gadfly), is a replacement for the SA-6 Gainful and was introduced into service in 1980. It is a medium-range radar-guided missile with a 90 percent kill probability against aircraft, 40 percent against cruise missiles. The target is acquired by a SNOW DRIFT warning and acquisition radar at ranges of up to 70km (43 miles), though the TELAR system takes over the tracking of the missile to target. The TELAR vehicle itself is a modified GM-539 tracked chassis carrying a Fire Dome radar unit and four missiles in a turntable launcher. The fully tracked configuration allows the Gadfly to keep up with Russian armoured units even in off-road manoeuvres.

Country of origin:	Russian Federation/Soviet Union
Crew:	4
Weight:	(launch vehicle) 32,340kg (71,309lb)
Dimensions:	Length: 9.3m (30.51ft); width: 3.25m (10.66ft); height: 3.8m (12.47ft)
Range:	500km (310 miles)
Armour:	Not applicable
Armament:	4 x Type 9M38M1 (SA-11) SAM missiles
Powerplant:	1 x V-64-4 12-cylinder diesel, developing 709hp (529kW)
Performance:	Maximum road speed: 65km/h (40mph)

Anti-aircraft vehicles

M1 Tunguska

The Tunguska is a low-level air-defence system introduced in 1986 which mixes SAM and cannon technology to make a versatile aerial-interception platform. Eight SA-19 Grison missiles are mounted on the turret for medium-range (up to 10,000m/32,800ft) interception, along with two twin-barrel 2A38M 30mm (1.18in) cannon for close-range (up to 4000m/13,100ft) targets. The Tunguska has full onboard fire-control, including target acquisition radar and automated cannon targeting. Mobility is provided by the chassis of a 34-ton GM-352M tracked vehicle, which has hydropneumatic suspension and full NBC protection for the crew. Tunguska is used by both the Russian military and the Indian Army.

Country of origin:	Russia
Crew:	4
Weight:	34,000kg (75,000lb)
Dimensions:	Length: 7.93m (26ft); width: 3.24m (10.63ft); height: 4.02m (13.1ft)
Range:	500km (310 miles)
Armour:	Classified
Armament:	2 x twin-barrel 2A38M 30mm (1.18in) cannon; 8 x SA-19 Grison SAMs
Powerplant:	1 x V-64-4 12-cylinder diesel, developing 709hp (529kW)
Performance:	Maximum road speed: 65km/h (40mph)

ADATS

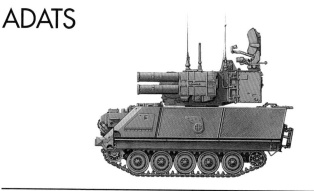

The Air Defense Anti-Tank System (ADATS) is a troubled experiment by the Swiss Oerlikon-Bührle-Gruppe and the US Martin-Marietta to produce a combined anti-tank/anti-aircraft missile system. Production began in 1989, but combat-conditions testing in the early 1990s led to the US Army abandoning the vehicle in favour of dedicated anti-tank/anti-aircraft weaponry. However, some remain in service with the Canadian Army and Swiss military forces. The chassis of the ADATS is a modified M113A2 APC. Eight ADATS missiles are mounted on the top of the hull with a Doppler pulse radar and an electro-optical target-acquisition system. ADATs missiles have a range of 10km (6 miles) and can penetrate 900mm (35in) of armour.

Country of origin:	Switzerland/United States
Crew:	3
Weight:	15,800kg (34,800lb)
Dimensions:	Length: 4.86m (15.94ft); width: 2.68m (8.79ft); height (with radar antenna): 4.48m (14.7ft)
Range:	400km (250 miles)
Armour:	12–38mm (0.47–1.49in)
Armament:	8 x ADATS SAMs
Powerplant:	1 x Detroit 6V-53N 6-cylinder diesel, developing 211hp (158kW)
Performance:	Maximum road speed: 58km/h (36mph); fording: amphibious; gradient: 60 percent; vertical obstacle: 0.61m (2ft); trench: 1.68m (5.51ft)

Anti-aircraft vehicles

Tracked Rapier

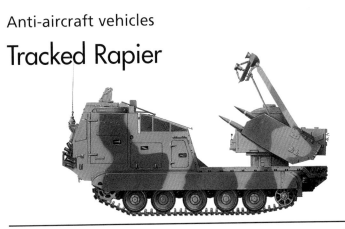

Tracked Rapier is the self-propelled version of the British Rapier SAM which first entered service with the British Army in 1971. The towed version consists of an optical tracker, power generator and the four-missile launch unit. In the case of the Tracked Rapier, all three of these elements are transplanted to the back of an M548 tracked cargo chassis, part of the M113 armoured vehicle series. The Tracked Rapier, however, carries eight missiles on its launcher, and the optical tracker is located in the cab, exiting to the outside through the roof. The tracking antenna elevates above the launcher itself. Protection for the Tracked Rapier crew is provided by a fully armoured cab.

Country of origin:	United Kingdom
Crew:	3
Weight:	14,010kg (30,892lb)
Dimensions:	Length: 6.4m (21ft); width: 9.19m (30.14ft); height: 2.5m (8.2ft)
Range:	300km (190 miles)
Armour:	Aluminium (details classified)
Armament:	8 x Rapier SAMs
Powerplant:	1 x GMC 6-cylinder turbocharged diesel, developing 250hp (186kW) at 2600rpm
Performance:	Maximum road speed: 80km/h (50mph); fording: amphibious; gradient: 60 percent; vertical obstacle: 0.6m (2ft); trench: 1.75m (5.74ft)

Armoured Starstreak

The Starstreak SAM is a close-range anti-aircraft missile designed for low-level defence against targets such as ground-attack aircraft and helicopters. It is a versatile missile which can be launched from multiple platforms: shoulder, attack helicopter, and a vehicular version, the Starstreak Self-Propelled High-Velocity Missile (SP HVM). The SP HVM entered into service with the British Army in 1997. Eight Starstreak missiles are mounted in a turntable launcher on top of an Alvis Stormer vehicle. A roof-mounted Air Defence Alerting Device (ADAD) performs infrared targeting. The missiles themselves break into three darts as they approach the target, each tracked to impact by a laser-guidance system.

Country of origin:	United Kingdom
Crew:	3
Weight:	12,700kg (28,000lb)
Dimensions:	Length: 5.33 m (17.49ft); width: 2.4m (7.87ft); height: 3.49m (11.45ft)
Range:	650km (400 miles)
Armour:	Aluminium (details classified)
Armament:	8 +12 Starstreak SAMs
Powerplant:	1 x Perkins T6/3544 6-cylinder turbocharged diesel, developing 250hp (186kW) at 2600rpm
Performance:	Maximum road speed: 80km/h (50mph); fording: amphibious; gradient: 60 percent; vertical obstacle: 0.6m (2ft); trench: 1.75m (5.74ft)

Anti-aircraft vehicles

M727 HAWK

In 1997, the US military disposed of the last of its HAWK ('Homing All the Way to the Kill') missiles after almost 40 years of service. It first entered US Army service in August 1960, the launcher unit first being towed by a 2.5-ton 6x6 truck. In the early 1970s, the HAWK was produced in a self-propelled version, the M727 SP HAWK. This used a modified M548 tracked cargo carrier, which supported the three-missile launcher mounted on its rear hull. HAWK missiles were tracked to their target by following electro-magnetic energy reflected off the target by a Continuous-wave Illuminator radar, part of the HAWK battery.

Country of origin:	United States
Crew:	4
Weight:	12,925kg (28,494lb)
Dimensions:	Length: 5.87m (19.26ft); width: 2.69m (8.83ft); height: 2.5m (8.2ft)
Range:	489km (304 miles)
Armour:	Not available
Armament:	3 x HAWK SAM
Powerplant:	1 x Detroit 6V53 6-cylinder diesel, developing 214hp (160kW)
Performance:	Maximum road speed: 61km/h (38mph); fording: 1m (3.3ft); gradient: 60 percent; vertical obstacle: 0.61m (2ft); trench: 1.68m (5.51ft)

M48 Chaparral

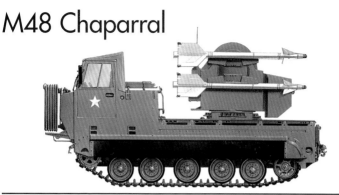

The M48 Chaparral went into production in the late 1960s using the MIM-72C SAM for short-range low-altitude interception missions. Guidance to target was via a fire-and-forget infrared system, later fitted with a Rosette Scan Seeker to resist enemy ECM. The M48 Chaparral system comprised a four-missile launcher on the back of an M-730A2 tracked cargo-carrier based on the M113 APC, with eight missiles stored. An amphibious capability was optional through a swim kit. An enemy aircraft warning system for the Chaparral was provided by a Forward Area Alerting Radar (FAAR) using a pulse-Doppler radar. All remaining Chaparral systems were deactivated in 1997.

Country of origin:	United States
Crew:	5
Weight:	11,500kg (25,360lb)
Dimensions:	Length: 6.06m (19.88ft); width: 2.69m (8.83ft); height: 2.68m (8.79ft)
Range:	489km (304 miles)
Armour:	Not applicable
Armament:	12 x MIM-72C SAM
Powerplant:	1 x Detroit 6V53 6-cylinder diesel, developing 214hp (160kW)
Performance:	Maximum road speed: 61km/h (38mph); fording: 1m (3.3ft); gradient: 60 percent; vertical obstacle: 0.61m (2ft); trench: 1.68m (5.51ft)

MIM-104 (GE) Patriot

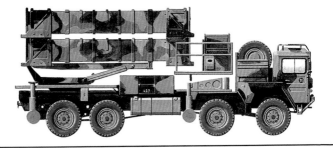

The Raytheon MIM-104 (GE) Patriot is an advanced SAM system introduced in the late 1980s. Using a track-via-missile (TVM) onboard guidance system in tandem with a ground-based tracking unit, each missile can engage aircraft targets and incoming ballistic and cruise missiles. Patriots were successfully used in the Gulf War to intercept incoming Iraqi Scud missiles fired at Israel, though their success did not equal media hype. Four pre-loaded Patriot missiles are transported in an M901 launcher fitted to an M860 two-axle semi-trailer. This in turn is pulled by an M818 6x6 tractor. A Patriot battery also features a MSQ-104 Engagement Control Centre (ECC) pulled by a M814 6x6 truck.

Country of origin:	United States
Crew:	2
Weight:	(M109 launcher) 26,867kg (59,241lb)
Dimensions:	Length: 10.4m (34.12ft); width: 2.49m (8.17ft); height: 3.96m (13ft)
Range:	800km (500 miles)
Armour:	Not applicable
Armament:	4 x Patriot SAM missiles
Powerplant:	1 x MAN D2866 LGF 6-cylinder diesel, developing 355hp (265kW)
Performance:	Maximum road speed: 80km/h (50mph)

BMS-1 Alacran

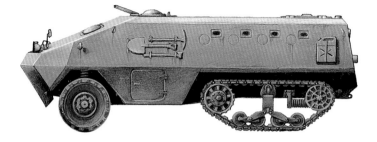

The BMS-1 Alacran is produced by the Chilean Industrias Cardoen company. It is unusual in being a modern armoured personnel carrier in half-track configuration, the product of a cancelled design initiative to update the World War II-era US M-3A1 half-tracks still in service with the Chilean Army. The Alacran can carry 12 fully equipped soldiers. It has an all-welded steel hull with the driver positioned on the front left and the commander just behind. Seven firing ports and eight vision blocks are provided around the troop compartment. Standard armament is a single machine gun, but cannon, ATGW systems and rocket launchers can be fitted.

Country of origin:	Chile
Crew:	2 + 12
Weight:	10,500kg (23,150lb)
Dimensions:	Length: 6.37m (20.9ft); width: 2.38m (7.81ft); height: 2.03m (6.66ft)
Range:	900km (560 miles)
Armour:	Not available
Armament:	1 x 7.62mm (0.3in) or 12.7mm (0.5in) MG
Powerplant:	1 x Cummins V-555 turbo diesel, developing 225hp (167kW) at 3000rpm
Performance:	Maximum road speed: 70km/h (43mph); fording: 1.6m (5.3ft); gradient: 70 percent

OT-810

Gerican half-track designs were so successful that after World War II many
countries adopted them their own armed forces. Czechoslovakia took over old
stocks of German Sdfz.251 half-tracks (Czechoslovakia was actually one of the
manufacturers of the Sdfz.251 chassis) and used them as armoured personnel
carriers. In the late 1950s, the vehicles were modified and were designated the OT-
810. The German engine was removed and replaced by a Tatra six-cylinder air-
cooled diesel. Armoured roof hatches were added to the troop compartment. Later,
an anti-tank variant was produced with an M59A 82mm (3.23in) recoilless rifle on
board, fired either from the vehicle or carried outside as an independent weapon.

Country of origin:	Czechoslovakia
Crew:	2 + 10
Weight:	9000kg (19,800lb)
Dimensions:	Length: 5.71m (18.73ft); width: 2.1m (6.89ft); height: 1.88m (6.17ft)
Range:	600km (370 miles)
Armour:	(Steel) 12mm (0.47in) maximum
Armament:	1 x 7.62mm (0.3in) MG
Powerplant:	1 x Tatra 928-3 6-cylinder diesel, developing 120hp (89kW)
Performance:	Maximum road speed: 55km/h (34mph); fording: 0.5m (1.6ft); gradient: 24 percent; vertical obstacle: 0.23m (0.77ft); trench: 1.98m (6.34ft)

M23

The origins of the M23 lie with Adolphe Kegresse, one of Russia's chief military vehicle engineers, who left to live in France in 1917. There, he began designing a series of half-tracks in cooperation with Citroën, and in 1923 a prototype of the Citroën-Kegresse AMC M23 was unveiled. It used the powerplant of the Citroën B2/10CV, a Kegresse P4 tracked mechanism, and an armoured hull built by Schneider. Kegresse used rubber tracks on the vehicle. The same track system on the Citroën B2/10CV was highly successful in the cross-Sahara desert rally of 1922–23. The M23 was armed with a 37mm (1.46in) SA-18 cannon or a single machine gun. Few were made and they were obsolete by World War II.

Country of origin:	France
Crew:	3
Weight:	2200kg (4850lb)
Dimensions:	Length: 3.4m (11.2ft); width: 1.4m (4.6ft); height: 2.3m (7.6ft)
Range:	200km (125 miles)
Armour:	Not available
Armament:	1 x 37mm (1.46in) SA-18 cannon or 1 x MG
Powerplant:	1 x Citroën 4-cylinder petrol, developing 17hp (13kW)
Performance:	Maximum road speed: 40km/h (25mph)

Half-Tracks

M28

The M28 was an 'improved' version of Kegresse's earlier M23. In effect, it was simply a larger vehicle, with the length extended out to 4.3m (14ft) and the height reaching 2.4m (8ft). The extended dimensions pushed the weight to 6000kg (13,200lb), and the power plant was upgraded from a four-cylinder engine generating 17hp (13kW) to a six-cylinder version developing 50hp (37kW). Armaments also changed. The M23 alternated between cannon and machine-gun armament, whereas the M28 combined the two. Its turret had a 37mm (1.46in) cannon extending from the rear and a single Hotchkiss machine gun at the front. Though more heavily armed, the M28 remained an impractical combat vehicle.

Country of origin:	France
Crew:	3
Weight:	6000kg (13,200lb)
Dimensions:	Length: 4.3m (14ft); width: 1.7m (5.6ft); height: 2.4m (8ft)
Range:	200km (125 miles)
Armour:	Not available
Armament:	1 x 37mm (1.46in) SA-18 cannon; 1 x 7.7mm (0.31in) MG
Powerplant:	1 x Citroën 6-cylinder petrol, developing 17hp (13kW)
Performance:	Maximum road speed: 45km/h (28mph)

Somua MCG/S307(f)

The French were extremely active in half-track design during the inter-war period. Though Somua specialized in civilian utility vehicles, in the 1930s it produced a series of artillery tractors using a Kegresse-type half-track configuration. In 1935, the Somua MCG went into production, and 2543 vehicles were built before World War II. The MCG had a rubber track like the Kegresse vehicles, though substantial metal reinforcing meant it could run for up to 8000km (4970 miles) before a track change. Under the Germans, requisitioned MCGs were designated S307(f) and many were converted into weapons platforms, carrying, for example, 75mm (2.95in) PaK 40 L/46 guns, 80mm (3.15in) rocket launchers and mortars.

Country of origin:	France
Crew:	4
Weight:	7300kg (16,100lb)
Dimensions:	Length: 5.3m (17.39ft); width: 1.88m (6.17ft); height: 1.95m (6.39ft)
Range:	170km (105 miles)
Armour:	Not available
Armament:	Various (see text)
Powerplant:	1 x Somua 4-cylinder petrol, developing 60hp (45kW)
Performance:	Maximum road speed: 36km/h (22mph)

Half-Tracks

SdKfz 10/4

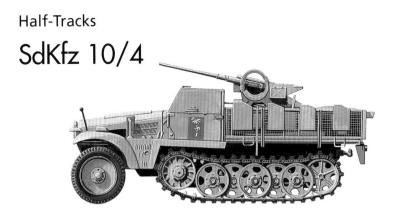

The SdKfz 10 was a general light utility vehicle/troop transporter introduced into the German armed forces in 1937. As an artillery tractor, it was used to draw weapons such as the 370mm (14.6in) PaK 35/36 or the 150mm (5.9in) sIG 33 field gun. It could also carry eight fully armed soldiers. Over 17,000 SdKfz 10s were produced between 1938 and the end of World War II, and many variants were designed for combat roles. The SdKfz 10/4, for example, was an anti-aircraft model. It initially mounted a single-barrel 20mm (0.78in) Flak 30 cannon, though many were subsequently upgraded to the Flak 38. The sides and rear of the hull could be folded flat to create an operating platform for the gun crew.

Country of origin:	Germany
Crew:	7
Weight:	4900kg (10,800lb)
Dimensions:	Length: 4.75m (15.58ft); width: 1.93m (6.33ft); height: 1.62m (5.31ft)
Range:	300km (190 miles)
Armour:	(Steel) 14.5mm (0.57in) maximum
Armament:	1 x 20mm (0.78in) Flak 30 or Flak 38 cannon
Powerplant:	1 x Maybach HL 42 TRKM 6-cylinder petrol, developing 100hp (75kW)
Performance:	Maximum road speed: 65km/h (40mph)

NSU Kettenkrad HK 101

The NSU Kettenkrad (SdKfz 2) was originally designed as a light artillery towing tractor for German airborne units, who needed a vehicle to pull the 37mm (1.46in) PaK 35/36 air-transportable anti-tank gun. In reality, it became a light utility tractor and was even used as a basic reconnaissance vehicle. The initial model was the NSU-101. One man drove the vehicle motorbike-style at the front, and two men sat facing backwards in the rear compartment. The Kettenkrad could pull a 450kg (1000lb) cargo, too little for it to make a serious logistical impact. This was a shame for the Germans, as the Kettenkrad could tackle extremely difficult terrain with ease. It became too expensive to make and production ceased in 1944.

Country of origin:	Germany
Crew:	3
Weight:	1280kg (2822lb)
Dimensions:	Length: 3m (9.9ft); width: 1.2m (3.9ft); height: 1m (3.3ft)
Range:	250km (150 miles)
Armour:	None
Armament:	None
Powerplant:	1 x Opel Olympia 38 petrol, developing 36hp (27kW)
Performance:	Maximum road speed: 80km/h (50mph)

Half-Tracks

SdKfz 250/3

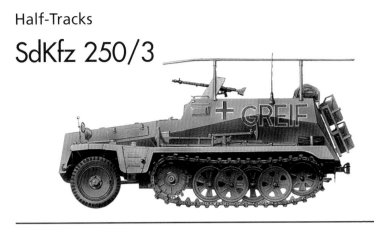

The basic SdKfz 250 was a one-ton half-track with an armoured hull and an open-top crew compartment occupying approximately half of the vehicle. It was one of the first half-tracks used by Germany in World War II, and 6000 were produced during the course of the war. It was conceived as an infantry carrier and support vehicle, and had a crew of six, armed with two 7.92mm (0.31in) MG34 or MG42 machine guns. The first version, the SdKfz 250/1, was only the first among 10 subsequent variants. The SdKfz 250/3 Leichter Funkpanzerwagen was an FuG12-radio vehicle used to control and coordinate motorized units. It was mounted with a large 2m (6.56ft) rod aerial, and later a 2m (6.56ft) star aerial.

Country of origin:	Germany
Crew:	6
Weight:	5340kg (11,775lb)
Dimensions:	Length: 4.56m (14.96ft); width: 1.95m (6.4ft); height: 1.66m (5.45ft)
Range:	350km (220 miles)
Armour:	(Steel) 15mm (0.59in) maximum
Armament:	1 x 7.92mm (0.31in) MG34 MG
Powerplant:	1 x Maybach hL 42 6-cylinder diesel, developing 120hp (89kW) at 3000rpm
Performance:	Maximum road speed: 65km/h (40mph); fording: 0.75m (2.46ft); gradient: 24 percent

SdKfz 4/1

The 15cm Panzerwerfer 42 (SdKfz 4/1) was a self-propelled version of the German 15cm (5.9in) Nebelwerfer rocket system. Opel was commissioned to build the vehicle in 1943 and did so by taking Opel and Daimler-Benz light trucks, removing their rear axles, and replacing them with the tracked assemblies from PzKpfw IIs. A fully armed superstructure protected the crew of four men, with a maximum armour thickness of 10mm (0.39in). The 10-barrelled Nebelwerfer 42 was set on the roof on a turntable fitting which could traverse 270 degrees and elevate 80 degrees. Secondary armament consisted of a single 7.92mm (0.31in) MG34 or MG42 machine gun. The Panzerwerfer 42 was mainly used on the Eastern Front from 1943.

Country of origin:	Germany
Crew:	4
Weight:	7100kg (15,650lb)
Dimensions:	Length: 6.02m (19.75ft); width: 2.26m (7.41ft); height: 2.17m (7.12ft)
Range:	Not available
Armour:	(Steel) 10mm (0.39in) maximum
Armament:	1 x Nebelwerfer 42 rocket launcher; 1 x 7.92mm (0.31in) MG34 or MG42 MG
Powerplant:	1 x Opel Olympia 6-cylinder petrol, developing 67hp (50kW)
Performance:	Maximum road speed: 40km/h (25mph)

Half-Tracks

Morris-Martel

The Morris-Martel emerged from the production facilities of Morris Commercial Motors and the creativity of Sir Gifford le Q. Martel. Martel was impressed by theories of armoured cavalry warfare in the post-WWI period. He subsequently designed a one-man armoured vehicle combining a Maxwell engine and the axle from a Ford truck for use in fast infantry assaults. Steering was done by the rear wheels. The War Office was initially enthused by this idea with the proviso that it became a two-man vehicle (one driver, one machine-gunner). Four prototypes were built by Morris, and eight more in 1927 for an Experimental Armoured Force, but this is as far as Martel's ideas went and the idea was soon dropped.

Country of origin:	United Kingdom
Crew:	2
Weight:	2200kg (4850lb)
Dimensions:	Length: 3m (9.9ft); width: 1.5m (4.9ft); height: 1.6m (5.3ft)
Range:	100km (60 miles)
Armour:	Not applicable
Armament:	1 x 7.92mm (3.1in) MG
Powerplant:	1 x Morris 4-cylinder petrol, developing 16hp (12kW)
Performance:	Maximum road speed: 25km/h (16mph)

Burford-Kegresse

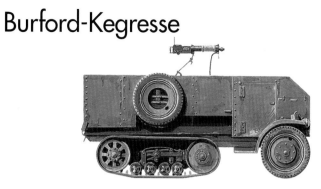

The French Kegresse half-track vehicle impressed many in the British forces with its great strength and sporting achievements. Yet Anglo-French relations dictated that the British would not simply buy French. Instead, Kegresse components were imported into Britain and assembled into similar vehicles at a factory in Slough, England. Three companies were involved in British production: Crossley, Vulcan and Burford. The Burford-Kegresse was directly based on the French M23 model, the tracked section featuring two main drive wheels with four minor wheels in between. The drive track was made of metal-reinforced rubber. The Burford vehicle could hold 12 infantry in addition to the two-man crew.

Country of origin:	United Kingdom
Crew:	2 + 12
Weight:	3500kg (7700lb)
Dimensions:	Length: 4.95m (16.24ft); width: not available; height: 2.1m (6.89ft) approx.
Range:	Not available
Armour:	Not available
Armament:	1 or 2 x Vickers 7.7mm (0.303in) MG
Powerplant:	1 x Burford 6-cylinder petrol
Performance:	Maximum road speed: 35km/h (22mph)

Bedford Traclat

The Bedford Tracked Light Artillery Tractor, or 'Traclat', was developed specifically as an artillery tow-vehicle for the 25pdr (87.6mm/3.45in) field gun, the 40mm (1.57in) Bofors anti-aircraft gun, and the 17pdr (76.2mm/3in) anti-tank gun. The Traclat's performance was impressive. Even towing a 25pdr gun weighing 1800kg (4000lb), it could travel at 48km/h (30mph) up a 1 in 30 gradient and even pull the gun up a 1 in 2 gradient. The tracked system enabled the vehicle to cope with muddy or snowy terrain with a ground pressure of only 3.67kg/sq cm (52.9lb/sq in). It was also waterproofed and fitted with air-intake extensions for fording operations. The war ended without the Traclat being tested in action.

Country of origin:	United Kingdom
Crew:	10
Weight:	6812kg (15,020lb)
Dimensions:	Length: 6.4m (20.9ft); width: 2.29m (7.51ft); height: 2.75m (9.02ft)
Range:	322km (200 miles)
Armour:	Not applicable
Armament:	None
Powerplant:	2 x Bedford 3500cc engines, developing 136hp (101kW)
Performance:	Maximum road speed: 48km/h (30mph)

Saurer RR-7

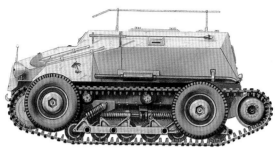

The RR-7 was developed by Saurer in 1937 as an artillery tractor for the Austrian Army. Distinctively, it used a wheel-and-track design, the wheels lowered to take over from the tracks when travelling on road surfaces. The design worked well, and 12 RR-7s entered service. After Austria was absorbed by Germany in the Anschluss of 1938, the German Panzer divisions found a different use for the RR-7. It was converted into an armoured observation post and given the designation SdKfz 254. Artillery observers would ride in the SdKfz 254 to the battlefront and direct fire for mobile artillery batteries. The SdKfz 254 saw service in the Balkans, Russia and North Africa and production reached 128 vehicles.

Country of origin:	Austria
Crew:	5
Weight:	6420kg (14,156lb)
Dimensions:	Length: 4.5m (14.76ft); width: 2.47m (8.1ft); height: 2.33m (7.64ft)
Range:	240km (150 miles)
Armour:	(Steel) 15mm (0.59in)
Armament:	None
Powerplant:	1 x Saurer CRDv 4-cylinder diesel, developing 70hp (52kW)
Performance:	Maximum road speed: 60km/h (37mph)

Renault Char TSF

The Renault Char TSF was derived from the FT 17 light tank. Most sources credit the FT 17 with being the 'most successful' of the World War I tanks, and it was still found in action as late as 1944 in the next world war. Its design was visually unusual, with a conventional top turret facing forwards while the rear of the hull formed a secondary turret facing backwards. Variants of the FT 17 included a 75mm (2.95in) self-propelled gun version, a bridge layer, and the TSF. The TSF was a radio-command vehicle. It was unarmed with a fixed casemate and a ER10 station radio installed. Crewed by three men, its role was to provide mobile battlefield communications amongst infantry and armoured units.

Country of origin:	France
Crew:	3
Weight:	7000kg (15,400lb)
Dimensions:	Length: 5m (16.4ft); width: 1.74m (5.7ft); height: 2.5m (8.2ft)
Range:	60km (37 miles)
Armour:	(Steel) 16mm (0.63in)
Armament:	None
Powerplant:	1 x Renault 4-cylinder petrol, developing 35hp (26kW)
Performance:	Maximum road speed: 8km/h (5mph)

Panzerbefehlswagen I

The Panzerbefehlswagen I (PzKpfw I) was actually designated a 'small armoured command vehicle'. It was created to allow Panzer formation commanders to keep pace with their units and maintain mobile communications. By removing the turret of the PzKpfw I training tank and replacing it with a fixed armoured box (experiments with a revolving-turret variant were later abandoned) greater space was provided internally for communications, signalling and navigation equipment. Some 200 Panzerbefehlswagen Is were produced and saw extensive service in the European and North African campaigns of 1939 to 1942. By 1943, however, most had been replaced by larger tank conversions which had better battlefield durability.

Country of origin:	Germany
Crew:	3
Weight:	5800kg (12,800lb)
Dimensions:	Length: 4.44m (14.57ft); width: 2.08m (6.82ft); height: 1.72m (5.64ft)
Range:	290km (180 miles)
Armour:	13mm (0.51in)
Armament:	1 x 7.92mm (0.31in) MG-34
Powerplant:	1 x Maybach NL38TR 6-cylinder petrol, developing 100hp (75kW) at 3000rpm
Performance:	Maximum road speed: 40km/h (25mph)

Type 82

The Type 82 emerged from Japanese Ground Self-Defence Forces trials in the 1970s for a new, wheeled reconnaissance vehicle. Trials of a 4x4 and a 6x6 vehicle resulted in the selection of the latter. This became the Type 82 Command and Communications Vehicle and production began in 1982. The vehicle transports a crew of eight, with two personnel responsible for driving and observation and the rest manning communications equipment in the raised rear of the vehicle. The front and back sections are connected by an inner gangway to the right of the hull. The Type 82 has side and rear doors set into the all-welded hull and armament is provided by roof-mounted machine guns.

Country of origin:	Japan
Crew:	8
Weight:	13,500kg (29,800lb)
Dimensions:	Length: 5.72m (18.77ft); width: 2.48m (8.14ft); height: 2.38m (7.81ft)
Range:	500km (310 miles)
Armour:	Classified
Armament:	1 x 7.62mm (0.3in) MG; 1 x 12.7mm (0.5in) MG
Powerplant:	1 x Isuzu diesel, developing 305hp (227kW) at 2700rpm
Performance:	Maximum road speed: 100km/h (62mph); fording: 1m (3.3ft); gradient: 60 percent; vertical obstacle: 0.6m (2ft); trench: 1.5m (4.9ft)

ABRA/RATAC

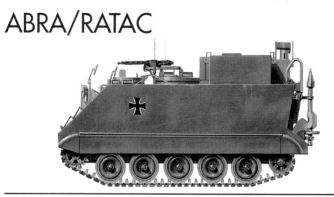

The ABRA/RATAC vehicle is a German M113 armoured personnel carrier converted to use the sophisticated RATAC artillery observation radar. RATAC is a French-designed system which can detect or calculate the positions of active artillery from the flight or burst of shells or through simple radar detection of the artillery piece's location. When fitted into the ABRA vehicle, the RATAC is deployed on a vertical telescopic pole 7.2m (23.6ft) high. In this position, the system can detect an artillery piece up to 18km (11 miles) away. In addition, it can monitor aerial targets up to 20km (12 miles) away. Once a target has been detected, the ABRA communications system relays the precise coordinates back to fire-control.

Country of origin:	Germany
Crew:	3 or 4
Weight:	13,000kg (28,700lb)
Dimensions:	Length: 4.86m (15.94ft); width: 2.7m (8.86ft); height: 7.16m (23.49ft)
Range:	300km (190 miles)
Armour:	Aluminium 12–38mm (0.47–1.5in)
Armament:	None
Powerplant:	1 x GMC Detroit 6V-53N 6-cylinder diesel, developing 215hp (160kW) at 2800rpm
Performance:	Maximum road speed: 68km/h (42mph); fording: amphibious; gradient: 60 percent; vertical obstacle: 0.61m (2ft); trench: 1.68m (5.51ft)

LGS Fennek

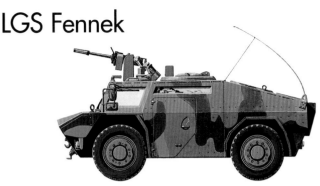

The LGS Fennek is a joint project of Krauss-Maffei Wegmann of Germany and SP Aerospace and Vehicle Systems B.V. of the Netherlands. It is an Armed Reconnaissance Vehicle, and uses the latest Tactical Command and Control System (TCSS). Battlefield observation is conducted using the STN Atlas Elektronik BAA technology. This combines a thermal imager, day camera and laser rangefinder in a single unit extended on a mast 1.5m (4.9ft) above the vehicle roof. A GPS system plots the position of enemy/friendly units on constantly updated digitized maps. Standard armament is an electrically controlled machine gun or 40mm (1.57in) grenade launcher. Some Dutch vehicles mount the Rafael Gill ATGW unit.

Country of origin:	Germany/Netherlands
Crew:	3
Weight:	7900kg (17,400lb)
Dimensions:	Length: 5.72m (18.77ft); width: 2.49m (8.17ft); height: 2.18m (7.15ft)
Range:	860km (530 miles)
Armour:	Details classified
Armament:	1 x 7.62mm (0.3in) or 12.7mm (0.5in) MG; or 1 x 40mm (1.57in) cannon
Powerplant:	1 x Deutz diesel, developing 240hp (179kW) at 2800rpm
Performance:	Maximum road speed: 115km/h (71mph); fording: 1m (3.3ft); gradient: 60 percent

M577

The M577 is one of the many variants of the ubiquitous M113 armoured personnel carrier. Its official designation is M577 Carrier, Command Post. The troop compartment is filled with communications and observation equipment which allows it to perform a multitude of command roles, including directing fire, acting as a centre of mobile communications and radio-listening, and operating as a tactical liaison vehicle. An external generator provides power for all the electronics, but in the latest versions of the M577 a hand-pump generator may be used to keep vital systems functioning in case of power failure. When at a standstill, a purpose-designed tent can be fitted to the vehicle to increase work space for the crew.

Country of origin:	United States
Crew:	5
Weight:	11,513kg (25,386lb)
Dimensions:	Length: 4.86m (15.94ft); width: 2.68m (8.79ft); height: 2.68m (8.79ft)
Range:	595km (370 miles)
Armour:	(Aluminium) 12–38mm (0.47–1.5in)
Armament:	1 x 7.62mm (0.3in) MG
Powerplant:	1 x GMC Detroit 6-cylinder diesel, developing 215hp (160kW) at 2800rpm
Performance:	Maximum road speed: 68km/h (42mph); fording: amphibious; gradient: 60 percent; vertical obstacle: 0.61m (2ft); trench: 1.68m (5.51ft)

Green Archer

The Green Archer is not a vehicle, but a mortar-detecting radar system. Germany, the Netherlands and the United Kingdom all developed an interest in the system in the mid-1960s. Both the Germans and the Dutch mounted the radar on modified M113 vehicles, whereas the British used the indigenous FV432 armoured personnel carrier to form the FV436 Self-Propelled Mortar-Locating Radar System, Green Archer. By detecting the firing and detonation of a shell, the radar could compute the location of an enemy mortar at ranges of up to 30km (18.6 miles). The main modification to the vehicles was the rerouting of the exhaust systems to avoid interference with the radar. Almost all these systems have now been replaced.

Country of origin:	Germany/United Kingdom/Netherlands
Crew:	4
Weight:	11,900kg (26,200lb)
Dimensions:	Length: 4.86m (15.94ft); width: 2.7m (8.86ft); height: 4.32m (14.17ft)
Range:	480km (300 miles)
Armour:	(Aluminium) 12–38mm (0.47–1.5in)
Armament:	1 x 7.62mm (0.3in) MG
Powerplant:	1 x Detroit Diesel 6V-53N 6-cylinder diesel, developing 215hp (160kW) at 2800rpm
Performance:	Maximum road speed: 68km/h (42mph); fording: amphibious; gradient: 60 percent; vertical obstacle: 0.61m (2ft); trench: 1.68m (5.51ft)

YP-104

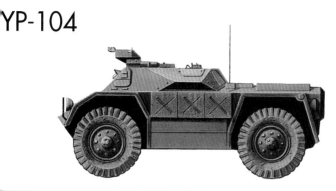

The YP-104 was a Dutch scout car developed in the early 1960s and it served until decommissioned in the late 1970s. Whereas most modern reconnaissance vehicles are armed, the YP-104 relied mainly on its top speed of 98km/h (61mph) for defence, though a single 7.62mm (0.3in) machine gun was an optional fitting. The design of the YP-104 was based closely on the British Daimler Ferret armoured scout car used in the British Army from 1952. Like the Ferret, the YP-104 had an all-welded steel construction with three windows set in a raised crew compartment. The armour was sufficient to protect against light small-arms fire, but not against heavy or persistent machine-gun bursts.

Country of origin:	Netherlands
Crew:	2
Weight:	5400kg (11,900lb)
Dimensions:	Length: 4.33m (14.21ft); width: 2.08m (6.82ft); height: 2.03m (6.66ft)
Range:	500km (310 miles)
Armour:	(Steel) 16mm (0.63in) maximum
Armament:	1 x 7.62mm (0.3in) MG (optional)
Powerplant:	1 x Herkules JXLD 6-cylinder petrol, developing 131hp (98kW)
Performance:	Maximum road speed: 98km/h (61mph); fording: 0.91m (2.99ft); gradient: 46 percent; vertical obstacle: 0.41m (1.35ft); trench: 1.22m (4ft)

Lynx CR

The Lynx Command and Reconnaissance Vehicle was based heavily upon the M113A1 armoured personnel carrier. The main similarities were in the all-welded aluminium hull and tracked configuration. Amphibious properties were also the same. The troop compartment, however, was occupied with communications equipment and troop carrying was restricted to the three-man crew. Armament consisted of a single 12.7mm (0.5in) Browning M2 HB at the front and a single 7.62mm (0.3in) Browning M1919 at the rear, both pintle-mounted. The Lynx was adopted in modified versions in Canada and the Netherlands. The Netherlands version had a 25mm (0.98in) Oerlikon cannon turret fitted.

Country of origin:	United States
Crew:	3
Weight:	8775kg (19,300lb)
Dimensions:	Length: 4.6m (15.09ft); width: 2.41m (7.91ft); height: 1.65m (5.41ft)
Range:	525km (325 miles)
Armour:	Aluminium (details not available)
Armament:	1 x 12.7mm (0.5in) MG; 1 x 7.62mm (0.3in) MG
Powerplant:	1 x Detroit Diesel GMC 6V53 6-cylinder diesel, developing 215hp (160kW) at 2800rpm
Performance:	Maximum road speed: 70km/h (43mph); fording: amphibious; gradient: 60 percent; vertical obstacle: 0.61m (2ft); trench: 1.47m (4.82ft)

M4 C2V

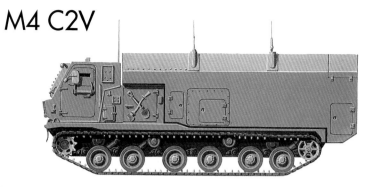

The M4 is a modern Command and Control Vehicle (C2V) manufactured by United Defense. It utilizes the tracked chassis of the M993 Bradley Fighting Vehicle, and consequently has the same performance as any modern main battle tank or infantry fighting vehicle. An armoured module containing advanced C2V electronics is mounted on the chassis, including the Army Battle Command System (ABCS) Common Hardware and Software (CHS) communications suite. The commander of the vehicle depends on a wireless Local Area Network (LAN) system so that communications can be made while mobile. The M4's principal role is to provide operational C2V coordination amongst armoured units. It has full NBC protection.

Country of origin:	United States
Crew:	1 + 8
Weight:	25,000–30,000kg (55,100–66,100lb)
Dimensions:	Length: 7.49m (24.57ft); width: 2.97m (9.74ft); height: 2.7m (8.86ft)
Range:	400km (250 miles)
Armour:	Details classified
Armament:	None
Powerplant:	1 x Cummins VTA-903T 8-cylinder turbo diesel, developing 590hp (440kW)
Performance:	Maximum road speed: 65km/h (40mph)

Steyr-Puch 700 AP Haflinger

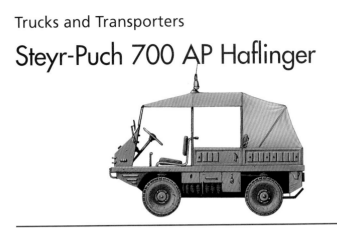

The Steyr-Puch 700 AP Haflinger was a light utility vehicle with extremely good off-road performance. It was originally designed for military mountain operations and came in a number of variants to aid small-unit manoeuvres. Its basic configuration was 4x4 with small 165mm x 12in tyres. There were two seats in the front of the vehicle and a flatbed cargo area to the rear. The entire vehicle could be covered with a canvas hood. In logistical roles, the Haflinger carried just under 500kg (1100lbs) of cargo. A winch with a 1500kg (3300lb) pull and a snow plough were optional fittings. After 1967, the Haflinger received a more powerful engine and models with a longer wheelbase were manufactured.

Country of origin:	Austria
Crew:	1 + 3
Weight:	645kg (1422lb)
Dimensions:	Length: 2.85m (9.35ft); width: 1.4m (4.6ft); height: 1.36m (4.46ft)
Range:	400km (250 miles)
Armour:	None
Armament:	1 x 12.7mm (0.5in) MG fitted on AA variant
Powerplant:	1 x Model 700 AP 2-cylinder petrol, developing 24hp (18kW)
Performance:	Maximum road speed: 75km/h (47mph); fording: 0.4m (1.3ft); gradient: 65 percent

Steyr 680 M3

The original Steyr 680 M vehicle was a fairly conventional 4x4 truck. It had a cab-over-engine configuration with an observation hatch in the cab roof (this accepted a machine gun on a pintle mount if desired). It could carry a 4.5-ton load or 20 soldiers sat on bench seats. Though the 680 M was a perfectly acceptable vehicle – many are still in use today – it had inadequate off-road performance. The Steyr 680 M3 resolved this. It was a larger 6x6 truck with independent suspension fitted to all wheels. Load-carrying capacity remained unchanged, but cross-country mobility was greatly improved. A 4.5-ton capacity winch was also fitted in the front of the vehicle.

Country of origin:	Austria
Crew:	1 + 17
Weight:	6500kg (14,300lb)
Dimensions:	Length: 6.73m (22.1ft); width: 2.4m (7.87ft); height: 2.63m (8.63ft)
Range:	500km (310 miles)
Armour:	None
Armament:	None (see text)
Powerplant:	1 x Steyr WD 610.74 6-cylinder diesel, developing 164hp (122kW)
Performance:	Maximum road speed: 80km/h (50mph)

Steyr-Puch Pinzgauer 716 M

The Pinzgauer series of light utility vehicles were first introduced in 1965 as simple 4x4 trucks, and over 20,000 vehicles have been sold to date. Today, Pinzgauers come in two basic versions: the 716 series (4x4) and the 718 series (6x6). An 8x8 version did not make it past the prototype stage. The Pinzgauer 716 M can take a load of up to 1400kg (3100lb) and carry it at 122km/h (76mph). Off-road mobility is excellent – a major client for the Pinzgauer is the Austrian alpine forces. An automatic level control system alters the cargo suspension according to the load. Apart from utility vehicles, Pinzgauers have also been configured for 20mm (0.78in) AA cannon, as command-and-control centres and as ambulances.

Country of origin:	Austria
Crew:	1 + 9
Weight:	2200kg (4850lb)
Dimensions:	Length: 4.48m (14.69ft); width: 1.8m (5.91ft); height: 2.04m (6.69ft)
Range:	1200km (750 miles)
Armour:	None
Armament:	None
Powerplant:	1 x 6-cylinder turbo diesel, developing 105hp (78kW) at 4350rpm
Performance:	Maximum road speed: 122km/h (76mph); fording: 0.7m (2.3ft)

BR-100 Bombi

The BR-100 Bombi entered production with Bombardier Limited of Quebec in 1978. Bombardier is one of Canada's premier manufacturers of oversnow vehicles. Usually these are destined for civilian markets, but military customers have been a growth area. The BR-100 is a small oversnow transport vehicle in service with the Canadian Armed Forces. It is capable of pulling a 450kg (1000lb) load over very soft snow conditions. With very wide tracks and a vehicle weight of just 1500kg (3300lb), the Bombi imparts a ground pressure of only 100g/sq cm (1.42lb/sq in) using summer tracks and 80g/sq cm (1.13lb/sq in) using winter tracks. The Bombi also has Middle Eastern customers, as it is ideal for travel over soft sand.

Country of origin:	Canada
Crew:	1 + 2
Weight:	1500kg (3300lb)
Dimensions:	Length: 3.15m (10.33ft); width: 2.2m (7.21ft); height: 2.01m (6.59ft)
Range:	Not available
Armour:	None
Armament:	None
Powerplant:	1 x Ford 4-cylinder petrol, developing 84hp (63kW)
Performance:	Maximum road speed: 22km/h (14mph)

Praga V3S

The V3S was developed in the early 1950s by the Prague Automobile Factory (Praga), specifically for military use. Such was the success of the design that it remained in production until the 1980s. With a slow top speed of only 62km/h (38mph) and a high diesel consumption, the V3S nonetheless compensated with good off-road handling by virtue of its 6x6 all-wheel-drive configuration (it came first in its class in a Paris–Dakar rally in the 1990s). The V3S could carry over five tons of cargo, but it was also fitted with a mobile office shell which gave 3.9m (13ft) of standing room. Its engine came from the Tatra company. The V3S chassis was later used to produce the M53/59 anti-aircraft vehicle.

Country of origin:	Czechoslovakia
Crew:	1 + 1
Weight:	5350kg (11,800lb)
Dimensions:	Length: 6.91m (22.67ft); width: 2.31m (7.58ft); height: 2.92m (9.58ft)
Range:	500km (310 miles)
Armour:	None
Armament:	None
Powerplant:	1 x Tatra T-912 6-cylinder diesel, developing 98hp (73kW)
Performance:	Maximum road speed: 62km/h (38mph)

Tatra T 148

The Tatra T 148 is another workhorse vehicle to emerge from the Eastern Bloc during the 1970s. It is far larger than the Praga V3S, weighing in at 25,640kg (56,540lb) fully loaded of which 14,580kg (32,150lb) is payload. To handle such weights, the vehicle uses a Tatra 2-928-1 eight-cylinder diesel engine with direct fuel injection, producing a slightly better road speed than the Praga V3S (71km/h/44mph). The T 148 uses three different brake systems to stop: (1) a pressurized airbrake which acts on all the wheels of the vehicle, including trailer wheels; (2) a mechanically applied emergency and parking brake; and (3) an exhaust brake which closes off the exhaust to increase the braking effect.

Country of origin:	Czech Republic
Crew:	1 + 2
Weight:	25,640kg (56,536lb) fully loaded
Dimensions:	Length: 9m (29.53ft); width: 2.5m (8.2ft); height: 2.44m (8ft)
Range:	500km (310 miles)
Armour:	None
Armament:	None
Powerplant:	1 x Tatra 2-928-1 8-cylinder diesel, developing 211hp (158kW)
Performance:	Maximum road speed: 71km/h (44mph)

Renault UE

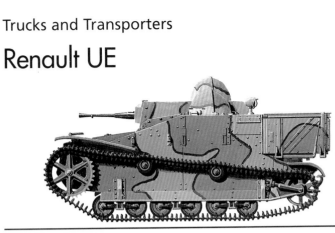

The Renault UE or 'Universal Carrier' was indebted in design to the British Carden-Loyd tankettes developed between the wars. With a two-man crew and a 38hp (28kW) Renault 85 engine, it could pull 600kg (1300lb) of trailer-mounted ammunition or weaponry or carry 350kg (775lb) of materials in its rear storage compartment. Thus laden, it travelled at a respectable 48km/h (30mph), powered by a Renault 85 four-cylinder petrol engine. Each crew member had a rounded dome cover to provide overhead protection. Following the German occupation of France in 1940, the Germans pressed the Renault UE into service and used it for ammunition carriage or for airfield security patrols.

Country of origin:	France
Crew:	2
Weight:	3300kg (7300lb)
Dimensions:	Length: 2.94m (9.64ft); width: 1.75m (5.74ft); height: 1.24m (4.07ft)
Range:	125km (80 miles)
Armour:	Not available
Armament:	None
Powerplant:	1 x Renault 85 4-cylinder petrol, developing 38hp (28kW)
Performance:	Maximum road speed: 48km/h (30mph)

Laffly W15T

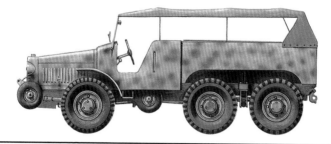

Laffly was founded in France in 1858, and specialized mainly in civilian haulage vehicles or utility vehicles for the fire service. In the first decades of the 20th century, it began to produce all-wheel-drive vehicles for military markets, particularly in collaboration with the Hotchkiss company in the 1930s. The W15T was one such vehicle. It was designed as an artillery tractor in 6x6 configuration and was manned by three crew, but three other soldiers could also be transported. Two small auxiliary wheels were placed at the front of the truck to facilitate climbing ditches. The W15T was a solid vehicle, and after German occupation in 1940, many were converted to Wehrmacht use, particularly as command vehicles.

Country of origin:	France
Crew:	3 + 3
Weight:	5000kg (11,000lb)
Dimensions:	Length: 5.4m (17.7ft); width: 1.9m (6.2ft); height: 1.8m (5.9ft)
Range:	280km (170 miles)
Armour:	Not applicable
Armament:	1 x 7.5mm (0.29in) MG
Powerplant:	1 x Hotchkiss 486 4-cylinder petrol, developing 51hp (38kW)
Performance:	Not available

ACMAT TPK 6.40

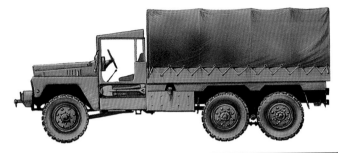

The ACMAT TPK 6.40 is part of a vast range of ACMAT utility vehicles developed on the basis of the ACMAT VLRA (Véhicule de Liaison, de Reconnaissance et d'Appui). VLRA vehicles come in either 4x4 or 6x6 versions. At the start of the range is the TPK 4.20, a two-ton vehicle which itself has radio command post, armoured personnel carrier and ambulance variants to name but a few. The TPK 6.40 is a much larger variant of the VRLA, with an unladen weight of 5700kg (12,600lb) and the capacity to carry over 4300kg (9500lb) of cargo, or 21 fully equipped soldiers. It has six variants including a tar spreader and a 4000-litre (880-gal) water carrier for fire-fighting support. ACMAT trucks have sold to over 30 countries worldwide.

Country of origin:	France
Crew:	3 + 21
Weight:	5700kg (12,600lb)
Dimensions:	Length: 6.94m (22.77ft); width: 2.25m (7.38ft); height: 2.64m (8.66ft)
Range:	1600km (1000 miles)
Armour:	None
Armament:	None as standard, though MGs optional
Powerplant:	1 x Perkins 6.354.4 diesel, developing 138hp (103kW)
Performance:	Maximum road speed: 85km/h (53mph)

Lohr Fardier FL 500

The Lohr Fardier FL 500 is a diminutive 4x4 vehicle developed to provide airborne forces with a basic form of transport and logistics at the battlefront. It is easily air transportable – the basic vehicle weighs only 680kg (1500lb) and is only 2.41m (7.91ft) long and less than 2m (6.6ft) high. During operations, its primary role is the transport of ammunition or other supplies, and it can tow guns or trailers up to its own weight. The FL 500 is both unarmoured and unarmed, though some have been fitted with MILAN anti-tank guided weapons as a more aggressive option. Currently the FL 500 serves with the French Foreign Legion and French and Argentine airborne units.

Country of origin:	France
Crew:	1
Weight:	680kg (1500lb)
Dimensions:	Length: 2.41m (7.91ft); width: 1.5m (4.92ft); height: 1.18m (3.87ft)
Range:	200km (125 miles)
Armour:	None
Armament:	See text
Powerplant:	1 x Citroën 2-cylinder petrol, developing 28hp (21kW)
Performance:	Maximum road speed: 80km/h (50mph)

Munitionstransporter IV

The Munitionstransporter IV was specifically designed to supply ammunition to the prodigious 'Karl' 600mm (23.62in) railway-transported heavy mortar. Each shell for this enormous weapon weighed up to 2.17 tons, and the Munitionstransporter IV could carry four shells in a specially designed ammunition rack. The vehicle itself was created using the chassis of a PzKpfw IV tank, and was fitted with a Maybach HL 120 TRM 12-cylinder petrol engine to generate enough power for its strenuous task. An electrically driven crane arm lifted the shells from the carriage to the loading platform. The power for this was provided by a two-cylinder motor/generator used in a PzKpfw IV to drive the turret traverse.

Country of origin:	Germany
Crew:	4
Weight:	25,000kg (55,100lb) fully loaded
Dimensions:	Length: 5.41m (17.75ft); width: 2.88m (9.45ft); height: not available
Range:	209km (130 miles)
Armour:	None
Armament:	None
Powerplant:	1 x Maybach HL 120 TRM 12-cylinder petrol, developing 299hp (223kW)
Performance:	Maximum road speed: 40km/h (25mph)

Raupen Schlepper Ost

The Eastern Front presented the German Army with severe environmental challenges: deep snow in the winter and deep mud during the autumn rains and spring thaw. In 1942, the Raupen Schlepper Ost (RSO) was developed to cope with these conditions. It was little more than a four-ton transport truck powered by a V8 petrol engine, but fully tracked to handle demanding off-road terrain. Production began in 1943 under several manufacturers, and 27,000 units were produced by the end of the war. Its duties were varied, and included gun tractor, snow plough, trailer tractor and even ambulance. Two main versions were produced, the RSO/01 with a solid and enclosed cab, and the RSO/03, which had a soft-top cab.

Country of origin:	Germany
Crew:	2
Weight:	5200kg (11,500lb)
Dimensions:	Length: 4.42m (14.5ft); width: 1.99m (6.53ft); height: 2.53m (8.3ft)
Range:	250km (150 miles)
Armour:	None
Armament:	None
Powerplant:	1 x Steyr 1500A 8-cylinder petrol, developing 68hp (51kW)
Performance:	Maximum road speed: 17km/h (11mph)

Daimler-Benz Unimog S 404 B

The Unimog S 404 B was a 1955 addition to a series of vehicles which entered development in 1946. 'Unimog' stands for Universal Motor Geräf, and the first of these general utility vehicles was put into production in the late 1940s. The basic Unimog vehicle was a 4x4 light truck carrying payloads of 1250–5000kg (2800–11,000lb). A 6x6 Unimog was also produced, which could carry a 8000kg (17,600lb) load. The S 404 B version was the standard 4x4 vehicle with a load-carrying capacity of 2300kg (5100lb). Some 65,000 vehicles have been produced, 35,000 of which went to the German armed forces. Modern Unimog variants are still in production today.

Country of origin:	Germany
Crew:	2 + 8
Weight:	2910kg (6417lb)
Dimensions:	Length: 5m (16.4ft); width: 2.05m (6.73ft); height: 2.74m (8.99ft)
Range:	570km (350 miles)
Armour:	None
Armament:	None
Powerplant:	1 x Daimler-Benz m 180/II 6-cylinder petrol, developing 80hp (60kW)
Performance:	Maximum road speed: 95km/h (59mph)

Ford G398 SAM

The Ford G398 SAM was part of the German Federal Armed Forces vehicle-procurement initiative after World War II. Like many designs for the cash-strapped force, the G398 was a modification of an existing design. However, of all the vehicles modified for service, the G398 was the one which gave least satisfaction. At its most basic, the G398 had an open cab for three crew, a hinged windshield, and a simple plank-bed cargo area. Some 5446 of these vehicles were produced between 1957 and 1961. A further 2582 were manufactured with enclosed cargo areas in various configurations. The G398 was high on fuel consumption and had poor, even dangerous, road handling and was quickly discontinued.

Country of origin:	Germany
Crew:	1 + 2
Weight:	7480kg (16,500lb)
Dimensions:	Length: 7.25m (23.79ft); width: 2.24m (7.35ft); height: 3.14m (10.3ft)
Range:	280km (175 miles)
Armour:	None
Armament:	None
Powerplant:	1 Ford G28T 8-cylinder petrol, developing 91hp (68kW)
Performance:	Maximum road speed: 85km/h (53mph)

Faun L912/45A

Fahrzeugfabriken Ansbach und Nürnberg (Faun) was born in Germany in 1918, though the company traces its history back to 1845, when the constituent companies began manufacturing horse-drawn or steam-powered fire-fighting vehicles. The L912/45A was born from Faun's post-World War II reconstruction. Remarkably for such a small company, Faun secured orders with the German Federal Armed Forces for logistics vehicles in the 10 to 12-ton class, of which the L912 series was one. The L912/45A was a three-axle 6x6 truck distinguished by a long cab and a short wheelbase. It was designed for heavy cargo transportation (up to 15 tons) or use as an artillery tractor pulling 155mm (6.1in) field howitzers.

Country of origin:	Germany
Crew:	1 + 2
Weight:	15,000kg (33,100lb)
Dimensions:	Length: 7.65m (25.09ft); width: 2.5m (8.2ft); height: 2.77m (9.09ft)
Range:	660km (410 miles)
Armour:	None
Armament:	None
Powerplant:	1 x Deutz F12 L714a 12-cylinder multi-fuel, developing 264hp (197kW)
Performance:	Maximum road speed: 77km/h (48mph)

MAN 630 L2

The MAN 630 L2 was one of the first logistical vehicles manufactured within Germany to equip the newly formed German Federal Armed Forces, the Bundeswehr. It is also one of the longest serving, with isolated examples still in use today (though the replacement for the 630 was officially completed during the 1990s). The basic vehicle in 1958 and 1959 had a cab-behind-engine configuration, was a 4x4 and featured a one-piece plank cargo bed 4.5m (14.8ft) long. Load-carrying capacity was around five tons. It was designed with a MAN D1243 MV3A/W multi-fuel engine which could burn diesel, petrol, kerosene and even waste-fuel mixtures (though impure fuels could adversely affect power output).

Country of origin:	Germany
Crew:	1 + 2
Weight:	13,000kg (28,700lb)
Dimensions:	Length: 7.9m (25.9ft); width: 2.5m (8.2ft); height: 2.84m (9.32ft)
Range:	420km (260 miles)
Armour:	None
Armament:	None
Powerplant:	1 x MAN D1243 MV3A/W 4-cylinder multi-fuel, developing 130hp (97kW)
Performance:	Maximum road speed: 66km/h (41mph)

Faun SLT 50-2 Elefant

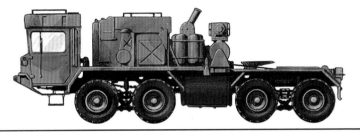

The Faun SLT 50-2 Elefant is, as its name suggests, a massive vehicle capable of hauling a Leopard 2 main battle tank, which weighs 54,981kg (120,960lb). Such a load takes the vehicle's maximum weight up to 107,400kg (236,800lb). Faun GmbH is one of the world's largest producers of military cranes and haulage vehicles and the Elefant, as well as the SaZgM FS 42 Franziska (also by Faun), are the German Army's main tank transporters. An 8x8 configuration is used in conjunction with an eight-axled semi-trailer to support the load. The Elefant relies on an MTU MB8837 Ea500 engine to draw its enormous load, with a power output of 729hp (544kW). Faun has recently introduced a new tank transporter, the MLC 100.

Country of origin:	Germany
Crew:	1 + 3
Weight:	107,400kg (236,800lb) maximum loaded weight
Dimensions:	Length with trailer: 18.97m (62.24ft); width: 3.05m (10.01ft); height: 3.24m (10.63ft)
Range:	600km (370 miles)
Armour:	None
Armament:	1 x 7.62mm (0.3in) MG
Powerplant:	1 x MTU MB8837 Ea500 8-cylinder diesel, developing 729hp (544kW)
Performance:	Maximum road speed: 65km/h (40mph)

MAN N 4510 5t mil gl

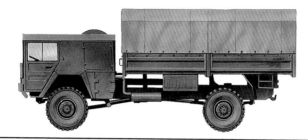

The MAN N 4510 5t mil gl is a 4x4 vehicle which emerged from a long development process by MAN during the 1970s. The German Federal Armed Forces had issued a requirement for a logistics vehicle to follow the Leopard main battle tank during operations. MAN produced several prototypes, but most were too expensive owing to features such as amphibious floats with propeller propulsion and sealed cabs. Once these features were dropped, however, a successful prototype emerged and MAN received orders for over 8000 vehicles in the five-, seven- and 10-ton classes. The MAN N 4510 represents the five-ton category, the 4520 the seven-ton, and the 4540 the 10-ton. All have a cab-before-engine configuration.

Country of origin:	Germany
Crew:	3 + 2
Weight:	14,460kg (31,880lb)
Dimensions:	Length: 8.01m (26.28ft); width: 2.5m (8.2ft); height: 2.85m (9.35ft)
Range:	750km (470 miles)
Armour:	None
Armament:	None
Powerplant:	1 x Deutz F8 L 413F 8-cylinder diesel, developing 252hp (188kW)
Performance:	Maximum road speed: 90km/h (56mph)

MAN 15 t mil gl A1

In the 1980s, the MAN 15 t mil gl A1 met the German Federal Armed Forces' requirements for a new series of high-mobility tactical trucks. The trucks had to be capable of multi-tasking logistical roles, have an armoured cab and offer a lifespan of 20 to 30 years. After extensive testing of various vehicles, the German military procurement agencies ordered 358 MAN 15 t mil gl A1 vehicles. Each vehicle can carry a payload of 18,200kg (40,100lb) and its Atlas Weyhausen trailer can be hydraulically raised to a 45-degree angle for the rapid unloading. The vehicle also has exceptional 8x8 manoeuvrability, and can cross ditches 1.9m (6.2ft) wide and tackle 60 percent gradients fully loaded.

Country of origin:	Germany
Crew:	1 + 2
Weight:	32,000kg (70,600lb) fully loaded
Dimensions:	Length: 10.27m (33.7ft); width: 2.9m (9.51ft); height: 2.93m (9.61ft)
Range:	750km (470 miles)
Armour:	Not applicable
Armament:	None
Powerplant:	1 x MAN D2566MF 6-cylinder turbo diesel, developing 394hp (294kW)
Performance:	Maximum road speed: 90km/h (56mph); gradient: 60 percent; trench: 1.9m (6.2ft)

MAN 40.633

The MAN 40.633 DFAETX was the winner of the competition to supply the United Arab Emirates with transporters for main battle tanks and heavy equipment. The 40.633 weighs 40,000kg (88,200lb); moving such weight across rocky desert terrain is especially hard on tyres, so the vehicle has a tyre-pressure adjustment system which works from a compressor mounted in the towing vehicle. The single-tyre format, rather than the European-variant double-tyre configuration, stops the vehicle sinking into soft sand, a problem which many double-tyre vehicles experienced during the initial competition. There are many rivers in the Middle East, so the 40.633 was constructed with a fording capability of 0.85m (2.78ft).

Country of origin:	Germany
Crew:	3 + 5
Weight:	40,000kg (88,200lb)
Dimensions:	Length: 8.22m (26.97ft); width: 2.9m (9.51ft); height: 3.17m (10.4ft)
Range:	1000km (620 miles)
Armour:	None
Armament:	None
Powerplant:	1 x MAN D 2840 10-cylinder turbo diesel, developing 621hp (463kW)
Performance:	Maximum road speed: 88km/h (55mph); fording: 0.85m (2.78ft)

Iveco 6605 TM

The Iveco 6605 TM is essentially a 6x6 artillery tractor, but its cab's capacity to hold 12 men almost makes it a troop transporter. An entire artillery unit can be carried by the vehicle, and in relative comfort – the cab has a canvas cover but is fitted with a ventilator and heater. Maximum load for the vehicle is five tons, though it can tow 15 tons if required. Usually, the artillery piece is towed and the crew and auxiliary equipment carried in the vehicle. An Iveco 6605 FH – an identical vehicle apart from weight and carrying capacity – often accompanies the TM, transporting the ammunition. The TM's cargo area can be separated into three areas by removable partitions, and can be used to carry 21 additional men.

Country of origin:	Italy
Crew:	1 + 11
Weight:	11,800kg (26,000b)
Dimensions:	Length: 7.33m (24ft); width: 2.5m (8.2ft); height: 2.92m (9.58ft)
Range:	700km (430 miles)
Armour:	None
Armament:	None
Powerplant:	1 x Fiat 8212.02.500 6-cylinder diesel, developing 219hp (163kW)
Performance:	Maximum road speed: 80km/h (50mph)

GAZ-AAA

The GAZ-AAA was one of the earlier offerings from the GAZ company. Production of the vehicle ran between 1933 and 1942. Like many Russian wartime trucks, the 1942 version has radically simplified bodywork – there are no bumpers, the wings and cabin have simplified lines, and there is only one headlight. Though the GAZ-AAA never reached the production figures of the ZiS-5 (qv), 37,373 were made in total. It was a 6x4 with a 2500kg (5500lb) payload capacity out of a total loaded weight of 4975kg (10,970lb). The gearbox consisted of eight forward gears and two reverse gears, and it could achieve a maximum road speed of 65km/h (40mph). The chassis of the GAZ-AAA was used to produce the BA-10 armoured car.

Country of origin:	Russia/Soviet Union
Crew:	2
Weight:	2475kg (5457lb)
Dimensions:	Length: 5.34m (17.52ft); width: 2.04m (6.69ft); height: 1.97m (6.46ft)
Range:	Not available
Armour:	None
Armament:	None
Powerplant:	1 x GAZ-M1 4-cylinder petrol, developing 50hp (37kW)
Performance:	Maximum road speed: 65km/h (40mph)

ZiS-5

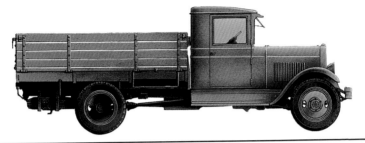

The ZiS-5 had its origins in the reformed Automobil Moscow Obshchestvo (AMO) company in 1931. AMO built a range of trucks between 1931 and 1933, at which point the company was renamed Zavod imeni Stalina (ZiS). The AMO trucks were relabelled and on 1 October 1933 production of the ZiS-5 officially began. It became one of the Russian Army's most prolific vehicles. Nearly one million were produced between 1933 and the mid-1950s. Its wartime service was crucial to Red Army logistics. Wartime vehicles can be spotted by austerity features, such as wooden doors and seats, the absence of bumpers and a fitting of only the left headlight. Production of the ZiS-5 ceased in 1958.

Country of origin:	Russia/Soviet Union
Crew:	2
Weight:	3100kg (6800lb)
Dimensions:	Length: 6.06m (19.88ft); width: 2.24m (7.35ft); height: 2.16m (7.09ft)
Range:	Not available
Armour:	None
Armament:	None
Powerplant:	1 x ZiS-5 6-cylinder petrol, developing 72hp (54kW)
Performance:	Maximum road speed: 65km/h (40mph); fording: 0.6m (2ft)

AT-P

The AT-P series of armoured artillery tractors entered service with Soviet forces in the early 1950s. It was developed mainly for towing anti-tank and anti-aircraft guns, but it was also capable of pulling larger-calibre weapons such as 155mm (6.1in) field howitzers and heavy-calibre mortars. The suspension was that of the SU-76/T-70, and the superstructure featured an open troop compartment holding six men – the three-man crew were inside an armoured compartment at the front. The AT-P was fast and durable, with solid torsion bar suspension. Several variants were produced, including the ASU-57 air-droppable vehicle armed with a 76mm (2.9in) airborne assault gun and a command-and-control version of the same, without gun.

Country of origin:	Russia/Soviet Union
Crew:	3 + 6
Weight:	7200kg (15,900lb)
Dimensions:	Length: 4.5m (14.76ft); width: 2.5m (8.2ft); height: 1.83m (6ft)
Range:	500km (310 miles)
Armour:	Not available
Armament:	None
Powerplant:	1 x ZiL-123F 6-cylinder petrol, developing 110hp (82kW)
Performance:	Maximum road speed: 50km/h (31mph)

Trucks and Transporters

GAZ-66

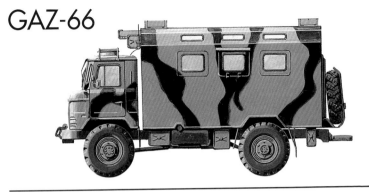

The GAZ-66 has been yet another successful Russian truck, running in production from 1964 until the present day. It is a 4x4 vehicle with a two-ton cargo capacity and a reputation for rugged reliability. Its engine is the same as that used in the GAZ-53, the ZMZ-66 8-cylinder overhead-valve diesel, providing 113hp (85kW). The basic GAZ-66 acts as the framework for many different specialist and utility vehicles, including engineer vehicles, troop transporters, and even a mobile NBC decontamination centre when fitted with the DDA-53C or DDA-66 decontamination unit. Modern versions like the GAZ-66-40 have special engines which allow them to operate at heights of 4500m (14,800ft) above sea level.

Country of origin:	Russia/Soviet Union
Crew:	2
Weight:	3470kg (7650lb)
Dimensions:	Length: 5.8m (19.02ft); width: 2.32m (7.61ft); height: 2.44m (8ft)
Range:	800km (500 miles)
Armour:	None
Armament:	None
Powerplant:	1 x ZMZ-66 8-cylinder diesel, developing 113hp (85kW)
Performance:	Maximum road speed: 90km/h (56mph)

KAMAZ-5320

KAMAZ-5320 trucks are general-purpose logistics vehicles from the Kama Motor Vehicle Plant at Naberezhynye Chelmy. They are simple 6x6 vehicles with a cab-over-engine configuration and an all-steel cargo unit (usually covered with a tarpaulin). Maximum road-load capacity is 8000kg (17,600lb), dropping to 6000kg (13,200lb) when travelling cross-country. The cargo unit folds down at the rear and the sides. Kama has also produced the 5320 in 8x8 and 6x4 configurations. KAMAZ-5320 vehicles are still in production and are as prevalent in civilian use as in military use (including applications as civilian passenger buses). Naturally there are numerous variants including a 6x4 fuel tanker, grain trucks and even milk tankers.

Country of origin:	Russia/Soviet Union
Crew:	3
Weight:	7080kg (15,611lb)
Dimensions:	Length: 7.44m (24.41ft); width: 2.51m (8.23ft); height: 2.83m (8.28ft)
Range:	485km (300 miles)
Armour:	None
Armament:	None
Powerplant:	1 x YaMZ-740 8-cylinder diesel, developing 209hp (156kW)
Performance:	Maximum road speed: 85km/h (53mph)

Trucks and Transporters

KAMAZ-4310

The KAMAZ-4310 derived from the civilian three-axle 6x6 KAMAZ-5320. In the late 1970s, this vehicle was modified for military use and renamed the KAMAZ-4310. The KAMAZ-4310 has proved itself an excellent logistics vehicle with a 6000kg (13,200lb) cargo capacity and a rugged off-road ability. It retains the 5320's 6x6 configuration, with all axles power-driven, and the central tyre-pressure regulation system ensures smooth travelling over the roughest of surfaces. Other features include a self-recovery winch. The 4310 comes in many variants, including the tanker version shown here. A more recent model – the 43114 – has seen the power plant upgraded from 206hp (154kW) to 260hp (194kW).

Country of origin:	Russia/Soviet Union
Crew:	3
Weight:	15,000kg (33,100lb)
Dimensions:	Length: 7.9m (25.92ft); width: 2.5m (8.2ft); height: 3.09m (10.14ft)
Range:	Not available
Armour:	None
Armament:	None
Powerplant:	1 x YaMZ-740 8-cylinder diesel, developing 206hp (154kW)
Performance:	Maximum road speed: 85km/h (53mph)

KrAZ-260

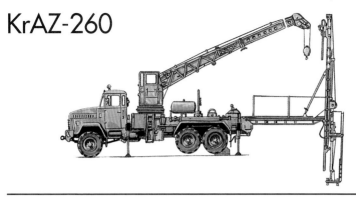

The KrAZ-260 was introduced in 1979 as a replacement amongst Russian forces for the KrAZ-255B, a 6x6 truck with an eight-ton load capacity and a 12-ton winch capacity. In basic format, the KrAZ-260 shows little change. The load weight, however, is upgraded to nine tons and 12.25 tons can be pulled with the front-mounted winch. Like the earlier vehicle, the KrAZ-260 has the option of locking the suspension when using the winch. The basic cargo body is an open bed with hinged tailgate. Weather protection is provided by a metal frame and canvas cover. The KrAZ comes in the usual range of variants and was first seen towing a 2A36 152mm (5.98in) howitzer in 1976.

Country of origin:	Russia/Soviet Union
Crew:	1 + 2
Weight:	12,250kg (27,000lb)
Dimensions:	Length: 9m (29.53ft); width: 2.72m (8.92ft); height: 2.98m (9.78ft)
Range:	700km (430 miles)
Armour:	None
Armament:	None
Powerplant:	1 x YaMZ-238L 8-cylinder diesel, developing 287hp (214kW)
Performance:	Maximum road speed: 80km/h (50mph)

Ural-4320B

The Uralsky Avtozavod OAO company has manufactured 1.2 million trucks since it was founded in November 1941. The first of the 6x6 Ural-4320 series came much later in 1977, and had a seven-ton carrying capacity or a towing strength of 18.5 tons. Durable and dependable, the 4320 quickly established itself as the market leader and the company began to add a string of variants and upgrades. The Ural-4320B entered production in 1983. It is a modern 6x6 vehicle designed for carrying cargo, people or towing trailers. Its maximum load is 5000kg (11,000lb) or 27 soldiers, who can be seated in the cargo compartment. Its body is fully armoured against small-arms fire up to 12.7mm (0.5in).

Country of origin:	Russia/Soviet Union
Crew:	2 + 27
Weight:	15,000kg (33,100lb) fully loaded
Dimensions:	Length: 7.6m (24.93ft); width: 2.7m (8.86ft); height: 2.8m (9.19ft)
Range:	1000km (620 miles)
Armour:	Details classified
Armament:	None
Powerplant:	1 x YamAZ-238M2 8-cylinder diesel, developing 236hp (176kW)
Performance:	Maximum road speed: 82km/h (51mph)

Bv 202

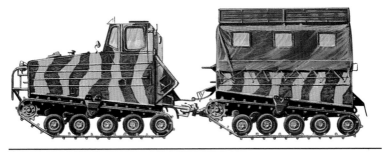

The Bv 202 entered production in 1961, made by the Bolinder-Munktell company. Only with the advent of the Bv 206 in 1981 did production of the Bv 202 cease. It was a double-unit vehicle, the front unit containing engine and crew, the rear unit carrying either a cargo load of 800 to 900kg (1800 to 2000lb) or 10 fully equipped soldiers. Unlike the later Bv 206, the rear unit was unheated with only a tarpaulin cover. Consequently winter travel in the Bv 202 could be icy, particularly during water crossings (the Bv 202 was fully amphibious). Later the rear unit was offered in a fully enclosed and heated version. Bv 202s have seen service across the world, and were used heavily by the British during the Falklands War.

Country of origin:	Sweden
Crew:	2 + 10
Weight:	2900kg (6400lb)
Dimensions:	Length: 6.17m (20.24ft); width: 1.76m (5.77ft); height: 2.21m (7.25ft)
Range:	400km (250 miles)
Armour:	None
Armament:	None
Powerplant:	1 x Volvo B18 4-cylinder diesel, developing 91hp (68kW)
Performance:	Maximum road speed: 39km/h (24mph); fording: amphibious; gradient: 60 percent; vertical obstacle: 0.5m (1.6ft)

Bv 206

The Bv 206 is found in service in the UK, US, Finland, Norway, Canada and Italy, as well as with Swedish armed forces. It has two units. The front unit contains the powerplant, transmission and operating crew. The rear unit is either an 11-soldier transportation vehicle or a cargo-carrying unit (maximum cargo haulage is 600kg/1300lb). The two are linked by a steerable connector and the climate inside the units is kept warm via an air heater. Appropriately for the Scandanavian environment, the Bv 206 is fully amphibious without preparation, propulsion coming from its extremely broad tracks. An anti-tank variant, the Pvbv 2062, has a Bofors 90mm (3.54in) recoilless rifle or Hughes TOW ATGW fitted to the roof.

Country of origin:	Sweden
Crew:	5 + 11
Weight:	Front unit 2740kg (6042lb); rear unit 1730kg (3815lb)
Dimensions:	Length: 6.9m (22.64ft); width: 1.87m (6.14ft); height: 2.4m (7.87ft)
Range:	300km (190 miles)
Armour:	None
Armament:	None
Powerplant:	1 x Mercedes-Benz OM603.950 6-cylinder diesel, developing 136hp (101kW)
Performance:	Maximum road speed: 55km/h (34mph); fording: amphibious; gradient: 60 percent; vertical obstacle: 0.5m (1.6ft)

Light Dragon Mk II

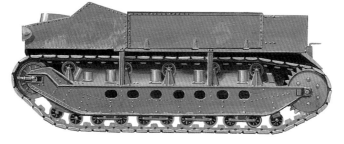

The Light Dragon Mk II was built from the chassis of the Vickers Mk II medium tank, of which about 200 were manufactured in the mid-1920s. The Light Dragon Mk I originally used the chassis of the Whippet, the British Army's first lightweight tank. The switch to the Vickers chassis made the Light Dragon Mk II more durable and gave the crew more armoured protection. An eight-cylinder Armstrong Siddeley petrol engine also produced the power to pull heavy field artillery. The Mk II was specifically an artillery tractor, with space for 10 artillery crewmen to sit in the troop compartment behind the driver and a capacity to carry/tow 118 shells. The Light Dragon was unarmed.

Country of origin:	United Kingdom
Crew:	1 + 10
Weight:	8000kg (17,600lb)
Dimensions:	Length: 5.33m (17.49ft); width: 2.78m (9.12ft); height: 2.17m (7.12ft)
Range:	300km (190 miles)
Armour:	Not available
Armament:	None
Powerplant:	1 x Armstrong Siddeley 8-cylinder petrol, developing 90hp (67kW)
Performance:	Maximum road speed: 35km/h (22mph)

Austin 10

The Austin 10 Light Utility Truck was developed directly from a civilian vehicle, the Austin 10 Saloon. Made in the late 1930s, the truck was specifically for military use. It was made at the Austin Motor Co. in Birmingham. A small canvas-covered cargo area was added to the rear of the vehicle, suitable for carrying a payload of up to 250kg (550lb). Nicknamed the 'Tilly' after its official military designation 'Car, Light Utility, 4 x2', the Austin 10 was ideal for staff duties, airfield duties and light ammunition carriage. Over 30,000 were produced during the war, recognizable by their angled front grille and cab-mounted spare wheel (though similar designs were produced by Standard, Hillman and Morris).

Country of origin:	United Kingdom
Crew:	2
Weight:	1003kg (2212lb)
Dimensions:	Length: 5.33m (17.49ft); width: 2.78m (9.12ft); height: 2.17m (7.12ft)
Range:	190km (119 miles)
Armour:	None
Armament:	None
Powerplant:	1 x Armstrong Siddeley 8-cylinder petrol, developing 90hp (67kW)
Performance:	Maximum road speed: 35km/h (21mph)

Humber Snipe

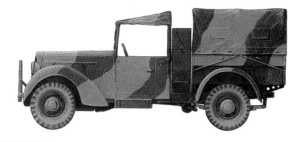

The Humber Snipe was one of several 0.4-ton utility vehicles which entered World War II service with the British Army (others included the Morris Commercial PU and the Ford WOC1). It was based on Humber's civilian vehicle, the Snipe sedan, directly utilizing the chassis, hood and radiator grille. To 'militarize' the vehicle, the bumpers were strengthened, storage boxes were added and a simple tarpaulin cover shielded the driver and passenger. Over 250,000 served British forces in World War II and many variants were produced. The 'General Service' version had seats in the rear area for troop transport or stretchers for medical evacuation. A communications vehicle designated FFW ('Fitted for Wireless') provided mobile radio facilities.

Country of origin:	United Kingdom
Crew:	4 or 5
Weight:	2170kg (4785lb)
Dimensions:	Length: 4.29m (14.07ft); width: 1.88m (6.17ft); height: 1.89m (6.2ft)
Range:	500km (310 miles)
Armour:	None
Armament:	None
Powerplant:	1 x Humber 6-cylinder petrol, developing 86hp (64kW)
Performance:	Maximum road speed: 75km/h (46mph)

Trucks and Transporters

Bedford OYC

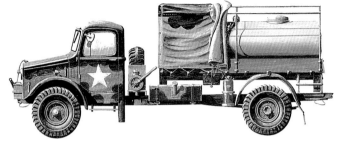

The Bedford OY was a 4x2 truck with a three-ton load capacity. It became a mainstay of British forces during World War II. Based directly on a US 2.5-ton truck design, the British appropriated the concept in 1940 in order to expedite development. The OY was a versatile, mass-produced truck capable of 80km/h (50mph). Bedford OYs cropped up in a bewildering array of variants. The OYC version shown here is a fuel carrier, the fuel containers shielded within a frame and tarpaulin cover, and a similar configuration was used to carry a 2046-litre (450-gal) water tank. A more unusual variant was a 4.3m (14ft) unit which contained X-ray facilities for use in battlefield medical emergencies.

Country of origin:	United Kingdom
Crew:	2
Weight:	7490kg (16,515lb) fully loaded
Dimensions:	Length: 6.22m (20.41ft); width: 2.17m (7.12ft); height: 3.1m (10.17ft)
Range:	300km (190 miles)
Armour:	None
Armament:	None
Powerplant:	1 x Bedford 6-cylinder petrol, developing 72hp (54kW)
Performance:	Maximum road speed: 80km/h (50mph)

Leyland Hippo Mk II GS

The Leyland Hippo was introduced into the British Army during the last two years of World War II. It was developed to increase the logistical capacity of Allied forces operating in northern Europe. Far larger than most other British trucks, the Hippo was a 6x4 vehicle with a 10-ton load-carrying capacity. The loading area at the rear was sunk low over the wheel arches to make a low loading height. In the Mk I Hippo, the cab was open, weather protection provided only by a canvas cover. The Mk II Hippo was an upgraded vehicle which featured an enclosed all-steel cab and a variety of van bodies, some including specialist facilities such as photo-processing and print machines.

Country of origin:	United Kingdom
Crew:	1 + 2
Weight:	8941kg (19,715lb)
Dimensions:	Length: 8.31m (27.26ft); width: 2.46m (8.07ft); height: 3.33m (10.92ft)
Range:	840km (520 miles)
Armour:	None
Armament:	None
Powerplant:	1 x Leyland Type L 6-cylinder diesel, developing 100hp (75kW)
Performance:	Maximum road speed: 60km/h (37mph)

M29C Weasel

The M28 Weasel was developed for use by Allied commandos and special forces soldiers in northern European theatres. It was envisaged that raids against German heavy water plants in Norway could be conducted using small and fast oversnow vehicles. Even when that threat receded in 1942 after Norwegian partisan raids, production continued and the vehicles found use as light cargo carriers in Europe, the Pacific and Alaska. A fully amphibious version, the M29C, became the most popular version with over 15,000 units produced. The M29C had excellent mobility over snow, mud and soft sand, and could transport loads of 900kg (1990lb). After the war, some Scandinavian countries adapted the Weasel for civilian use.

Country of origin:	United States
Crew:	1 + 3
Weight:	1800kg (4000lb)
Dimensions:	Length: 4.79m (15.72ft); width: 1.7m (5.58ft); height: 1.82m (5.97ft)
Range:	280km (170 miles)
Armour:	None
Armament:	None
Powerplant:	1 x Studebaker Champion 6-170 6-cylinder petrol, developing 65hp (48kW) at 3600rpm
Performance:	Maximum road speed: 58km/h (36mph); maximum water speed: 6km/h (4mph); fording: amphibious

Mack NO

The Mack NO became legendary amongst Allied troops during World War II for its great strength and reliability. It was a 7500kg (16,500lb) 6x6 vehicle over 7.5m (24.6ft) long, making it one of the largest straight trucks used by any side during the war. Artillery towing was its primary duty, usually pulling large guns such as 155mm (6.1in) or 203mm (8in) field howitzers. Though Mack produced another artillery tractor, the NM6, the NO was fitted with special equipment for the task as standard. At the rear of the cargo area was a chain hoist for lifting the gun's trail-clamp ready for towing. The Mack NO also had a Garwood 5 MB winch fitted at the front with a 11,300kg (25,000lb) pulling strength.

Country of origin:	United States
Crew:	4
Weight:	7500kg (16,500lb)
Dimensions:	Length: 7.5m (24.6ft); width: 2.67m (8.76ft); height: 3.1m (10.17ft)
Range:	650km (400 miles)
Armour:	None
Armament:	None
Powerplant:	1 x Mack EY 6-cylinder petrol, developing 159hp (118kW) at 2100rpm
Performance:	Maximum road speed: 54km/h (33mph)

M274 Mechanical Mule

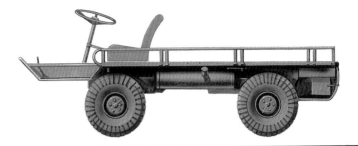

The M274 Mechanical Mule was a dimunitive utility vehicle developed by Willys for US forces in the mid-1950s. Its was designed to transport ammunition, personnel, cargo and heavy infantry weapons. The Mule satisfied this requirement admirably, being able to carry a 450kg (1000lb) cargo on a small flatbed area behind the driver, who was seated on the left of the vehicle. While the A1 version had a four-cylinder petrol engine, later models had a two-cylinder powerplant. The materials used to make the Mule varied. Some were made from steel, others from aluminium or magnesium alloy. All models had four-wheel drive and most (the A5 being the exception) had four-wheel steer.

Country of origin:	United States
Crew:	1
Weight:	380kg (840lb)
Dimensions:	Length: 2.98m (9.78ft); width: 1.78m (5.84ft); height: 1.19m (3.9ft)
Range:	180km (110 miles)
Armour:	None
Armament:	None
Powerplant:	1 x Willys A053 4-cylinder petrol, developing 21hp (16kW)
Performance:	Maximum road speed: 40km/h (25mph)

M561 Gama-Goat

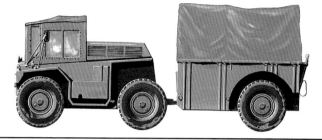

The M561 Gama-Goat is so called because its mobility was meant to be goatlike, and its creator was called Roger Gamaunt. It is a six-wheel-drive utility vehicle capable of tackling the roughest terrain and consists of two sections – a front section containing the engine and crew cab and a rear section for the cargo. The two sections are connected by a flexible coupling which allows the carrier body to pitch plus or minus 40 degrees and roll plus or minus 30 degrees in relation to the front vehicle. Fully amphibious capability is available without preparation, and the M561 can achieve 3km/h (2mph) on the water. Propulsion is provided by the wheels only. The M561 can pull 1.25 tons of cargo.

Country of origin:	United States
Crew:	2
Weight:	4630kg (10,200lb)
Dimensions:	Length: 5.76m (18.89ft); width: 2.13m (6.99ft); height: 2.31m (7.58ft)
Range:	840km (520 miles)
Armour:	None
Armament:	None
Powerplant:	1 x GM 3-53 3-cylinder diesel, developing 103hp (77kW)
Performance:	Maximum road speed: 88km/h (55mph); fording: amphibious

M992 FAASV

The M992 Field Artillery Ammunition Support Vehicle (FAASV) goes beyond the tradition of ammunition supply trucks by being as fast and manoeuvrable as the self-propelled artillery piece it supports (usually an M109A2). It can move off-road at 56km/h (35mph) and can travel on all terrains, whether mud, snow, rock or sand. It can also ford water obstacles up to 1.06m (3.48ft) deep. The M992's ammunition supplies are stored in racked containers behind the driving position, with separate compartments for shells and fuses. An extendable conveyor belt moves the shells from the racks to the artillery crew. The M992 has a crew of two men, but six other personnel can also be carried.

Country of origin:	United States
Crew:	2 + 6
Weight:	25,900kg (57,100lb) fully loaded
Dimensions:	Length: 6.27m (20.57ft); width: 3.15m (10.33ft); height: 3.24m (10.63ft)
Range:	Not available
Armour:	Not available
Armament:	None
Powerplant:	1 x Detroit Diesel 8V-71T 8-cylinder diesel, developing 398hp (297kW)
Performance:	Maximum road speed: 56km/h (35mph)

Oshkosh PLS

The Oshkosk Palletized Load System (PLS) is a heavy load-carrying system fitted to the Oshkosh High Expanded Mobility Tactical Truck (HEMTT). Since the US Army placed a large order in 1981, HEMTT has become a principal US military transport vehicle with over 11,000 units in use. The basic HEMTT vehicle is an 8x8 M977 with a maximum cargo capacity of 11,840kg (26,100lb). PLS vehicles differ by having an extra axle, making a 10x10 configuration. The vehicle works with a variety of trailers and flat-track load-carrying systems. Using an M1076 three-axle trailer, for example, the PLS can add an additional 16.5 tons to its load, with a combined truck and trailer payload of 33 tons.

Country of origin:	United States
Crew:	2
Weight:	17,600kg (38,800lb)
Dimensions:	Length: 10.67m (35ft); width: 2.43m (7.97ft); height: 3.28m (10.76ft)
Range:	540km (340 miles)
Armour:	None
Armament:	None
Powerplant:	1 x Detroit Diesel 8V-92TA 8-cylinder diesel, developing 500hp (373kW)
Performance:	Maximum road speed: 91km/h (57mph)

Glossary

AP: Armour-Piercing; munitions designed for maximum penetration using chemical, kinetic or explosive means.

APC: Armoured Personnel Carrier; a vehicle designed to transport a small unit of soldiers and protect them from small-arms fire.

APFSDS: Armour-Piercing Fin-Stabilized Discarding-Sabot; a tank shell with a diameter smaller than the gun barrel. During firing the shell is encased in a sleeve to make up the gun bore, but which falls away outside the barrel to leave the inner shell travelling with extreme kinetic force. Fins are attached to the round provide a more stable and accurate flight.

APHE: Armour-Piercing High-Explosive; an armour-piercing shell with an enhanced high-explosive content.

ARRV: Armoured Repair and Recovery Vehicle.

ARV: Armoured Recovery Vehicle.

ATGW: Anti-Tank Guided Weapon; an anti-tank missile which is guided to its target from the moment of launch to the point of impact.

AVLB: Armoured Vehicle Launching Bridge.

Central tyre-pressure regulation: A system allowing a driver to inflate or deflate his or her tyres electronically without exiting the vehicle. Used to improve handling on different terrains.

Composite armour: Armour constructed from several different metals and materials. Contrast with homogenous armour.

Explosive-reactive armour: Armour which explodes outwards when struck by a shell. The explosive blast of the armour is designed to counteract the inward force of the shell and leave the crew compartment intact.

GPMG: General-Purpose Machine Gun; a 7.62mm (0.3in) weapon manufactured by FN Herstal and commonly called FN MAG.

HESH: High-Explosive Squash Head; a shell which plasters high explosive onto armour plate then detonates it. Shockwaves travel through the armour and blow off a piece of metal on the inside that destroys interior equipment and personnel.

Homogenous armour: Armour made of a single metal.

Howitzer: a short-barrelled field gun which fires shells on high trajectories at fairly low velocities.

ICBM: Intercontinental Ballistic Missile.

IFF: Identification Friend or Foe; a electronic device which distinguishes enemy vehicles from friendly vehicles. Friendly vehicles are fitted with a special transmitter which transmits a recognition code back to the receiving station.

LST: Landing Ship Tank; a ship designed to transport armoured vehicles from ship to shore.

MBT: Main Battle Tank; a well-armoured vehicle designed purely for heavy combat roles.

MICV: Mechanized Infantry Combat Vehicle.

NBC: Nuclear, Biological, Chemical.

Recoilless rifle: A large calibre anti-tank weapon with no recoil upon firing. The recoilless mechanism works by venting the rocket gases through a small aperture at the back of the weapon and creating a forward thrust equal to the backward recoil of the weapon.

Run-flat inserts: solid rubber sections inside pneumatic tyres which maintain vehicle mobility even if the pneumatic tyres are flat.

SAM: Surface-to-Air Missile.

Scarifier: A toothed digging device used to rip up road surfaces.

Stabilising spades: Extendable blades which dig into the ground and give the vehicle greater static stability.

Submunition: An explosive device contained within a larger shell or bomb, usually a small air-dropped mine or cluster bomblet.

TELAR: Transporter, Erector, Launcher; a ballistic missile vehicle which contains all the facilities for moving, preparing and launching its weapon.

TERCOM: Terrain Contour Matching; a system used in cruise missiles using terrain features for guidance to the target.

TOW: The Hughes Tube-Launched, Wire-Guided, Optically Tracked anti-tank missile.

Trim vane: A panel fitted to the front of an amphibious vehicle to prevent water flooding over the bows into the troop/crew compartment.

Index

Page numbers in **bold** type indicate a feature article which includes an illustration and technical specification. Page numbers in italics refer to illustrations only. The following abbreviations are used: s-p=self-propelled; APC=armoured personnel carrier.